Cuthbert Grant of Grantown

Cuthbert Grant of Grantown:

Warden of
the Plains of
Red River

Margaret Arnett
MacLeod
and
W.L. Morton
(assisted by Alice R. Brown)

WITH A NEW INTRODUCTION BY
W.L. MORTON

The Carleton Library No. 71

McClelland and Stewart Limited

THE CARLETON LIBRARY

A series of Canadian reprints and new collections of source material relating to Canada, issued under the editorial supervision of the Institute of Canadian Studies of Carleton University, Ottawa.

The Canadian Publishers
McClelland and Stewart Limited
25 Hollinger Road, Toronto 374.

Cuthbert Grant of Grantown was originally published in 1963 by McClelland and Stewart

Printed and bound in Canada

Introduction to the Carleton Library Edition

Cuthbert Grant of Grantown was published in 1963 by McClelland and Stewart aided by a grant from the Historical and Scientific Society of Manitoba, and that body distributed the edition, now exhausted. As there is still some interest in this study of one of the personalities of early western Canadian history, the surviving author, the present writer, and Mrs. A. E. Annetts, daughter of Margaret Arnett MacLeod, welcome a second edition of the original text in the Carleton Library. Such a re-issue will make the story of the first leader of the Métis people more accessible than it could be in the first and limited printing.

The History Editor of the Library has decided to attempt no revision or abridgement, but only the necessary and minor corrections critics have revealed. He has, however, asked the writer to say something of Margaret Arnett MacLeod, whose undertaking the book was, and of why she laid certain emphases on aspects of Grant's life and saw it in a light particularly her own. This is, of course, a task of some delicacy for a collaborator and one to whom Margaret MacLeod was a very dear friend. Because the enterprise was one she had made her own, because her knowledge of the man and his local background was unrivalled, the present writer out of respect for those facts and Margaret MacLeod's deep-felt enthusiasm, collaborated in the book as printed, with certain clear reservations as to Grant's character and career, reservations expressed to Margaret MacLeod and discussed with her, but which she declined to accept. To have done so would have destroyed her concept of the man. Now it seems that, in a second issue, the writer, while respecting Margaret MacLeod's version, and leaving it unaltered, owes the reader a clear statement of what his reservations were. They will be given below.

The Preface to the first edition sets out adequately the part of the book for which one writer or the other was researcher and author, and acknowledges the assistance of Mrs. Alice Brown and Mr. Douglas Kemp. The reservations spoken of apply only to Margaret MacLeod's own explicit work. The writer has found no occasion to alter the chapters he composed, *III*, *IV*, *V*, and the larger part of *X*, but it will be noted that they are for the most part descriptive and not interpretative. The figure of Grant which emerges is Grant as Margaret MacLeod saw him, and it is the presentation of Grant's personality and career about which the writer had reservations.

As the Grant of *Cuthbert Grant of Grantown* was Margaret MacLeod's Grant, so her work on Grant and her background was very much part of her own life. Indeed, her historical work was more intimately a fact of her life than a career as writer or historian can commonly be part of a person's inner life. Her work on Grant was at once a process of identification with a land to which her family were newcomers and with her husband's family background. A few lines of biography are in place therefore to reveal why Margaret MacLeod worked so intensively on Cuthbert Grant and felt so intensely about him.

Margaret MacLeod was born in Kerwood, Ontario, not far from London, Ontario, on January 14, 1877, daughter of Thomas Lewis Arnett who had emigrated from London, England, and Angelina Hughes, born near Kerwood of Irish and Welsh descent. Her father had established a dry goods store at Kerwood. In 1880 he moved with his family of six children to Winnipeg on the eve of the great railway boom and opened a large and superior dry goods and haberdashery store at the corner of Main Street and McDermot Avenue, known as "Arnett's Golden Lion." When the boom collapsed, the Arnetts moved to Brandon, and Thomas Lewis Arnett opened a store there. In Brandon Margaret attended school, and at the age of fifteen took a course to prepare for teaching.

The following year she taught a primary class in the school at Stonewall, Manitoba, but like many another youthful school marm had her career cut short by marriage. Her husband was Dr. Alexander Neil MacLeod, a recent graduate of the Manitoba Medical College, itself a very recent institution, who was practicing in Stonewall. He was himself the child of a mother who was born in Red River and a father who settled there after serving in the Hudson's Bay Company. To the background of Dr. MacLeod's people Margaret was introduced not so much by her husband as by stories of Red River days gleaned from an old friend and neighbour, J. P. Matheson. This was the beginning of that historical knowledge which in time was to do so much to recover the texture and sentiment of old Red River.

Before the years of heavy historical work came, however, there were years of happy marriage during those golden pre-1914 times, when at long last the great West was opened and began to prosper in the hopes long nurtured for it. Three children were born to the marriage, Alan Arnett, who was to win the Victoria Cross in the First World War, Marion, now Mrs. C. W. Adams of Arvida, Quebec, and Helen, now Mrs. A. E. Annetts of Ottawa. It is the latter to whom thanks for most of the above information are owing. Two great losses were to interupt that happiness, Alan's tragic death by influenza in 1918, and the death of Dr. MacLeod in 1940.

Margaret MacLeod left the writer with the impression that her own historical work began after the loss of her husband. This was mistaken, except in the sense that after 1940 she took up again an occupation already long pursued—her interest in history, its study and composition. As a member of the Executive of the Women's Canadian Club of Winnipeg she took part in the collection of material for *Women of Red River* published in 1923. After Dr. MacLeod's appointment as Executive Secretary of the Faculty of Medicine of the University of Manitoba in 1923, the family lived in Winnipeg, and Margaret was in touch with the gifted and eager women writers and historians of the 1920's and 1930's, of whom Margaret Stovell McWilliams is perhaps best known. Certainly it seems that Margaret MacLeod got her first training and experience in that collective effort to gather reminiscences before it was too late; her work on Grant was of the same kind. Her own part in *Women of Red River* is not known, as no credit was given to any member of those who took part in assembling the material for the book.

It is not certain when Margaret MacLeod began her research on Grant, nor what drew her to him and his career. In general, however, the reason is quite clear, and was explained by the historian to the present writer. Her work for *Women of Red River* revealed to her that among those of English speech Grant was something of a figure of fear—the man of Seven Oaks—while among those of French descent he was an admirable, even a heroic man. It was this difference she set out to investigate by interviewing the old timers of Saint-Boniface and Saint-François-Xavier and by archival research. In the course of her work she became convinced that the Selkirk Settlers' image of Grant was mistaken and that that of Saint-Boniface and Saint-François-Xavier was nearer to the truth. Her work, therefore, was to examine the career of Grant as leader of the Métis not only in the fur trade war that led to the collision at Seven Oaks, but also as leader and moderator of his semi-nomadic people—people both of the river lot and the buffalo hunt. The present book is only to be understood in terms of that search for the true and whole Grant and the evidence Margaret MacLeod assembled to bear witness to the character of his role in Red River after 1816.

It would be quite misleading, however, to leave the impression that Margaret MacLeod was a partisan researcher, or that she abandoned her feeling for English Red River. Such an impression is quickly removed by reading the extensive list given below, probably by no means complete, of her writings in the Winnipeg newspapers and Canadian periodicals from the 1930's to the 1960's, and her speeches and addresses in the same period. The subjects of these occasional pieces, occasional but often her best work, cover the whole of Red River history, English as well as French, fur trade and buffalo hunt, Selkirk Settler and Métis, Company and colony, explorer and missionary. Their wonderful catholicity exhibits the range and eagerness of Margaret MacLeod to know, feel and live every aspect of that strange colony's unique way of life. In her work on Grant the point of her endeavour was to correct a distortion which the fears and horrors of Seven Oaks had wrought in the course of Red River history. It is, after all, the historian's supreme task to put right the distortions history itself has made.

By the end of the 1930's Margaret MacLeod was wholly embarked on a strongly running tide of research. Every research student knows the many centrifugal pulls any significant piece of research sets going, and the search for Grant led her to the Hargrave Papers in the University of Toronto Library. Her research was so compelling, her published work so authentic, that it came to the notice of two eminent historians, both great helpers of other historians, J. B. Tryell and W. Stewart Wallace. Through them Margaret MacLeod was invited by the Council of the Champlain Society to prepare a selection and edition of the letters of Letitia Hargrave. It was a collection central to the history of the Canadian Northwest in the first three quarters of the nineteenth century. Letitia, for example, who was the daughter of Dugald Mactavish of Campbeltown, niece of Chief Factor John George Mactavish, and sister of Chief Factor William Mactavish, Governor of Rupert's Land, became wife of Chief Factor James Hargrave, and mother of the fur trade clerk and historian, Joseph James Hargrave. In her work on the volume Margaret entered the inner recesses of that history, gaining knowledge of personalities and private thoughts that satisfied her deep sense that history is a personal experience of the historian, and that it is by the conviction created of having been present, and seen and heard and felt that the historian wins the attention and confidence of the reader. The volume appeared in 1947, and took its place gracefully among the more delightful reading of the great volumes in the red and gold of the Champlain Society.

The experience of editing the *Letters of Letitia Hargrave* confirmed Margaret MacLeod's place among historians who can do work that will last, even if she was too modest to feel the assurance the successful experience should have given her. But the work on Grant, if not discontinued, had been set back. She strove to get back into the swing of research and did indeed publish pieces which were to be incorporated into the present book, or used to support it, such as "Dickson the Liberator," *The Beaver*, 1956, and "Red River Buffalo Hunt," *The Canadian Historical Review*, 1957. But her many interests, her occasional writings and speeches, the effort of living alone in her own home, as she chose to do, and partial loss of vision, made it at length an impossible hope to arrange the boxes of notes and compose a firm narrative from scattered and often discordant evidence.

The writer did not know Margaret MacLeod until those later years, although he remembers well his first meeting. It was, probably in 1938, in the office of the late Professor R. O. Macfarlane, who was assisting Margaret with some part of her work. The writer at that time had done little on the history of the West in the last century, and it was some time before his own interests and increasing acquaintance ripening into friendship made it possible for him to suggest the collaboration in the late 1950's out of which the present volume came.

The part the writer played in the preparation of *Cuthbert Grant of Grantown* is specified in the first edition. In addition to the composition of the chapters designated, the writer did the annotation of Margaret MacLeod's text from her notes, with the aid of her devoted assistant, Miss Mabel Finch, it being impossible for Margaret to do such close and tedious work. Everything was read to and checked with her, and had her approval.

The work was done to ensure the survival and publication of what Margaret had done over the years, and for the honour of collaboration with such a gifted historian.

Anyone who has collaborated with another author, particularly with one handicapped as Margaret was, will realize the difficulties. The writer had reservations as to the character of Grant which he expressed to Margaret, but did not push. Acceptance of them would have so affected her idea of the man and his work as to make necessary a re-consideration plainly beyond her strength. The writer therefore kept silent because the book as it is contains a needed correction of a historical misunderstanding, and because his role was to ensure the publication of Margaret MacLeod's work and her conclusions from it.

Now, however, it does seem right, with all respect to Margaret, to state those reservations in order that readers of the second edition may use it more critically, and perhaps with greater profit.

The writer's general reservation is that whereas Margaret MacLeod saw Grant as a heroic figure whose services to his people and to the Red River settlement had been under-estimated by the English-Canadian public, and particularly by the English people of Red River and their descendants, the writer was and is unable to see Grant as being what he has termed "heroic."

His reasons for the reservation are the following:

First, Grant was used by the North West Company to lead the

Métis in their cause in the fur trade war with Lord Selkirk and the Hudson's Bay Company. Grant, of course, was very young at the time and his father had been a Nor' Wester. But heroes, even when young, are not used; they pursue their own objects. He was used also by George Simpson to conciliate the Métis.

Secondly, there is considerable evidence that Grant, on occasion at least, drank more than his position of responsibility allowed. His intervention, when by no means sober, against the Sioux visiting party of 1836, for example, was an embarrassment and might have had dangerous consequences.

Thirdly, it may at least be disputed, since in fact it never actively performed the role, that Grantown was a barrier against Sioux attack on Red River. The Sioux never attacked, and it is not known positively that they were deterred by the war-like reputation of Grant and his Métis warriors. On the contrary, the Red River buffalo hunt, one party of which came from Grantown, was pushing more and more into territory admitted to be Siouian, and might well have provoked retaliation against the settlement.

Fourthly, there is little evidence that Grant was a folklore figure of the Métis. He is, for example, mentioned only once in the known Métis ballads.

Fifthly, Grant did absolutely nothing to foil the assault by James Sinclair in 1849 on the Hudson's Bay Company's monopoly of the fur trade. He could not presumably because his people were in sympathy with Sinclair, and the assault ended the monopoly he had helped maintain, to the Métis cry of *"le commerce est libre."*

Finally after 1849, to his death in 1854, Grant was a nonentity in Red River affairs.

These reservations are considerable and, if accepted, affect to a major degree the view to be taken of Grant. They leave him a respectable local leader, and a convenient representative for the Hudson's Bay Company of his people.

That is not to say that he was unworthy of the work Margaret MacLeod expended upon him. As Alexander Ross pointed out in his time, and as Marcel Giraud has echoed with great anthropological learning in this century, the essential history of Red River was how to maintain a civilized and orderly society on a borderland of civilization—settled life—and wilderness-nomadic life. Grant was an interesting example of the persons of mixed blood, educated, travelled, yet accepted by his own people, as were similar men, James Sinclair, James Ross and Louis Riel, *fils.* All had ability, education, background in the fur trade or the Colony. All knew the hazards and uncertainty of a wilderness background, drink, tuberculosis, psychic instability, even sudden death such as terminated Sinclair's career.

Grant lacked the brilliance of the others, but his stability, if sometimes sodden, did help give the Métis place and assurance in the Colony, and it is a pity he left no son to give leadership in 1869, to head the "Cuthbert Grant party" of Saint-François-Xavier against the "Lagimodière-Riel party" of Saint-Boniface for the leadership of the Red River Resistance. Had the Grant party prevailed, there might have been no shooting of Thomas Scott. Margaret MacLeod was basically correct. "Mr. Grant" stabilized his people in his lifetime, and history errs in forgetting that not all Métis left Manitoba for the Saskatchewan or the Missouri. Those who followed the tradition of settlement which Grant had striven to develop remained, as their descendants remain to-day.

W.L. MORTON.
1972

PREFACE

This biography of Cuthbert Grant is the result of researches carried out by Margaret Arnett MacLeod in the 1930's. Mrs MacLeod assiduously collected reminiscences of Grant and Grantown from his descendants and those of his friends and relatives. This material she corroborated and increased by study of the sources of fur trade history between 1750 and 1850.

Mrs MacLeod's research at that time, however, led to the publication only of her "Cuthbert Grant of Grantown" in the *Canadian Historical Review* for March, 1940, and of occasional articles in the local press. Then her work in editing *The Letters of Letitia Hargrave* for the Champlain Society, which appeared in 1947, took Mrs MacLeod's attention from Grant and his people.

Not until some time later did her friends, among whom was W. L. Morton, begin to fear that the labour already invested in Grant might not come to fruition, and an unusual knowledge of the man and his period be lost. Mrs MacLeod was pleased with their encouragement to take up again the unfinished work of some twenty years before, and to see it to completion despite other tasks.

After many delays, the outcome is the present volume. It is as a whole the fruit of Mrs Macleod's research; a good portion of it her original composition; much of it she revised and worked up from preliminary sketches based on her notes by those assisting; all of it she has heard read, and approved in general.

Chapters III, IV, V, and most of Chapter X, are from research done by W. L. Morton, were composed by him, and for them he is responsible.

The assistance of Mrs Alice Brown and Mr Douglas Kemp in research, writing and revision are gratefully acknowledged by both Mrs MacLeod and myself. Our thanks are also owing to the Canada Council for a grant in aid of composition, and to the University of Manitoba for stenographic assistance. Both Mrs MacLeod and I wish to record reciprocally how rewarding an experience our collaboration has been for us both. If our efforts explain and vindicate the character and career of the chief of the Métis and the defender of Red River Colony, we shall be doubly rewarded.

W. L. MORTON

CONTENTS

INTRODUCTION

Cuthbert Grant is best remembered in history as the leader of the *bois-brûlés* in the massacre of Seven Oaks, and as such he has not been kindly remembered by the descendants of the Selkirk settlers, or by western Canadians generally.

Yet the same Cuthbert Grant was the founder of Grantown, which became the mission and parish of Saint-François-Xavier on the Assiniboine. That settlement of his folk, the Métis buffalo hunters of the plains, some of whom had been the warriors of Seven Oaks, became the bulwark of the settlement against the Sioux. Its presence for almost fifty years gave the colonists of St James, St Johns, Kildonan and St Andrews an ever present sense of security. They slept more quietly in their beds knowing that to westward lay those hunter-warriors and their chief who were the terror of the Sioux. And well they might, for Grant not only made his own people friends of the Red River Settlement, but his influence with his Indian kin, the Assiniboines and Crees of the plains, helped to keep those tribes at peace with the white men; he was a warrior feared and respected by the untamable Sioux.

It is this contrast between the surviving memory of Cuthbert Grant and the history of the greater part of his life which prompts this book on the man's life and the settlement he founded. That his name should be cleared, if cleared it can be, of the opprobrium of the massacre, is only right. The work he did in founding the second colony in Red River and bringing the nomad hunters of the plains to settle and take up the tasks of agriculture ought to be set beside the brief tale of violence which was his youthful career. These things must be done if justice is to be done Grant. He merits justice, not only as all men do, but because historically he was one of the founders and leaders of the Red River Settlement.

Justice must be done to Grant also if the history of the Red River Settlement is to be seen in its proper proportions. That history has always been distorted by a natural but unhistorical emphasis on Selkirk and his colonists. It has been distorted also by the fact that Red River was a colony of French and English people, and its history has been recorded not only in two languages but, it almost may be said, in two histories. If a true proportion is to be achieved, the role of the French half-breeds, the Métis, must be given its proper place in Red River history. And Grant was the leader, in some sense the maker, of the Métis nation.

This book, then, is not only the life of a man, but a history of his settlement of Grantown on the White Horse Plain which became the parish of Saint-François-Xavier. There can be no doubt that only the influence and example of Grant, with the urgings of Rev. J. N. Provencher and Rev. Picard Destroismaisons, brought the Métis to accept the Red River Settlement and to become a colony within it. Without such an example the great majority of them would have remained nomads of the plains and, perhaps, enemies of the Settlement. But once committed to the cause of the colony, the Métis became its protectors and one of the factors which explain its survival. In leading his people to throw in their lot with the colony and become its defenders, Grant was fulfilling his role of leader of the Métis nation. He was able to persuade them to settle because of the completeness of his identity with them. And because his leadership was effective, Grant himself through his care for his people was transformed from the youthful scourge of the colony to its friend and defender. His story is not to be separated from that of his people and his settlement. They are interwoven from beginning to end.

The picture of Grant that this book offers, then, is not only that of the dashing youth who brought the wild *bois-brûlés* down the Assiniboine to the clash at Seven Oaks. It is a picture of "Mr Grant" the pacifier and civilizer, the leader of the settlement, the western seignior placing his people around him on his fief of six mile frontage of the Assiniboine, the farmer, the miller, the leader of the hunt, the dispenser of medicine, the magistrate, the Councillor of Assiniboia, the correspondent of Simpson and Donald Ross, the bane of the free trader, the friend of white and half-breed, the defender of Red River.

Cuthbert Grant of Grantown

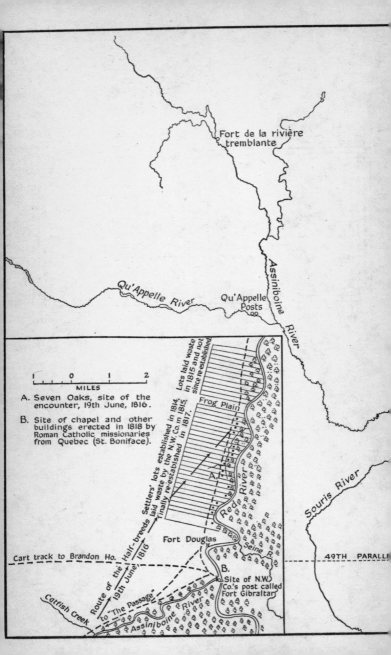

Fort de la rivière tremblante

Assiniboine River

Qu'Appelle River

Qu'Appelle Posts

1   0   1   2
MILES

A. Seven Oaks, site of the encounter, 19th June, 1816.

B. Site of chapel and other buildings erected in 1818 by Roman Catholic missionaries from Quebec (St. Boniface).

Lots laid waste in 1815 and not since re-established

Frog Plain

Settlers' lots established in 1814, laid waste by the N.W.Co. in 1815, finally re-established in 1817.

A.

Red River

Cart track to Brandon Ho.

Route of the Half-breeds 19th June 1816

Fort Douglas

Seine R.

49TH PARALLEL

B. Site of N.W. Co.'s post called Fort Gibraltar

to "The Passage"

Catfish Creek

Assiniboine River

Souris River

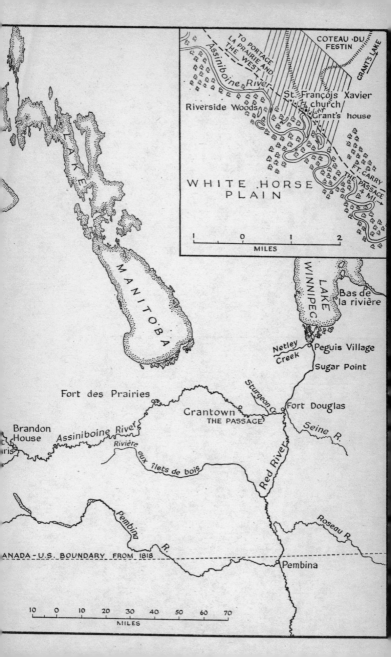

COTEAU DU FESTIN

GRANT'S LAKE

TO PORTAGE
LA PRAIRIE AND
THE WEST

Assiniboine River

St. François Xavier church

Grant's house

Riverside Woods

WHITE HORSE PLAIN

PT. CARRY
THE PASSAGE
4 MI

1   0   1   2
MILES

LAKE MANITOBA

LAKE WINNIPEG

Bas de la rivière

Netley Creek

Peguis Village

Sugar Point

Fort des Prairies

Sturgeon C.

Grantown
THE PASSAGE

Fort Douglas

Brandon House

Assiniboine River

Rivière aux îlets de bois

Seine R.

Red River

aris

Pembina R.

Roseau R.

CANADA-U.S. BOUNDARY FROM 1818

Pembina

10   0   10   20   30   40   50   60   70
MILES

CHAPTER I

GRANT'S ANCESTRY AND UPBRINGING,

1793-1812

Young Cuthbert Grant came into the spotlight as a romantic and intriguing figure in 1816, during the last bitter struggle between the North West and Hudson's Bay Companies for supremacy in the fur trade in the Canadian northwest. Later, from 1824 to the time of his death in 1854, as holder of the only seigniory in the west, on which he planted his outpost settlement of Grantown, and as Warden of the Plains, he made a notable contribution towards the establishment of the first permanent settlement in Western Canada, that of the Red River colony. Indeed the settlers at The Forks of the Red and Assiniboine rivers, where Winnipeg now stands, acknowledged that in their most critical years his settlement of Grantown afforded the infant colony much-needed protection from the Sioux.[1] His buffalo hunters supplied them with "plains provisions" – practically the only food obtainable in the country.

Isaac Cowie was to write in later years that this was so.

> Under Grant, the Métis of the buffalo hunting brigades were organized as a disciplined force, which repelled every hostile Indian attack so successfully as to win renown as the most skilful and bravest warriors of the Prairies.
>
> . . . They protected themselves from overwhelming numbers of Sioux . . . guarding the agricultural settlers of the Red River Colony from molestation by the bloodthirsty "Tigers of the Plains" and other warlike tribes.
>
> The warlike qualities of the Métis often were most favourably commented on by military men who hunted and travelled with them. . . . They expressed surprise at the excellent discipline they maintained among themselves when on the grand annual buffalo hunt. British officers mention them in their reports as magnificent horsemen, and splendid marksmen, whose services would be invaluable in war on the frontier.[2]

Moreover, as chief of the people of mixed blood, the Métis hunters of the plains, he kept them reconciled to the government and monopoly of the fur trade by the Hudson's Bay Company.

Cuthbert Grant of Grantown was born in 1793 at Fort Tremblante in what is now Saskatchewan. The fort was located on the north bank of Rivière Tremblante or Aspen Creek about a half-mile east of its confluence with the Assiniboine. At this point there is a ridge running parallel with the river, and here "on a beautiful slope where the hill slips into a wide river flat"[3] stood Grant's boyhood home. It was a "paradise of the traders." Here young Cuthbert Grant was born – of Scottish, Cree, and perhaps French descent.[4] The boy was named for his Scottish father, Cuthbert Grant, a trader and partner of the North West Company.[5] Little is known of his mother, the daughter of a white trader and an Indian woman from the Qu'Appelle region of Cree or Assiniboine stock. It is not known whether his maternal grandfather was a Frenchman or another trader like his father.[6] Cuthbert was the second son of the family, an older brother, James, having been born two years earlier. The register of the Scotch Presbyterian Church of St Gabriel Street, Montreal, has the following entries:

> James, son to Cuthbert Grant, Indian trader, the Mother unknown, aged seven years, was baptised in the presence of Messrs. James Grant and James Laing of Montreal, merchants, this seventh day of November in the year of our Lord, one thousand seven hundred and ninety-eight, by
> > James Laing
> > James Grant.   J. Young Minister.

> Cuthbert, son of the deceased Cuthbert Grant, late Indian Trader, aged eight years, was baptised this twelfth day of October in the year of our Lord, one thousand eight hundred and first.
> > W. McGillivray
> > Rod. Mackenzie.   J. Young. Minst.[7]

Besides the two boys there were three sisters among the children who played around the log walls of Fort Tremblante. They were to marry and settle with Cuthbert Grant at Grantown: Mrs John Wills, Mme François Morin, and Mme Pierre Falcon.

Nothing further is known of Cuthbert's mother, but something has been discovered of the origin and life of his father, Cuthbert Grant, Sr. He was a member of the Clan Grant of Strathspey in the county of Inverness in Scotland. In the second half of the eighteenth century many members and connections of the Grant clan were sent to trade in Canada by the London firm of Robert Grant and Company. Among them was one Charles Grant who came to Canada some time before 1768 and entered the fur trade. He died in Quebec in 1784, but apparently not before he had introduced some of his relatives into the Canadian trade. One was his cousin, Robert Grant of Lethendry, a partner of the North West Company of 1779. Robert, it may be assumed, brought his brother Cuthbert into the service of the new company.

W. S. Wallace in his "Strathspey and the Fur Trade" notes that Donald A. Smith, later Lord Strathcona, was connected with the Grants, and was indeed brought out by John Stuart, a cousin of our Cuthbert Grant, Sr. Smith thus had relatives in the northwest when he came out as special commissioner in the Riel Resistance. Wallace wonders whether these connections were among the reasons for Smith's appointment.[8] Certainly Smith at that time referred publicly to his "cousins."[9] When Mrs MacLeod's article on Cuthbert Grant of Grantown appeared in the *Canadian Historical Review* in 1938, it attracted the attention of the late Mr J. D. McGrigor, of Whitehouse, Reading, England. As a result of a correspondence of some years with Mr McGrigor fresh light was thrown on the ancestry of Cuthbert Grant. Mr McGrigor sent to Mrs MacLeod the researches of Miss Evelyn Grant on the Grants of Letheredie,[10] from which branch of Clan Grant Cuthbert Grant was descended as follows:

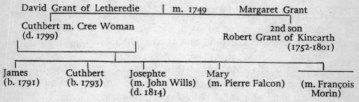

David Grant of Letheredie | m. 1749 | Margaret Grant

Cuthbert m. Cree Woman
(d. 1799)

2nd son
Robert Grant of Kincarth
(1752-1801)

James
(b. 1791)

Cuthbert
(b. 1793)

Josephte
(m. John Wills)
(d. 1814)

Mary
(m. Pierre Falcon)

(m. François
Morin)

Not a great deal is known of the elder Cuthbert Grant's career in the fur trade, although his importance is recognized. He was among the first Nor'Westers to reach Great Slave Lake in 1786,[11] where with Peter Pond he established a post – later Fort Resolution – in opposition to John Ross and Laurent Leroux, independent traders.[12] It was while Grant was there that Peter Pond prepared his papers on Great Slave Lake and began his map to lay before Catherine, Empress of all the Russias. Grant was at Fort Chipewyan in 1789 when Alexander Mackenzie returned to it from his voyage down his "River Disappointment."[13] He must indeed have contributed something at least to Pond's knowledge, and perhaps to Mackenzie's. From 1791 to 1793, if not longer, he was in charge of the North West Company post at Aspen Creek on the Upper Assiniboine where his boys were born. In the summer of

1793 he established the first North West Company fort on the Assiniboine in the Souris mouth area in opposition to independent traders. This post, in turn, was opposed later that year by the establishment of the Hudson's Bay Company's Brandon House a few miles upstream.[14] That he was a solid family man despite his life in the wilderness is suggested by his subscription of three guineas to the building fund of the St Gabriel Street Presbyterian Church of Montreal,[15] as well as by the baptism there of his boys. In 1798 he was made a partner of the North West Company. It had taken him some time as a "winterer" to become a *bourgeois*, but with his partnership Cuthbert Grant had definitely arrived. With his success came membership in the famous Beaver Club of Montreal.

But only a short time was left Grant to enjoy his newly won position. His health was failing. This no doubt explains why in 1798 he sent his elder son James, then aged seven, to Montreal to be baptized, and then to Scotland to be educated. That year John McDonald of Garth, whose *bourgeois* he was, related:

> He was a good man but not active enough for such a department. He saw that and told me to act as I thought proper. I stayed at Fort de Isle and he proceeded to Fort Augustus [Edmonton] and wintered there with Mr. Hughes. Spring came on and Mr. Grant feeling quite ill I had to fit him out a comfortable awning in one of the boats to take him down the river to Cumberland House. . . . We got Mr. Grant to Kaministiquia where he soon died.

Grant was spoken of as a man of great influence in the fur trade and the position to which he had risen in the company is indicated in McDonald's next sentence. "Mr. Grant recommended me to replace him so I thus took my departure as master of the largest department in the North."[16]

Thus when he was only six, young Cuthbert was left an orphan. For the next two years he remained with his sisters in his mother's country, bereft now of the protective aura of importance which his father's position had provided for his children. These were impressionable years for the little lad for, insecure and threatened with the possibility of abandonment by his father's people, he was probably closer to the wild life of the plains than at any other time in his life.

His father had willed, however, unlike some of his colleagues, that his children should be reared as Christians and his sons educated. The little lad became the concern of one of the great men of the North West Company. William McGillivray, his guardian and executor of his father's will, was a man of wealth and influence. In fact, when he was made superintendent of the North West Company seven years later he was regarded as the most powerful man in the fur trade.

In June 1801 McGillivray was at the Grand Portage to meet the wintering partners from the fur country and receive their reports. No doubt it was at this time that young Cuthbert was brought to him from the west. McGillivray took the child with him to Montreal. He arranged for his baptism in the St Gabriel Street Presbyterian Church on October 12, as recorded above. Associated with him was Roderick Mackenzie who had been with Cuthbert's father at Great Slave Lake, and was in 1801 an agent of the North West Company.

One sees the small boy from the empty prairies, dressed suitably for the occasion, standing in the big church, his mind filled with awe and wonder as he gazed about him. He had seen nothing in his few short years to give him any conception of such grandeur. He must have had a lost feeling, and one hopes that the grand gentleman, William McGillivray, or Roderick Mackenzie, held his hand.

After baptism, young Cuthbert may have gone to school in Montreal.[17] But it is probable to the point of certainty that Cuthbert Grant was brought east and baptized as preparation for his being sent to relatives in Scotland to be educated. It was not uncommon for the *bourgeois* of the fur trade to do so. They had the means, and an education in the Old Country helped to offset the child's Indian ancestry and early upbringing in the wilderness. John Stuart, a cousin of the elder Grant and uncle of Donald A. Smith, sent his two sons to Scotland in this fashion. In the instance of both young James and Cuthbert Grant, there is a definite tradition, remembered identically in branches of the family now separate, that both boys were sent to Scotland to be educated. There James indeed remained.

Probably he had preceded Cuthbert by the two years' difference in the date of their baptisms. But both, it seems, were sent to live with their father's nearest kin, the Stuarts. John Stuart, mentioned above, had entered the service of the North West Company in 1799. He was the companion of Simon Fraser during the descent of the Fraser River in 1806. In 1813 Stuart became a partner in the North West Company, and a Chief Factor in the Hudson's Bay Company at the union of the companies in 1821. In Scotland John had left a brother Peter, who never came to Canada.[18] While it it doubtful whether the Stuart brothers were closer kin than second or third cousin to the young Grants, and while there is no documentary evidence of a connection of any intimacy, still less of the boys having resided in the Stuart home, there is some evidence which does seem to indicate that the connection was an active and intimate one. Two wills of Cuthbert Grant have survived. One was made in 1818 in Montreal. In it John Stuart, who had been for many years resident in New Caledonia, or British Columbia, was named executor.[19] In 1822 Grant made a second will in which he named Peter Stuart his executor, and made him a bequest of five hundred pounds.[20]

A still further evidence of intimate kinship is given in yet another and thought-provoking way. John Stuart was uncle to Donald A. Smith, as noted above, and in fact was instrumental in bringing young Smith into the service of the Hudson's Bay Company. Thus Cuthbert Grant was a cousin, Scots fashion at least, of Donald Smith, and so of course was his younger sister Mary, who was to marry the Métis poet, Pierre Falcon. The family tradition is that when Smith visited Mary Falcon after he first came to the northwest in 1870, he was always greeted by her as "little Donald" though a man of fifty and high in the service of the great company. At meeting he called her "cousin," in reply to her embraces and the fond repetition of "little Donald, little Donald." Probably this relationship aided Smith in his mission to the people of Red River during the troubles of 1869-70.

The evidence, then, is slight and scattered, but it does serve to confirm the family tradition that Cuthbert Grant was sent to Scotland to be educated.

The upbringing and schooling in Scotland, however, were only preparatory to a career in the North West Company. It is not known at what age Grant returned to Montreal from Scotland. Young men entered the services of the fur companies at the age of fifteen or sixteen years. William McGillivray knew that young Cuthbert's future would best lie in the company in which his father had been so influential. Also, the lad had no ties of close kin in Scotland; so it is probable that he began his career in the North West Company at a fairly early age.

Grant had lived among gentlefolk since he was eight years old. There was no lack of means. McGillivray dispensed his friend Cuthbert Sr's legacy to meet all the boy's needs. Like other sons of fur-trade officers who were sent to the Old Country for their education, he would attend a school for gentlemen's sons. He would naturally spend his holidays among his father's relations and no doubt often wandered along the banks of the beautiful river in Grantoun-on-the-Spey.

It was therefore a young gentleman, the product of this Scottish environment, who returned to Montreal to begin work at the North West Company headquarters. He now found himself among his father's old associates and his heart must have been warmed by their interest and patronage. He made his friends among their families and had entrée to such homes during the three or four years he spent in Montreal.

It would appear that the only existing photograph of Grant was taken during this period. It shows him as a well-dressed young gentleman of the period, with nothing to suggest the rough manners of Fort Tremblante and the wilderness life of the Upper Assiniboine. The boy from the Indian country is revealed as a self-possessed young gentleman, at home in society and among gentlefolk.

One who was to know him later stated that Grant was "protected and educated by the North West Company at Montreal"; and no doubt his education was furthered by the training he received there. By 1812 he had reached the status of clerk and was appointed to the Upper Red River District in the northwest.[21]

To Grant and the other young men at company headquarters in Montreal, life in the western fur trade must have taken on a romantic aspect. In spring the gay brigades with much ceremony and jollity, their canoes laden with goods for the trade, started off on their long journey to the northwest. The gentlemen, the *bourgeois*, dressed in fine garb and seated luxuriously in their canoes, disappeared in the distance to the lilting songs of their canoe-men. In autumn the rich packs of furs arrived from the west to fill the warehouses. The lads then listened to breath-taking tales of adventurous travel, of victorious contests with fur trade rivals, and of gay revels at the western posts.

It would thus be in a spirit of high adventure, with his imagination fired by thoughts of a romantic life before him, that young Cuthbert Grant left that spring of 1812 for his post in the northwest. He was then nineteen. For eleven years he had known only the firm gentleness of a Scottish home and school, the quiet life of the Highlands, the steady discipline of the desk, and the decorum of a Montreal counting-house. He had been bred a gentleman to serve as a clerk and perhaps to rise to a partnership in the North West Company. As a boy of eight he had left the life of the fur trade country behind him. Its ways had been laid aside as his Indian blood had been ignored. Grant, though a native of the Indian country, was coming back to it a *moonias*, a greenhorn, with all to learn of how to manage the trade and the wayward people, the Indian and Métis of the northwest. But he was the son of a *bourgeois*; the old winterers would welcome him as Cuthbert Grant's son. And in the tepees of the Assiniboine and Plains Cree and the cabins of the Métis the word would pass that his mother's son had come back to the plains of the Upper Assiniboine. As the *bourgeois* down at Montreal intended, the Indian country would claim its own, however much the gentleman he might be.

CHAPTER II

THE RED RIVER COUNTRY IN

1812

In May of 1812 young Mr Grant rode out from Montreal along the shores of the St Lawrence to Lachine. He was to embark in the canoes for the Red River country. The brisk little city under the forested mountain, and its shipping on the broad river, were quickly left behind as the gentlemen trotted under the great elms of the island of Montreal. The river was busy with traffic, timber rafts bound for Quebec, and Durham boats coming down from Upper Canada. Trade was good, for Canadian timber and wheat were in demand in Britain, locked in the last round of the great contest with Napoleon. That man of destiny was that very spring preparing his invasion of Russia. But Canada was a land at peace, and the only threat to its peace and prosperity was the growing anger of the American government at the British violations of neutral rights and at British friendship with the western Indians. That anger was to bring war with the United States in June of 1812, and the North West Company was already prepared for it. The news of war would be the occasion for seizing the key to that southwest country lost to the United States in 1783, the great post of Michilimackinac.

Young Mr Grant, however, was bound for the northwest where as yet the Americans were not to be feared. He went gladly, for a period of service in the interior was the way to promotion in the company. As an apprentice clerk he had his foot on the ladder of promotion, and was a gentleman among the gentlemen of the company. Being such, he made no concessions to the wilderness voyage. He rode dressed in his frock coat, beaver hat, breeches, and boots as though he were going down to the counting-office. His ample baggage had already gone up to Lachine by wagon, and in it, too, no concession had been made to the wilderness. Gentlemen travelled as gentlemen in the canoe brigades, with robe, tent, travelling-desk, preserved foods, wines, and every comfort obtainable. The canoe-men and personal servants would do all the work of travel and making camp along the rivers and lakes.

At Lachine the party found the canoes afloat, the men waiting. The great master canoes, six fathoms in length, rode heavily on the water, the great up-curved bows and sterns with their painted stars and animals giving them grace. These wonderful craft, the work of Canadian canoe-builders, were the explanation of the operation of the

eat company from Montreal to the Pacific. Their combination of
ghtness with strength alone made possible the swift transport of men,
oods, and furs across the continent in the brief northern summer.

Now the partners came down to the water's edge, exchanged
reetings with the guide of the brigade and the steersman and bowman
f their canoes, and settled themselves comfortably in their places in
he centre. Grant as a clerk took his seat with a *bourgeois*. Then the
middlemen thrust off and the paddles took up the beat. The bowman
f the lead canoe struck up a *chanson*, and the line of canoes filed out
nto the broad expanse of the Ottawa.

For a month thereafter from dawn to dusk the brigade swung up
he Ottawa and the Mattawa, over the height of land into French River,
long the broad reaches of Georgian Bay, up St Mary's River to the
ault, and by the looming capes and deep bays of Superior to Fort
William. At dusk the gentlemen were carried ashore on the backs of
middlemen, and stretched their legs while the servants prepared the
upper and raised their tents. Before the sun rose, they would be
oused by the guide's cry of *lève! lève!* and would drowsily take their
laces once more, to recline, smoke, talk or write as hour by hour the
weating *voyageurs* drove the great canoes.

At Fort William on the Kaministiquia River the Montreal partners
with whom Grant came met the wintering partners who had come
down from the interior. They brought their furs from the Red River
ountry, the Saskatchewan, and the Athabasca, where they had traded
during the winter. For a few boisterous days there was much talk,
xchange of news, and festive dining and drinking in the great hall of
Fort William. Ross Cox in his book *The Columbia River* described the
western headquarters of the North West Company at Fort William in
816 in part as follows:

> The dining hall is a noble apartment and sufficiently capacious
> to entertain two hundred. A finely executed bust of the late
> Simon McTavish is placed in it, with portraits of various pro-
> prietors. A full-length likeness of Nelson, together with a splendid
> painting of the battle of the Nile, also decorate the walls, and
> were presented by the Hon. William McGillivray to the Com-
> pany.[1]

Grant must have lingered in this great room, already full of memories
of the fur trade, and gazed at the hero of the Nile.

The Montreal and wintering partners met in council there to discuss the next year's trade, the prospect of war with the United States,

and the purpose of the colony Lord Selkirk of the Hudson's Bay Company was about to begin on the Red River. Grant as a clerk of course took no part in the council, but he would know the tenor of the discussion, and would be told that he had been assigned to the North West post on the Qu'Appelle, in his father's old district.

By the time the council ended, the packing of the "pieces," the ninety-pound bales of goods, was completed, and once more the brigades moved out from Fort William, and passed slowly up the winding Kaministiquia. The canoes now were not master canoes, but north canoes, shorter and slimmer, and designed for the faster water and frequent rapids of the voyage to Lake Winnipeg and over the height of land to the Athabasca. It was harder travel now, and Grant fought the mosquitoes as he waited while the men trotted with the canoes and pieces over the long portages at Dog Lake and the Savanne portage. Then came the broad stream of Rainy River, the Lake of the Woods, and the fierce plunging of the Winnipeg over its thirty waterfalls, each marked by the many crosses set up for *voyageurs* who had perished in their currents. At the mouth of the Winnipeg in Traverse Bay stood Fort Bas de la Rivière, the provision depot of the canoe brigades. Here the Red River canoes turned south for Red River. In two days they reached The Forks of the Red where stood the new North West Company post of Fort Gibraltar, the home of Cuthbert's sister Josephte, wife of John Wills, the master of the fort.

Wills had spent many years in the fur trade. He had been with the XY Company and was one of the six wintering partners of this concern who entered the North West Company as partners when the two amalgamated in 1804. He then became an outstanding Nor'Wester, and a member of the exclusive Beaver Club in Montreal.[2]

The fort stood high above the surrounding country at the junction of the Red and Assiniboine rivers, the name, no doubt, being an allusion to its position at a strategic point on the country's water communications. It was an impressive establishment of considerable size which had taken twenty men nearly a year to build.

Within its stout palisades, eighteen feet high, were numerous buildings. Two houses, respectively thirty-six and twenty-eight feet in length, accommodated forty servants. There were stables, a carpenter and blacksmith shop, a meat-house, kitchens, and a store thirty-two feet long. On top of an icehouse was the fort's wooden watchtower, and in a central position stood the *bourgeois*'s large and comfortable house, sixty-four feet long. There, Grant's sister, Mrs Wills, reigned as chatelaine of the fort and there she entertained him as befitted a gentleman and her brother.

No doubt Grant had heard, in Montreal and at Fort William, rumours of the Hudson's Bay Company's scheme for an agricultural settlement in the vicinity of Gibraltar which was to be carried out by Lord Selkirk. He might even have heard that settlers from Scotland with their Governor, Miles Macdonell, were already on their way up the Red River.[3] But as he gazed over the prairies about him there was as yet no indication of the coming settlement – this threat to his company's trade that was also to influence his own life so largely.

During his first year in the west Grant was placed in charge of a small post attached to the Nor'Westers' Fort Espérance on the Qu'Appelle River.[4] There he was under the instructions of its master, John Pritchard.[5]

Grant must early have shown qualities of leadership, since, from the first, his company used him increasingly for special missions in their watch – it was not yet war – on the Hudson's Bay Company and on Selkirk's settlers.

Consequently, he was much at Fort Gibraltar, the Nor'Westers' headquarters in Red River.[6] Along his route, between Qu'Appelle and Gibraltar, lay the Hudson's Bay Company's Brandon House. There he met John Richards McKay whose father, John McKay, had been master of the post until his death in 1810. With John Richards was his sister Elizabeth, and the place soon became Grant's stopping place for more than one reason.

The two young men found many interests in common as both had been educated in the Old Country. McKay was blond, well set up, good-looking, and a general favourite. It was said that he was more popular with his customers than with his company who considered him too liberal a trader. He was also noted for his expert swordsmanship. The art of fencing had evidently been included in John Richards's education, since some years later when he proposed to open an academy in Red River he listed fencing in his curriculum. One can easily imagine the two young men testing each other's strength and skill with the sword, and one wonders if this facility had been part of Grant's education too.[7] At any rate it would be an excellent skill to practise in a country menaced by the Sioux, and any athletic or military prowess was useful in impressing the Indians and Métis. Grant in this sport was already showing those manly qualities which were to win him the admiration and respect of the native people. His quickness of motion and his light complexion led the Indians to call him "Wappeston," which means "White Ermine." The Indians intended this name as a tribute to Grant's agility and his fairness of skin.[8]

Cuthbert Grant and John Richards McKay became firm friends. It was a lasting friendship, one that was not to be terminated by the business conflicts or the family disruption of a later period.

The second attraction for Grant at Brandon House – one which, no doubt, came first with him – was McKay's sister Elizabeth, the "Bethsy" of Grant's later letter. His frequent journeys gave ample opportunity for their courtship, a courtship which reached its climax in 1814 with the only marriage possible at this time, a *mariage du pays*, since there were no clergy in the country.

In 1815 we have only a slight glimpse of the young couple. Peter Fidler, master of the Red River Colony's Fort Douglas, recorded that Bethsy, who had been staying there, had now gone over to be with Grant at Fort Gibraltar.[9] She probably went home to Qu'Appelle for the summer as this was the year their son was born, and Grant was much occupied with work for his company at the posts.

One wonders what Grant's thoughts and sentiments were as he returned to his native country, a grown man and an educated gentleman. As he was a bright boy of eight years when he left it, he must have remembered much. Perhaps in Scotland and Montreal he had remembered and longed for his boyhood way of life. Certainly he quickly adapted himself to fur trade life again. Not only did he win friendship and approval in the trade; he also quickly won the respect and loyalty of the Métis and the Indians. He won their hearts, not only as a *bourgeois* but as one proficient in the way of life of the plains, as horseman, hunter, and warrior. That he should have done so indicated unusual gifts of person and of mind. All these he was to need in the warfare that was kindling in the fur trade.

The background of that war was simple and written on the face of the country. The fur-traders regarded the Red and Assiniboine rivers as one system. The former was known as Lower, the latter as Upper, Red River. Lower Red River had never been a rich fur region, and its course from south to north had not made it of much use to the westward-pressing traders. But Upper Red River, curving as it did from north to east, with the wooded Duck and Riding Mountains to the north and the buffalo plains and the timbered plateau of Turtle Mountain to the south, drained a country rich in furs. But all the Red River country was now an inferior fur district. Its fur-bearers had been trapped since the 1680's when the French traders established themselves on Lake Superior and the English on Hudson Bay. Twice its beaver had been cleaned out, once by the French under La Vérendrye and once by the first North West traders in the 1770's and 1780's. When Hudson's Bay Company traders came in from Fort Albany on Hudson Bay by the Albany and English rivers in 1793 the pressure on the wild life of the region became very severe. John Tanner, the white boy raised as an Indian, tells in his *Narrative* of year after year of scanty hunting and frequent famine.[10]

As the fur resources of the Red River country dwindled, however, the traders pushed northwestward along the way opened by the elder Cuthbert Grant and Peter Pond to the Athabasca country. As the line of communication lengthened and the canoe brigades grew, it became more and more necessary to furnish food from the country for the brigades and the posts. A staple food was found in the pemmican made from the meat and fat of the buffalo on the plains of the Red River country. Thus as the country declined in importance as a fur region, it became more and more necessary to the trade as a source of provisions. It was its buffalo plains rather than its fur forests that made the Red River country significant to the fur-traders in 1812.[11]

It was for its provisions, then, more than for its furs that the two great fur companies maintained their rival posts in the Red River country. Since 1804 the North West Company had combined in one great concern all the fur-traders of Montreal. With plenty of capital, a strong and loyal corps of *engagés* from Lower Canada, the peerless Canadian canoe-men, and its hard-driving, confident partners and clerks kept eagerly loyal by hope of rising to be *bourgeois*, it held the Athabasca country and was occupying the Columbia River basin. Bold and aggressive, the partners claimed the northwest as their own by right of the French title of exploration and occupation. They denied the claim of the Hudson's Bay Company to Rupert's Land by its charter of 1670, but were content in practice merely to meet their slow-moving rivals in commercial competition. As the Bay men came in and built their posts one by one opposite the posts of the Nor'Westers, no such fierce or, occasionally, bloody rivalry broke out as had occurred among the competing Montreal traders before 1804. The men of the two companies traded post by post in watchful rivalry, often cloaked in forced conviviality as each strove to discover the other's plans. But the Nor'Westers were too sure of their superiority to resort to sterner measures against their weaker competitors. The "North West spirit," they were confident, would carry all before it as in the past.

It was this rivalry and the needs of provision and the fur trade which determined the distribution of posts in the Red River country. On Lower Red River above The Forks, there was the North West post and the Hudson's Bay Fort Skene where the Pembina River joined the Red.[12] Here the furs of the Red River country were collected, and buffalo hunted towards the Pembina hills.

Along the Upper Red the old posts at Portage des Prairies were abandoned, as was the post at Pine Creek in the Sand Hills. On the southern loop of the Assiniboine where it bordered the buffalo plains, the only active parts in 1812 were the Hudson's Bay Company's Brandon House on the north bank and the North West Company's La Souris on the south. This North West post took its name from the Souris River which joins the Assiniboine a few miles below the fort.[13] Higher still in the upper reaches of the Assiniboine were the two old posts, the North West's Fort de la Rivière Tremblante, Grant's birth-place, and the Hudson's Bay Company's Fort Hibernia. With them the borders of the Swan River country were reached. Westward up the Qu'Appelle stood the North West Fort Espérance and, close by, one of the Hudson's Bay Company. It was there that Grant was making his way in the summer of 1812.

At the posts on the edge of the plains, Espérance, La Souris, Brandon, Pembina, the pemmican was collected. The buffalo were hunted in the summer by the *engagés* of the posts and by their friends and relatives, the "freemen" and their half-breed sons. The freemen were *engagés* who had taken their discharge and remained in the northwest, held there by an Indian wife and half-breed children and the wild life they had come to prefer. Their children were called Métis, and sometimes *bois-brûlés* from their swarthy complexion. Even in their freedom they retained much of their dependence on the North West Company and remained in many ways its servants and natural allies. Casual workers, trappers and hunters like their Indian kin, the Métis had their sense of identity preserved by the connection with the company. As buffalo-hunting became more important, they began to specialize in it and to conduct their expeditions out onto the plains in an organized way.

More and more they gave up the stalking of the buffalo by indi-vidual hunters and began, like the plains Indians, to "run" the buffalo on horseback, shooting down the great beasts one after the other from the saddle. After a run, their women had days of work before them, cutting and drying the meat, pounding it to flakes, and stirring it with melted fat, tallow, and sometimes berries, in bags of green buffalo-hide.

Each spring the provisions posts would ready the rough boats made each winter by the post carpenter and send the pemmican down by them on the receding high waters of May and early June. Down the great valley of the Upper Red the brigades would file, through the narrow gorge of the Sand Hills and around the wandering loops of the flat Red River plains from Portage des Prairies. All, with those from Pembina, had to pass The Forks of the Red, dominated since 1810 by the high bastions of Fort Gibraltar. Here was the key to the rivers, to the pemmican trade and, in a measure, to the northwest fur trade.

From The Forks the North West boats went on to Bas de la Rivière, where their cargoes were stored for the brigades east and west. There the boats were burned, the nails collected from their ashes, and taken back to the Upper Red for use again in a country where iron was scarce.

Even with their growing trade in a rich food taken from the swarming buffalo of the plains, the food supply of the Red River country was precarious at best. Game and fish supplemented the diet of the posts, but the supply of both was subject to wide fluctuations. Even the buffalo were sometimes elusive, or the plains tribes hostile. Indian corn had just recently been introduced, and was seldom available. Potatoes and vegetables were grown at the posts, and by freemen, for sale at one or two places, such as The Forks. But all these additions to the staples of dried meat, meat frozen in the ice-houses, and pemmican, were slight and uncertain. The food resources of the Red River country would soon be severely strained if there should be any considerable increase in the number of mouths to be fed. Yet it was in the Red River country that the Hudson's Bay Company decided, with the help of Lord Selkirk, to found a colony. The colonists were, it is true, to grow food for the use of the Hudson's Bay Company in an effort to challenge the North West Company even in its preserve of the Athabasca. But they might not succeed at once, and would become dependent on the buffalo hunt for the means of survival.

To Selkirk the Hudson's Bay Company had granted a great tract of territory, to be called Assiniboia. It included, roughly speaking, the Red River country described above, down to the watershed of the Missouri and the Mississippi, eastward to the head of Rainy River, and with a northern boundary along the Rainy and Winnipeg rivers to the middle of Lake Winnipeg and westward across Winnipegosis to the headwaters of the Assiniboine. It included, in short, the country of Grant's birth and early childhood and of his adult life subsequent to 1812.

The North West Company viewed Selkirk's grant and his projected colony as a threat to their claims in the northwest and to their trade. In Scotland Alexander Mackenzie had tried strenuously to stop the recruiting of colonists for Red River. Despite his efforts, the first party had sailed in 1811, but had to winter on the Bay near York Factory. In the spring they came south to Red River, which they reached only in August, after Grant had ridden westward to Qu'Appelle.

The first party was made up of Scots and Irish labourers, who might or might not become colonists. Their leader was the colony's Governor, Miles Macdonell. Macdonell was a Canadian Scot from Glengarry. He was a Roman Catholic of Loyalist stock, and had served in the Canadian militia. Selkirk had come to know him while in Canada seeing to his colony at Baldoon.[14] He chose him as a man used to exercising authority, and as one knowing the country, although Macdonell had never been in the northwest or served in the fur trade. It was to prove a not altogether happy choice. Macdonell was to reveal himself as loyal, but not capable of inspiring loyalty; as reliable, but not too discerning of unreliability in others; as dogged in enterprise, but somewhat erratic in judgement. While familiar enough with the character of the men he commanded, he failed either to manage them by persuasion or to impose his personal authority upon them. In consequence, his government of the colony was to prove slack from the first and quite inadequate when difficulties developed.

This the future was to reveal. For the moment, the dominating fact was that he had reached Red River too late in the season to have much hope of growing a crop to feed his party or the first band of colonists, which sailed in the spring of 1812. Macdonell had to turn at once to the fur traders of both companies for succour, and to plan to have his people support themselves through the winter by hunting buffalo at Pembina. Thus the colony at once became a charge on the food supply of the Red River country. The scene was now set for the conflict with which the career of Mr Cuthbert Grant, clerk of the North West Company, was to be deeply involved for the next ten eventful years.

CHAPTER III

A LEADER OF THE MÉTIS,

1813-1815

W hile Grant was learning his new duties on the Qu'Appelle, and tasting in buffalo-hunt and prairie-ride the life of the plains and the fur trade, Miles Macdonell was busy making preparation for the first band of settlers to pass the winter at Pembina. He had chosen The Forks as the site of the colony. On Point Douglas, a broad point of land in a loop of the Red a mile north of The Forks, he had placed the colonial establishment which consisted of stores of goods and houses for the labourers and colonists. Some ground had been broken on the Point with the hoe and late sowings attempted. North from Point Douglas he planned to have the settlers' lots surveyed. Thus at the very key to the rivers, along the provision route from Qu'Appelle, Selkirk's colony was taking shape. In its labourers and settlers was a force which might, if Selkirk's purpose was antagonistic to the interests of the North West Company, stop the movement of pemmican from the Upper Assiniboine to Bas de la Rivière. And every new band of settlers would increase the threat.

Grant and his superior officer, John Pritchard, must have discussed from time to time the purpose of the colonizer and the prospects of the colony. Pritchard was a garrulous, optimistic man, whom his colleagues viewed with a slight distrust. He was skilful in all the ways of the fur trade and adept at wilderness life and travel. He had come to love the northwest, and to him the colony offered the possibility of retirement from the trade and a chance to live out his life in the Red River country. In fact Pritchard was a colonist at heart, eager to till the western soil, and he watched the colony with an anxious and growing affection.

To Grant it probably had no such appeal. Reared as a gentleman, he was content with the routine of the office, the management of free-men and their half-breed sons, and the sport of riding over the plains to shoot buffalo on the prairie or ducks along the lakes of the Qu'Appelle. To his youthful eyes the colony must have seemed not an interesting experiment in agriculture in a land where no one farmed but a mad venture which might become a nuisance, or even a danger, to the company. Such certainly was the Nor'Wester view, and Grant identified himself heart and soul with the company of which his father had been a *bourgeois*, which had seen to his own bringing up, and which had now opened a career to him. The colony he would watch with a personal indifference, but also with the hostility of a Nor'-Wester.

There is no mention of Grant visiting Selkirk's colony in the following summer of 1813, but it is probable that he did so. The labourers and colonists returned from Pembina in the spring of that year. The former were set to rearing the colonial establishment on Point Douglas, and the latter were assigned to the river lots laid out by Peter Fidler, surveyor and sometime postmaster of the Hudson's Bay Company's Brandon House. Fidler was now practically in charge of building and settlement, and in the following year he became a member of Macdonell's council.[1] The settlers, once on their lots, began to break land and sow. That done, they turned to building cabins; and soon a row of squat log houses ran from Point Douglas down the west bank of the Red.

The sowings of 1813, however, were to prove no more successful than the hurried efforts of 1812. Fortunately, perhaps, no colonists arrived to swell the number of mouths to be fed. Those who came in 1813, the Kildonan Settlers, were held at Churchill all winter. There was nothing for Macdonell to do, then, but to take his people once more to Pembina to live by the buffalo hunt.[2]

All this news, of course, would be brought to the Qu'Appelle by the express couriers of the Nor'Wester mail service, or learned from the gossip of the Red River freemen and Métis who had come out to the plains for the summer's hunting and trading. Grant would hear from Wills of Fort Gibraltar particularly; and Pritchard, longing to hear of the colony's growth, would canvass every traveller from The Forks. But there was in the news nothing to suggest that the colony was meant to harm the Nor'Westers' trade. The one great concern was how all the people were to be fed when the provisioning of the fur trade called for so much pemmican.

Grant had other things to do than worry about the future of Selkirk's colony. One by one he met his sisters as their husbands' affairs brought them to the Qu'Appelle. Awed as they might be by this brother who was a gentleman and a clerk of the company, they would question him about where he had been, the relatives who had befriended him, and all the treasured Scottish connection. Grant's brothers-in-law, François Morin and Pierre Falcon, proud men though they were in their own right and among their own people, looked up to the young man who had so high a place in the world of the company. The word went round that young Cuthbert had come back a *bourgeois* like his father, and once more the name of Grant was uttered in respect around the summer camp fires and in the winter cabins of the Upper Red River country. Young Mr Cuthbert Grant had come back to his own country, and the people who had known his father were slyly measuring the son to determine whether he was the man his father had been. As they talked with him at his post, and traded their pemmican, and watched him in the saddle and at the hunt, they found him to be a man they could trust, a real *bourgeois* who, while he kept his distance, would never forget them and never turn them away. And this knitting of bonds of trust between Grant and the *bois-brûlés* was just what the partners of the North West Company had had in mind when they sent Grant back to Upper Red River.

Grant's own loyalty to the company was kept bright by the presence of a similar post of the Hudson's Bay Company, a mere musket-shot from the Qu'Appelle. There the master of the post was now John Richards McKay, who struggled manfully to induce the Indians and Métis to bring their furs and pemmican to his trading room rather than to that of the Nor'Westers.[3] Even when he had scant success, his presence kept prices up, because both Indians and Métis had a keen sense of the value of competition to the seller's market. And sometimes an offended or cunning Indian would trade at the other post, leaving his debt to the rival unpaid. Then there might be trouble between the traders, and renewed efforts to win over the clients of the other with drink and cajolery.

The rivalry was keen, however, only when the winter's packs were brought in in the spring and the summer's pemmican in September. During the long winters the rivalry would become only a concealed watchfulness, and there would be much visiting back and forth, exchange of books, long hours of talk and, when a visit from another post gave occasion, night-long dancing and revelry. As McKay had as housekeeper his sister Elizabeth, the bachelors of the North West Company often drifted down to the Hudson's Bay trader's house and spent long hours by the fire, smoking their pipes and talking with the men – but really there to enjoy the company of the women. But Grant was secure in the possession of Bethsy's affection, and before long it was known through Upper Red River that they were lovers.

Little more is known of Grant and Bethsy's love, and there is no need to imagine that it in any way differed from the other quick, responsive romances of that wild country where civilized young people of the same station in life were so few. But if Grant and Bethsy were lovers in 1813, their romance was soon to be thwarted. Selkirk's colony came into conflict in 1814 with the North West Company, and a fur-traders' war was to be waged with mounting violence until the summer of 1816. In that war Grant was to emerge as leader of the half-breeds of Upper Red River.

The war between the Nor'Westers and the colony was not intended by either side. It grew out of the colony's need for food threatening the supply of pemmican for the North West brigades. It soon flared into a dispute between the rival claims of the North West and Hudson's Bay Companies to the Red River country. And as that country was the region which supplied provisions for the fur trade of the Athabasca country, where the Nor'Westers got the richest part of their furs, and which the Hudson's Bay Company now proposed to invade with the help of supplies from Red River, the war in the Red River country merged with the rivalry of the two great companies for the trade of the whole northwest.

It all began innocently enough with a measure taken by the worried and headstrong Governor Miles Macdonell. The winter at Pembina had been a difficult one. The buffalo had kept far out on the plains and the hunters had failed to do more than barely keep the colonists alive. They and the labourers were bitterly discontented. And the fur-traders of both companies were naturally preoccupied with ensuring that they had enough provisions to keep the trade going. Ahead was the summer of 1814, with the uncertainty of the pioneer crops at The Forks and the certainty of the arrival of a new band of colonists. How was the colony to be fed until the crops were harvested, and how was an increased body of settlers to be carried through the winter of 1814, especially if the crops failed? These were the worries that harassed Macdonell, and he set himself to meet his difficulties by acting without consultation and without due regard to the interests of the Nor'-Westers.

In January, 1814, as Governor of Assiniboia he issued a proclamation by which he prohibited the export of pemmican from Assiniboia except by licence from himself. The results of this act were two. One was to place the supply of pemmican for the North West Athabasca brigades at the discretion of the Governor of Assiniboia, which to the Nor'Westers meant at the discretion of the Hudson's Bay Company. The second was to assert the authority of the Governor of Assiniboia in an inescapable manner over the Red River country. That authority, in the eyes of Macdonell and his employer, Lord Selkirk, derived from the Hudson's Bay Company's charter of 1670. By that charter the officials of the Company were lords of the soil and rulers, under the British Crown, of all Red River. Macdonell and his officers could enforce their proclamation by arrest and deportation for trial in the courts of the United Kingdom.

This claim to jurisdiction and proprietorship the Nor'Westers flatly denied. The Red River country, they claimed, was French-Canadian by right of French exploration and occupation. It had passed with Canada to the British crown by the Treaty of Paris in 1763. Almost at once it had been reoccupied by their predecessors from Montreal—twenty-five years before a servant of the Hudson's Bay Company had set foot in the Red River country. They could point to the Canada Jurisdiction Act of 1803, by which crimes committed in "the Indian country" were to be tried in the courts of Canada. If Macdonell could arrest and deport for that cause, so could they under commissions as Justices of the Peace obtained in Lower Canada.

Because of the Athabasca trade, because of their claim to trade in Red River, the Nor'Westers could not but view Macdonell's proclamation as a challenge which must be met promptly and forcefully. Indeed they had other reasons for concern. The War of 1812 was now two years old and, while Detroit and Michilimackinac had fallen to British troops and North West Company volunteers in 1812, by 1813 Detroit had been recaptured by the Americans and the supply of corn for Fort William cut off. Red River pemmican would be needed for the route from Rainy Lake to Fort William as well as for the Saskatchewan. For these reasons the Nor'Westers resolved, when the news of the Pemmican Proclamation came down to Fort William, to act with all the old North West spirit.[4]

Commissions as Justice of the Peace were obtained for certain of the partners under the Canada Jurisdiction Act. Commissions such as Archibald Norman Macleod[5] held in the Voyageurs Corps, although it was already disbanded, were obtained for others. Duncan Cameron, practically in charge of Fort Gibraltar as John Wills was ill, was made a captain. Alexander Greensfield Macdonell,[6] a cousin of the Governor in the service of the North West Company, was made a lieutenant. He was ordered to Fort Espérance to succeed Pritchard, who had retired to become a colonist. Thus on the eve of the fur-traders' war Grant acquired a daring, aggressive man as his new superior. Finally, Seraphim Lamar, a Canadian clerk posted at Gibraltar, was made an ensign. These titles, however dubious and eked-out by borrowed regimentals such as the major's uniform A. N. MacLeod lent Cameron, were meant to equal Miles Macdonell's commissioned rank as captain, and to impress the Indians and *bois-brûlés*.[7]

The partners doubtless felt more than justified in having taken these measures when they learned how vigorously Miles Macdonell had proceeded to enforce his proclamation. When he learned that the Nor'Westers had decided to defy it, he blocked the passage of the

Assiniboine above Fort Gibraltar with a battery of guns, no less.[8] This was war indeed. When a party of Nor'Westers coming down with pemmican discovered the obstacle and cached their cargo up the river at a place known as White Horse Plain, Macdonell sent the Sheriff of Assiniboia, John Spencer,[9] to discover and seize it. Early in June the sheriff was also sent up the river to the Souris, where he seized more of the Nor'Westers' pemmican. The Nor'Westers reacted by collecting their servants and some *bois-brûlés* at Fort Gibraltar. Under the command of Duncan Cameron, Cuthbert Grant and William Shaw were active in an attempt to capture Miles Macdonell.[10] When the Fort William brigade arrived under John McDonald of Garth,[11] Macdonell was outnumbered. McDonald then proceeded to negotiate an agreement by which Macdonell licensed the export of two hundred bags of pemmican by the North West Company, in return for an undertaking that he should be given an equivalent supply of fresh meat for his colonists in the coming winter.

The first trial of strength thus ended peacefully and indecisively. But the Nor'Westers had not the least intention, once the provisions for the brigade of 1814 were assured, of acknowledging the pretensions of Miles Macdonell and his superiors. Duncan Cameron at Gibraltar, with Alexander Macdonell at Qu'Appelle, at once began a campaign planned earlier in Montreal and Fort William. Their strategy was simple. The Hudson's Bay Company officers and men, with the colonists, outnumbered the Nor'Westers at all seasons but June, when the brigades were passing The Forks and Bas de la Rivière. At all other seasons the key to the situation was therefore the adherence of the freemen and their half-breed sons, the *Jeunes Gens*, the "Young Fellows," of the Red River country. Most of them were attached by tradition and casual employment to the North West Company. The policy of the Nor'Westers was to use the freemen and the Métis to drive out the colonists and the Hudson's Bay Company.

It was not an easy matter to arrange. Not all the freemen and natives were Nor'Westers in sympathy. There were already some Hudson's Bay Company half-breeds attached to that company either by birth or employment. The freemen, especially the older men from Lower Canada, were quite independent. They knew their rights. They also knew and feared the law under which they had grown up and for which they preserved, even in the Indian country, an abiding respect. Their disposition, then, was to avoid trouble and to remain neutral in the conflict they saw beginning. Often in the next two years the freemen would slip quietly away to the plains to spend the summer peacefully hunting and trading, away from the warfare along the rivers.

Their half-breed sons, however, were wilder by disposition and more easily influenced. It was to win their loyalty and to inflame their feelings against the colony that Cameron and Alexander Macdonell now addressed themselves. Almost at once Governor Macdonell played into their hands. As has been noted, the *bois-brûlés* hunted the buffalo by running them on horseback, as did the plains Indians. This was their preference and, they held, their right. The effect, however, was to drive the buffalo away from Lower Red River, and make it difficult for the colony's hunters to stalk the herds and bring in the meat. Another result, perhaps intended, was that hunting buffalo was becoming the monopoly of the Métis horsemen. Governor Macdonell was afraid that the colony's food supply would suffer. In July, acting on a sly suggestion from Cameron,[12] he issued a second proclamation by which he forbade the running of buffalo. The Métis were furious at this interference with their rights, and began to see the colony and Macdonell's claim to govern the Red River country as a menace to their way of life.

Their anger was fed by Cameron and Alexander Macdonell. These two, in long talks with the *bois-brûlés*, pointed out that the colony was founded on two claims. One was the ownership of the soil of the Red River District, the other a right to govern all who lived in the country. But, they went on, were not the *bois-brûlés*, through their Indian mothers, participants in the Indian title to the land, which had not been extinguished by treaty? And were not the *bois-brûlés*, like the Saulteaux, or the Crees, or the Assiniboines, their mothers' people, themselves a tribe with rights like the Indians, a free people not to be governed but to be treated with? Were they not the new nation of the northwest? The Métis listened and talked over among themselves these exciting new ideas.[13] They liked them. The suggestions accorded with their idea of themselves. They assented. And so the alliance between the Nor'Westers and the *bois-brûlés* against Selkirk's colony began.

It was, however, as yet but a vague and wavering thing, a matter of hint and insinuation only. It had to be cemented.

To this work Cameron and Macdonell bent themselves in the fall of 1814. If they were to make a new nation, they must provide it with leaders. Who could be better than the half-breed sons of partners of the company? And what better way to make a man an acceptable leader than to bestow on him a military title like their own, if of even more doubtful validity. Duncan Cameron, whether at Gibraltar or Qu'Appelle is not known, now made Cuthbert Grant "a captain of the Métis." He seems also to have made William Fraser, Angus Shaw, and

Nicholas Montour, other sons of partners, and clerks or interpreters of the company, officers at the same time.[14]

Even if Grant was only one of four captains of the Métis, however, he was now cast for the role he was to play in the fur-traders' war. A clerk of the company, he had been chosen both because of his standing as a clerk and a gentleman and because of his ties of blood with the Métis to lead them in their alliance with the Nor'Westers in the fur-traders' war. He was to help bind the *bois-brûlés* to the cause of the company, and with their help to remove from the life-line of Upper Red River the menace of the colony at The Forks. He was to lead the Métis in rejecting the claims of Selkirk to the Red River country by asserting those of the Métis. With the eagerness of youth and the unquestioning loyalty of the clansmen, he made his *bourgeois'* cause his own and passionately identified himself with the campaign to drive the colonists from Red River. By so doing he was also to identify himself with the new Métis nation, and stands at the beginning of their history as Louis Riel stands at the end.

But at the same time, Grant was to make himself and the *bois-brûlés* the dupes and tools of the Nor'Westers. It was a fact he did not perceive in his youthful enthusiasm, because the North West Company and the *brûlés* seemed to have a common interest in resisting the establishment of the colony. So Grant thought, and so he acted. Later, when he found the Nor'Westers disposed to shift the blame for the violence that arose out of the resistance, his loyalty began to falter, and he was to become in the end the champion of the Métis, and of the Métis alone.

The bond that was knitting between Grant and the Métis was one of sympathy and mutual loyalty, founded on respect. As the Métis gave him their trust which once given to anyone was rarely withdrawn, so he responded with his own most outstanding trait, a simple, unswerving fidelity. Just as it was natural for sons of his father's companions and servants to give him the loyalty their fathers had given his, so it was natural for him to return an equal loyalty. And that loyalty to his Métis followers was of a piece with his allegiance to the North West Company. A youthful and impetuous loyalty to the company and the Métis is the key to the part he played in the stormy events of the next four years.

It is, in fact, not too much to say that the loyalty of Grant to the company, and of the Métis to Grant, was the decisive element in the course of the next two years. That the Métis would support the Nor'-Westers in driving out the colonists was by no means certain in 1814. The Hudson's Bay Company men and Miles Macdonell might well have induced some of the Métis and freemen to defend the colony. Grant's readiness to follow the plans of his superiors and to use his growing influence with the Métis to rally them to the cause of the North West Company and of their own rights in the soil was to be the principal factor in the Nor'Westers' harrying of Selkirk's colony.

The Nor'Westers under Duncan Cameron and Alexander Macdonell began their campaign in the fall of 1814. They did not use the methods of open warfare. What they employed were the old tactics of the competitive fur trade. Their rivals were to be cajoled, bribed, badgered, and intimidated into withdrawing. It was their hope that such methods would suffice, as indeed they might unless met by a determined resistance. If that occurred, then the harrying would result in actual war.

Accordingly Duncan Cameron arrived at Fort Gibraltar on September 1 with a flag flying and himself in regimentals, as were his officers, Grant among them. He began to urge the Métis to run the buffalo as he, Cameron said, not Macdonell, was chief in Red River.[15] After thus rousing the Métis, he spent much of the winter talking with those colonists who remained at The Forks. His door was always open, his fire blazing, his bottle near, for those who chose to call. He welcomed them open-armed, talked to them in the Gaelic and pressed them to come again. When need arose, he gave them supplies. And the talk always came around to the rigours of the iron country to which they had come, the folly of Lord Selkirk's experiment, the tyranny of Miles Macdonell, and the fairer prospects of a settler's life in Canada. But it was far away: there would be room in the company's canoes. But one had no silver: the company would make advances and not press too hard for repayment. By June 1815, forty-two had agreed to accept passage to Canada, and were warmly attached to the cause of Cameron, their deliverer from the wiles of Selkirk and the snows of Red River.[16]

While Cameron persuaded his colonists at The Forks to desert, Miles Macdonell was striving to provide for those at Pembina. The Métis had continued to run the buffalo, defying the Governor's proclamation. Meat became scarce at Pembina in January 1815, in part because the buffalo herds had been driven off by the Métis running them. Macdonell went up the Red to the Métis camp at Turtle River to obtain meat and to warn the Métis of the penalties of defying his proclamation. But Grant had preceded him and encouraged them to continue to disobey. In consequence, they refused to listen to Macdonell, and ran John McLeod of the Hudson's Bay Company service out of their camp. When the Métis' leader, Peter Pangman, commonly known as Bostonais after a Yankee father, was arrested by Macdonell's officers on McLeod's complaint on March 19, Grant with a party of twenty-seven men retaliated by seizing four of the Governor's men, including an officer of the colonial establishment, Mr John Warren. Both sides now had hostages, and the matter might well have led to violence. But neither the harassed Macdonell nor the cool-headed Grant wished to proceed to extremes. Civilities were interchanged, and Grant on March 31 politely carried out an exchange of the prisoners.[17] So the affair ended, but the Métis had been championed by Grant in their right to run the buffalo. And in April there was open resort to violence at Red River.

It began when a body of the colonists who had agreed to go to Canada were persuaded by Cameron to seize a large part of the guns and a number of muskets in the colonial establishment at Point Douglas and remove them to Fort Gibraltar. He had little difficulty persuading them, as they were exasperated by Miles Macdonell's vacillating rule and by the harsh discipline of his lieutenant at The Forks, Archibald Macdonald. They said they took the arms to prevent a repetition of the dangerous and illegal violence Macdonell had used when he planted his battery in 1814 to block the pemmican-boats on the Assiniboine. Macdonell retorted by arming his men. There were arrests, forced releases, and renewed arrests. On April 5 Grant led a party to Point Douglas to liberate a servant of the establishment who had helped carry away the artillery and had been confined for so doing. Grant hotly denied that the man could be held without warrant. A period of demonstrations and threats followed. Both Cameron and Macdonell paraded their men on the plain between the establishments in threatening demonstration of their military might. Reinforcements of officers and servants of both companies came in from the posts on the Red and Assiniboine.[18]

Miles Macdonell and Archibald Macdonald proved no match for the clever and slippery Cameron, and for Grant with his command of the Métis. Not only had they failed to keep the loyalty of a large part of the colonists, they now failed to rally any of the English half-breeds to their side, either as allies or as intermediaries between them and the unattached Métis. Their only staunch friend outside the colonial establishment on Point Douglas and the loyal colonists was the Indian chief, Peguis – "Peguis, the Cutnose Bungee chief," as Fidler described him.[19] Peguis was chief of the small band of Saulteaux and Swampy Cree Indians who had themselves recently settled near the mouth of the Red River, and who welcomed the colonists as friends and helpers in the unfamiliar task of leading a settled life. As a result of the failure to win recruits, the colony's forces failed to grow as April and May passed and the Nor'Westers grew steadily stronger.

Grant remained at Fort Gibraltar during these spring months, rally-ing the Métis with the aid of the three other half-breed clerks who, like himself, were sons of North West *bourgeois* – William Fraser, Angus Shaw, and Nicholas Montour. They drove home to the minds of their wild Young Fellows the idea that Cameron and Alexander Mac-donell had begun to circulate the autumn before. The Métis were, they assured them, lords of the soil and a new nation not bound by the pretended laws of Miles Macdonell and his colony, whose claim to the land and to the power to make laws was a violation of their rights in the soil and of their liberty as a free people. The Métis listened and were convinced, and Grant himself, who may well have believed all he said, did certainly think that the claims of the Hudson's Bay Company and Selkirk were a usurpation.

During the violence of these spring days, his romance with Bethsy McKay once more enters the story. At Point Douglas Peter Fidler was at work on the buildings of the colonial establishment, and daily wrote up his journal. On May 22 he wrote that Elizabeth McKay had run off from Point Douglas to join her lover, Cuthbert Grant.[20]

By the end of May the Nor'Westers were ready to begin the actual harrying of the colonists from Red River. On May 28 the sentries in the colonial buildings on Point Douglas fired on a band of Nor'Westers prowling near-by. On June 7 Grant and his fellow chiefs established a camp of Métis at Frog Plain (later Kildonan) four miles below Point Douglas. Here the prairie ran down to the west river-bank to a point where a slight curve gave command of a broad stretch of the river. The camp was set up to blockade the colony and prevent either escape to Lake Winnipeg or reinforcement from the north. The reason the Nor'Westers gave was that they had a warrant for the arrest of Miles Macdonell and desired to prevent his escape. On the same day, June 7, forty-two colonists left for Canada in North West canoes, and no doubt Grant's march to Frog Plain covered their departure.[21]

Now the Métis began to invest Point Douglas, not by a close siege, but by ambushes and skirmishings. Settlers were fired at, cattle driven off, the sowers frightened from the fields. On June 10 there was an exchange of fire at Point Douglas, and the next night the colonial estab-lishment was fired on by the Métis. Grant was later named as one of the attackers. Macdonell replied with musketry and his remaining artillery. Three of the defenders were wounded, and John Warren died from the explosion of a swivel-gun.[22]

It seems that these manoeuvres and brushes had two purposes: to cover the passage of the pemmican-boats and canoe brigades, and to harry the colonists out of the country.

The North West officers protested, however, that they desired only the surrender of Macdonell to their warrant, not the destruction of the colony. Macdonell disbelieved this but, to satisfy his worried council and to expose the deceit, he left Point Douglas and went into hiding. Despite his disappearance, the Métis continued to harass the settlement, stealing horses and dragging off the ploughs and harrows left in the fields. Desertions from the colony were resumed under this terror. When Macdonell had come out of hiding, only sixteen settlers with eighteen Hudson's Bay Company men were left, and the council insisted that Macdonell surrender in return for a promise to spare the settlement. Macdonell at last agreed, and on June 17 gave himself up. The North West partner present at Gibraltar, Hugh McKenzie,[23] agreed that the attack on the colony would cease. On June 22 Macdonell left for Canada under arrest.[24]

The Métis and their leaders were not a party to the agreement. Grant and the other captains were in fact under North West orders to destroy the colony and restore the old state of affairs. But the orders were to be carried out through the Métis and in their name as a free native people. The left hand was not to know what the right hand had done. It would seem that there can be little doubt that there was conscious duplicity. Grant was a party to this ruse of war, and saw it as a legitimate means of defence for the rights of the company and the Métis.

The result after Macdonell's arrest on June 17 was, therefore, that his successor as head of the colony, Peter Fidler, had to negotiate a new agreement with the leaders of the Métis. In their camp at Frog Plain they held the colony in their grip, and they now demanded the evacuation of the colony and the departure of the Hudson's Bay Company. But some English half-breeds, prompted by Peter Fidler, induced them to moderate their demands, probably by pointing out the advantage to the Métis and Indians of having rival companies to trade with. On June 20 Pangman told Fidler that no colonists would be allowed to remain, but that a limited number of Hudson's Bay Company servants might do so, if the company's officers would undertake to pay an annual tribute to the Métis. The leaders and Métis in council would yield no more, however, and on June 22 the attacks on the settlement were renewed. This time the purpose was destruction. Several of the colonists' houses were fired, and men later deposed that Grant and Shaw were the first to set the torch to the cabins.[25]

Chief Peguis now tried to intervene on behalf of the colony, but without effect. He was made bearer on June 24 of an order to Fidler to leave with the colonists. It was signed by the four chiefs: Cuthbert

Grant, William Shaw, Peter Pangman, and Bonhomme [Nicholas] Montour. On June 25 Fidler replied by proposing the following terms:

Proposals of Peace delivered by us to the Half Breeds, 25th June, 1815.

Peace.

In the year of our Lord 1815 this 25th Day June & of His Majesty's Reign the Fifty Sixth. 1st. It is hereby promised that peace & amity shall hereafter ever exist between the people of this Settlement and the Half Breeds & that all that has been done on both sides shall be forgiven.

2nd. It is furthermore agreed that the Half Breeds shall ever enjoy the full liberty of running Buffalo and living according to the custom in which they have been brought up.

3rd. And it is also agreed that they shall not be subject to any Local Laws that may be hereafter established unless they finding the good effects of living a civilized life shall come forward and ask to be admitted into our society, then they shall be considered as one of us and shall enjoy all the Privileges we may possess.

4th. And it is further promised that whatever presents may be given annually to the Indians, that the Half Breeds shall have an equal share in them.

Red River Settlement, 25th June, 1815.[26]

Grant and the other captains rejected Fidler's proposals and sent back a copy of their own. They were in fact an ultimatum, and Fidler and his lieutenant, Surgeon James White,[27] had no choice but to sign, with the victorious captain of the Métis, the terms of a treaty which asserted the rights of the Métis and achieved the aims of the North West Company.

1. All settlers to retire immediately from this river, and no appearance of a colony to remain.

2. Peace and amity to subsist between all parties, traders, Indians, and freemen, in future, throughout these two rivers, and on no account any person to be molested in his lawful pursuits.

3. The honourable Hudson's Bay Company will, as customary enter this river with, if they think proper, from three to four of their former trading boats, and from four to five men per boat as usual.

4. Whatever former disturbance has taken place between both parties, that is to say, the honourable Hudson's Bay Company and the Halfbreeds of the Indian territory, to be totally forgot and not to be recalled by either party.

5. Every person retiring peaceable from this river immediately, shall not be molested in their passage out.

6. No person passing the summer for the Hudson's Bay Company, shall remain in the buildings of the company but shall retire to some other spot, where they will establish for the purpose of trade.

> Cuthbert Grant,
> Bostonais Pangman,
> Wm. Shaw,
> Bonhomme Montour,
> The four chiefs of the
>   Half-breeds,
> James Sutherland,
> James White.[28]

Red River Indian Territory, Forks, Red River, 25 June, 1815.

When the treaty was signed, Fidler ordered the settlers to get their effects together and muster at the boats, one of which was the colony's schooner, *Cuchillon*. John McLeod and some Hudson's Bay men were left to watch the goods of the Hudson's Bay Company and, as it turned out, the crops.[29] Then, as the boats dropped down the Red, the colonists watched the smoke rolling up from the last of their cabins and the whooping *brûlés* racing their buffalo-runners through the plots of tender wheat and barley. The Nor'Westers, the *brûlés*, and Mr Cuthbert Grant — clerk, captain, and chief — had "cleared the two rivers" of colony and company.[30]

Thereafter, except for the establishment at Fort Gibraltar, the Nor'-Westers and most of the Métis left The Forks. Grant returned with Bethsy to his post on the Qu'Appelle. The site of the colony was deserted during mid-summer of 1815. Only John McLeod of the Hudson's Bay Company at Point Douglas saw that the Métis had not done their work of destruction well. The trampled wheat and barley shot up strongly in the Red River sun, and the potatoes made dark green patches on the prairie.

The work of destruction was indeed soon to be undone. The colony so pitilessly destroyed was suddenly restored. On August 19 a brigade of boats filed slowly up the Red, bringing back the colonists. They were led by Colin Robertson. Robertson was a former Nor'Wester, a bold, restless, self-confident man, whom the Hudson's Bay Company had engaged to assist in its great enterprise to invade the Athabasca.[31] When Robertson found the ejected colonists at the north end of Lake Winnipeg, he decided that the restoration of the colony was a vital part of the Athabasca campaign. Accordingly he led them back, along with eighty-four new colonists and forty labourers. And Robertson came not only with reinforcements, but with ideas. He knew how to handle the Métis. He knew they were the key to victory in the war of the fur companies in the Red River country. He would win them away from the Nor'Westers. Grant now had a rival far more formidable than the uncertain Macdonell or plodding Fidler.

Robertson soon met the freemen and Métis at Red River, some thirty men in twelve lodges, encamped at Frog Plain. He blandly told them that he had come to Red River to hire Canadians for an expedition to the Athabasca. The man's policy was embodied in this casual explanation of his presence in Red River. Robertson, as an old Nor'Wester, knew the Métis, and he would treat them as the Nor'Westers did, as an independent third party who were to be consulted, flattered, and engaged on their own terms. He saw that if they could be won from their old alliance with the North West Company, the Nor'Westers would be easily defeated. Accordingly, when he had resettled the colonists, Robertson proceeded to woo the Métis.

The colony, he assured them, was not a threat to their existence, but an alternative market for the produce of the hunt. The Métis listened. They complained that Miles Macdonell had never given them a drink or asked them in to warm themselves.[32] Robertson gave them drink and kept an open house. Tongues loosened, and even the Nor'Wester, Seraphim Lamar,[33] confessed that Cameron had induced Macdonell to prohibit the running of the buffalo.[34]

Then on September 4 Cuthbert Grant came down from Qu'Appelle to see what mischief was afoot. The Métis flocked to greet him, but he received them coldly. He knew that they were wavering in their allegiance. When old Deschamps, a freeman, told him what Robertson had told them, that Cameron had put the whole blame for the destruction of the colony on the Métis, Grant replied that he would not believe Cameron guilty of such a thing.[35] And after Grant came Cameron himself, who proceeded to praise the Métis for their good work of the spring and to distribute presents among them. But his efforts, like those of Grant, failed to lure the Métis away from Robertson's new-won influence. Robertson was aided by the fact that the Nor'Westers, thinking they had Red River to themselves, had stripped it of goods for the Athabasca, and the Métis could not obtain the supplies they wanted. Accordingly they were annoyed.[36]

Robertson's tactics at Red River, the separation of the Métis from the Nor'Westers, soon affected the strategy of the great struggle. He was responsible for the provisioning and defence of the colonists and the few servants of the Hudson's Bay Company. Robertson now converted the buildings on Point Douglas into Fort Douglas by building a palisade with a watch-tower. He did this in order to be able to concentrate the colonists for defence. He then carefully collected the crops whose yield was still heavy in spite of the trampling of the Métis and the flocks of birds. With his growing influence on the Red River Métis he was thus secure at The Forks. But the main staple of the colony would still have to be the meat and pemmican of the plains hunt, and the Nor'Westers might yet starve Red River into submission by cutting off the supplies from Pembina and the Qu'Appelle.

Meantime Alexander Macdonell and Grant had returned from Red River and taken up their winter headquarters at the Qu'Appelle post. James Sutherland of the Hudson's Bay Company's near-by post described their coming.

> Freemen and Half Breeds forming two distinct companies. Macdonell led one of these consisting of Canadians with colours flying, the other Company were Half Breeds headed by Cuthbert Grant, a Half Breed who has been regularly educated at Canada and has acted for several years as clerk, and still continues to act as such, to the N.W. Co. This Tribe had another Flag hoisted of what Nation I know not. It is red with a figure of 8 placed horizontally in the middle of it and is said to be a present from the N.W. Co. along with Some Swords and a few pairs of Pistols to these deluded young men, the Half Breeds as a recompense for their exertions against the colony, Spring 1815 . . .[37]

After this colourful arrival, Grant settled down for the winter. With him was his wife, Bethsy, and his sister Mrs Wills. In the face of North-West opposition Bethsy's brother, John Richards McKay, had rebuilt the Hudson's Bay post, burned – allegedly by accident – in the summer, and was now maintaining it despite threats and pressure.[38] Even in the comfort and peace of the winter and across the bonds of kinship the fur-traders' war went on; for the pemmican McKay traded was needed to feed the colony, and if Macdonell and Grant could prevent it reaching The Forks, the re-established colony would be in jeopardy.

When therefore Robertson received word on October 14 that Alexander Macdonell of the North West Company had attacked the Hudson's Bay Company's provisions post on the Qu'Appelle River (an exaggerated report, no doubt, of the arrival described above) he reacted sensitively and decided to strike. The next day he seized Fort Gibraltar in retaliation. No Métis stirred to help the Nor'Westers at this bold stroke. Duncan Cameron submitted meekly, and promised that the Qu'Appelle post would not be molested again. Robertson thereupon restored Gibraltar to Cameron and Lamar.[39]

Robertson was then well in command of the situation at Red River when in November there arrived the new Governor-in-Chief of Rupert's Land, Mr Robert Semple,[40] and his staff — the Sheriff of Assiniboia, a second Alexander Macdonell,[41] Lieutenant Holte,[42] late of the Swedish Navy, and Captain Rogers[43] of the Royal Engineers — together with a new party of colonists. Semple was of American birth, a travelled man, an author of some experience in business, and of a capacity not unequal to the responsibilities of his position. He was, however, somewhat impulsive, yet at the same time stiff and unimaginative. Holte and Rogers were to prove to be narrow-minded and hard-drinking fellows. The success of Robertson's policy, so far effective, would now depend upon whether Semple and his officers could at least refrain from destroying Robertson's influence over the Métis.

That influence was now considerable. At Fort Daer on the Pembina, Bostonais, or Pangman, the Métis chief, was hunting for the colonists and was entirely reconciled to the colony. Robertson was therefore pleased to see Semple begin to pay attention to the Métis as well as to the Indians. ". . . separate these men," he wrote gleefully, "from the N. W. Co. and they are gone."[44]

To these efforts of Robertson's, Grant had to make such opposition as he could from Qu'Appelle. From there he and Macdonell were rallying the North West brûlés to assemble in the spring for the destruction of the colony. The fur-traders' war on the Red now embraced all the northwest fur country. But the bois-brûlés of Red River must be kept from Robertson's wiles. In December Alex Fraser was sent to Gibraltar to help Cameron and Lamar, and Grant wrote the latter urging him to keep the brûlés true to the North West cause.

Fort John, 2nd December, 1815

My dear sir,

As Mr. Fraser goes down the river I shall not attempt to give you any news, as Mr. Fraser will inform you better than I can hope to do. But speaking of this new Governor, he gives every indication that we shall really be forced to shut him up if we are to spoil his game – he has indeed attempted everything he can, but what most annoys me at present is the advantage he takes of your want of everything. But we must hope that our turn will come when that he will be paid with a vengeance. As for McLean, he will laugh on the other side of his face. Give my best wishes to all the Young Fellows of the *bois-brûlés* that you see and you must impress on them that they keep up their courage and take good care what they do for come spring we shall see the *bois-brûlés* from Fort des Prairies [Edmonton] and from all sides. Impress on them too that I hope that their behaviour during the winter will not be dishonourable on their side. Send my very best regards to old Hesse and tell him to do his utmost to hearten the Young Fellows. As I have no special news to tell you, I shall close by wishing you a peaceful winter.

I am

My dear sir,

Your most obedient Servant,

Cuthbert Grant.[45]

Mon. Seraphim Lamar
N.W. Co.,
The Forks.

The winter passed without event on the Red River. Bostonais Pangman was almost won over to become an active defender of the colony. At Fort Douglas in March Robertson could report that the freemen, some Métis, and all the Indians had adopted the cause of the colony. But he was worried about the situation on the Qu'Appelle. If provisions were short there, he would have to seize Fort Gibraltar for its provisions, for the supplies of the colony were already running low, and word came in at the end of February 1816 that Métis at Pembina were driving buffalo away.[46]

On December 17 Semple set out from The Forks on a tour of inspection of the Hudson's Bay Company posts in Assiniboia. By January he had reached Brandon House. On February 2 he wrote to Grant, who was in charge at Qu'Appelle while Macdonell was absent, requesting that the cannon taken in the spring of 1815 be returned. He threatened decisive measures if they were not.[47] Macdonell on his return replied that the guns would not be supplied unless those taken from the North

West Company were also returned. When Semple himself went to Qu'Appelle early in March, he tried once more, sending John Richards McKay and Chrysologue Pambrun to demand the restoration of the guns and the surrender of the post. Grant told them: "Come and get it. You will meet with the reception such conduct deserves."[48] Semple then wrote to The Forks expressing fear that the Nor'Westers intended trouble. He was right in his fears, as two letters of Grant's written on March 13 clearly indicated.

River Qu'Appelle, 13th March, 1816

My dear sir:

As the express is to start tomorrow morning I shall take the liberty of addressing you a few lines and at the same time to inform you of our countrymen at Fort Despreries [des Prairies] I am happy to inform you that they are all [illegible] and staunch and ready to obey our commands [.] They have sent one of them here to see how things stood and to know weather [sic] it was necessary that they should all come which of course I send [sic] word that they should all be here about the first of May. The Half Breeds have killed 3 Stone Indians at Fort Despreries which were come to steal their Horses. As for the Half Breeds of the English [Churchill] River Mr. Shaw [h]as gathered the whole of them, as they come by water, I do not know which time they will be at the Forks.

You must know that Robertson's famous Clarke is gone to pot his men have all left him tired of their diet of hunger and the rest are always in danger of being cut of [sic] by the Natives there which will give Robertson a terrible fever when he'll hear of it.

All I have to say now is that [illegible] of you and Bostonais to help the Half Breeds below [illegible] if possible. As for those here I am sure of them excepting Mr. Hoole which I gave a set down this morning and Broke him. You will please to give my respectful compliments to Bostonais and to Mr. Seraphim as I have no time to write him.

Mr. McDonnel from Swan River arrived here the day before yesterday he's always playing the Fiddle and he's 90 — to give us a Kick up tonight — will receive better information from Cameron of the News from the North than I can pretend to give you, I shall conclude wishing you health and happiness.

I remain,

Mr. Alex. Fraser,   Yours sincerely
Forks, Red River.   Cuthbert Grant.[49]

At the same time Grant wrote his oft-quoted letter to J. D. Cameron at Sault Ste Marie:

> River Qu'Appelle 13th March 1816
>
> My Dear Sir
>
> I received your generous & kind letter last fall, by the last Canoe; I should certainly be an ungrateful being, should I not return you my sincerest thanks; altho a very bad hand at writing Letters, but I trust to your generosity; I am as yet safe and sound thank God, for I believe its more than [Colin] Robertson or any of his suit dare to offer the least insult to any one of the Bois Brûlés; altho' Robertson made use of some expressions, which I hope he shall swallow in the Spring – he shall see that it is neither 15, thirty nor fifty of his best Horsemen that can make the Bois Brûlés bow down to him – The Half Breeds of Fort Dauphin, de Pra[i]ries & English river are all to be here in the spring, it is hoped we shall come off with flying colours and never see any of them again in the Colonizing way in Red River, in fact the Traders shall pack off with themselves also, for having disregarded our orders last spring; according to our arrangements, we are to remain at The Forks & pass the Summer for fear they should play us the same trick as last Summer of coming back, but they shall receive a warm reception. I am loth to enter into any particulars as I am well assured you will receive a more satisfactory information than I have had from your other correspondents – Therefore I shall not pretend to give you any; at the same time begging you will excuse my short Letter, I shall conclude wishing you health and happiness
>
>> I shall ever remain
>> My Dear Sir
>> Your most obedient Humble Servant
>> (Signed) CUTHBERT GRANT
>
> My sister & Betsy
> return their most
> respectful compliments[50]
>
> To J. D. Cameron Esqr.

The young chief might boast of how his people would conduct themselves, but he also referred to a well-planned campaign that was designed to destroy the Red River colony beyond renewal. And Grant by his education, his firmness and his loyalty, was now to be chief of the Métis, who were lords of the soil of the northwest and its masters. At the end of March his position was formally recognized.

The occasion for the announcement of his appointment was the arrival of John McDonald (le Borgne) of Swan River at Qu'Appelle. "On his arrival," James Sutherland narrated, "two flags were hoisted that is the N.W. Co's flag at the Flag Staff and the Half Breeds flag on a pole erected on the top of their Bastion. This was the first time they had shown the half breed flag since my arrival which indicated something."[51]

On the same day Grant attempted ("with a good deal of arrogance, more than usual," commented Sutherland) to arrest one of the Hudson's Bay Company men, in order to try him for horse stealing. Sutherland refused to allow it and prepared to defend himself.

But the Nor'Westers were rejoicing, not making war, that day, and Sutherland learned why from an inebriated Canadian who came over to his post:

> The flag was flying in honour of Cuthbert Grant having been appointed Captain-General of all the Half Breeds in the country, and likewise as a rejoicing for the news brought by Swan River MacDonald that the Half Breeds in Athabaska, English River, Saskatchewan and Swan River were collecting under their several chiefs and had sent information that they would all join Grant early in the spring to sweep Red River of all the English.[52]

Sutherland did not take this drunken talk too seriously, but later learned that it was indeed intended to renew the war against the colony in the spring. The crisis of the fur-trade war was near.

CHAPTER IV

THE COLLISION AT SEVEN OAKS,

1816

The appointment of Cuthbert Grant as Captain-General of the Métis was obviously part of a plan by Macdonell and Cameron of the North West Company for dealing with the assembling of the Métis of the northwest at which Grant had been at work all winter. Grant had shown himself so superior at once in education and boldness and in his influence over the Métis, that he now emerged as first of the four chiefs of 1815. Thenceforward Grant was to be the chief of the Métis nation.

If Grant's appointment was part of a plan prepared during the winter by Macdonell and Cameron, by March 26 there was reason for the Nor'Westers and their allies to gather. They learned that day that Colin Robertson, left in charge of the colony during Semple's tour, had no doubt as to the hostility of the Nor'Westers. He saw clearly that they could starve the colony by seizing Hudson's Bay Company pemmican on the Qu'Appelle and the Souris. The obvious counteraction was to deny pemmican to the North West Athabasca brigades by seizing Fort Gibraltar and stopping the passage of their pemmican boats at The Forks. When Semple wrote on March 10 of his concern at the temper and preparation of the Nor'Westers, Robertson thought the time had come to act. Gibraltar should be seized, while still relatively defenceless, "for the Papers it contains and the Expresses about to arrive"[1] (from Fort William). These, he was confident, would furnish evidence of the North West designs. For the next week Robertson fretted, hoping Semple would write ordering the seizure; the Nor'-Westers, he wrote, had "struck the first blow at Qu'Appelle. They shall not be the first at The Forks."[2] Finally, he was stung to action on his own initiative by the sight of a letter of humble submission from John Richards McKay of the Hudson's Bay Company post at Qu'Appelle to Grant, described by Robertson as "a native chief and clerk in the N.W. service."[3] On the night of March 17 Robertson seized Fort Gibraltar by surprise with a mere twelve men, despite its two square bastions and eighteen-foot palisades.[4] He then obtained the papers which revealed the motives and actions of the Nor'Westers in the attack on the colony in 1815, possession of which might act as a deterrent to an attack in 1816. Robertson also seized the North West expresses as they came in, with the evidence which they contained of the attack preparing for 1816.[5]

For the moment then, Robertson was master of the situation at Red River. But his success depended on the continued alienation of the freemen and Métis at Red River from the North West Company. Robertson's influence was soon endangered. On March 23 the North West post at Pembina was captured, on Robertson's orders, to complete the blockade of the rivers, and the Métis leaders Fraser, Hess and Bostonais [Pangman], who were no doubt acting for Grant, were arrested by Chrysologue Pambrun and Alexander McLeod, leaders of the colonists' party.[6] Robertson feared this act would drive the ordinary Métis back to their old allegiance. He was soon also to be worried by Semple's stiffness in dealing with the natives and by the frankly contemptuous attitude of his lieutenants, Holte and Rogers, towards them.

Warlike preparations on the Qu'Appelle were thus matched by those on Lower Red River. Both sides thought its own acts defensive and read those of the other through a mist of mounting fear and anger. Robertson and Semple, who had returned to The Forks on March 28, were also faced by the possibility in early summer of attack in the rear by the North West brigade from Fort William. For this danger they were soon to be prepared. The colony's schooner, *Cuchillon*, had been fitted out in the Seine River in the winter with a deck and a piece of artillery. Of thirty-five-foot keel and eleven-foot beam, the *Cuchillon* had been built as a sailboat at Fort Daer in the winter of 1813. In the summer of 1815 her sides had been raised at Norway House, and her construction and armament were to be completed early in June.[7] She was, Lieutenant Holte reported, "to be fitted out man-of-war style and moored at the bottom [mouth] of the Red River to intercept the N.W. canoes." "I will be," he declared, "in my proper glory and will give the N.W. scoundrels a drubbing if I can."[8]

At Qu'Appelle the effect of the seizure of Gibraltar was to precipitate the rallying of the Métis to their flag and the proclamation of Grant as Captain-General. Alexander Macdonell now tried to hasten their coming and increase their numbers, for his position was desperate. Robertson had seized "the key of the river"[9] and lay between him and the brigades he was to provision for the long haul to the Athabasca. Somehow he must pass The Forks to meet the canoes from Fort William. He and Grant, as they guarded Qu'Appelle with posted sentries, must have discussed long and anxiously how they could break Robertson's blockade of the rivers. The contending forces were nicely poised. Semple and Robertson by their blockade could deny passage to the North West pemmican. But they themselves needed for the support of their garrison and the colony the pemmican of the Hudson's Bay post on the Qu'Appelle. This, as James Sutherland was only too painfully aware, lay within a musket-shot of Grant's assembled *brûlés*. Thus Macdonell and Grant could retaliate for the blockade of The Forks by seizing the Qu'Appelle pemmican and denying it to the colony. The weakness of their position was that they probably could not starve the colony into submission in time to provision the Athabasca canoes.

Both sides were aware of the evenness of the balance. Semple, who had officially approved the seizure of Gibraltar, was critical of Robertson's general policy and conduct and was determined to follow his own line. He moved first to end the developing stalemate. On April 10 he wrote Macdonell to assure him that his person and property would be allowed to pass The Forks if the Qu'Appelle post were not molested.[10] He was, in short, prepared to let the North West pemmican pass if assured of the pemmican the colony needed before the crops ripened. There was no reply. Either Macdonell, who does not mention it, did not receive the letter or chose to ignore it. But James Sutherland had already written for reinforcements.[11]

So April passed, each party endeavouring to rally the *brûlés* of Red River to its side, or at least to keep them neutral. Some of the freemen and older Métis indeed began to prepare quietly to slip away to the plains to hunt during a summer which promised to be troubled along the rivers. Most of the young men, however, responded to Grant's call, or waited his coming. Robertson began to doubt the result of his efforts to win the *brûlés* from their old allegiance to the North West Company.

For this he blamed Semple's aloofness and the brutal contempt Holte and Rogers showed to the natives at The Forks. But part of the cause of the growing rift between Semple and Robertson was undoubtedly Semple's determination to be master. He had refused to accept Robertson's proposition that "if the N.W. Co. gain over the natives, the colonists must raise the first years crop on Douglas Point."[12] Robertson thought that, if his policy of winning the Métis away from the Nor'Westers failed, the colonists must be concentrated under the guns of Fort Douglas. But Semple refused to agree, on the urging, Robertson believed, of Sheriff Alexander Macdonell. Semple actually was anxious not to alarm the colonists by so drastic a precaution, and perhaps drive them to desert to the North West Company. And it must be added that no doubt Semple and his officers found the bold, assured Robertson – Mr Lofty, as they called him – a trying and uncomfortable associate.

Finally, the two men quarrelled over the issue on May 1. Things then went from bad to worse. On May 10 Rogers challenged Robertson

a duel, and Semple took Rogers's part. Robertson resigned his office
be able to meet Rogers. When Holte was insolent over the affair,
.obertson kicked him out of his room. In the upshot the duel was
ostponed, and Robertson and Semple were reconciled. These diffi-
ulties indicate, however, that the definite policy and strong line of
.obertson, which might have seen the colony through the summer of
816, were giving way to impulse and vacillation on the part of
emple and his hard-drinking aides.[13]

It was no time for the commanders at The Forks to be quarrelling,
or at Qu'Appelle Macdonell and Grant had struck. In mid-April
emple, in response to Sutherland's appeal and in an endeavour to
nsure the safe transport of the pemmican from the Hudson's Bay
Company post on the Qu'Appelle, had sent Pambrun up the Assiniboine
vith a party. They arrived early on April 20. Macdonell interpreted
heir arrival as preparation for an attack, and rejoiced that a reinforce-
nent of brûlés arrived at precisely the same time to strengthen Grant's
orce. The truth was simply that Pambrun and Sutherland hoped to
get the pemmican away from under Grant's guns while such a move
night yet be attempted.[14]

Macdonell, however, was now determined to attempt negotiation
as Semple had done a month before. His intention was veiled, and so
remains, but probably he was moved to write Semple and interview
Sutherland on May 4 to propose an arrangement, by the fact that
Qu'Appelle pemmican was still within reach but might yet be removed
by Sutherland's growing force. But Sutherland refused to treat, and
Semple thought fit to reply with a threat that if Macdonell seized
the pemmican "a blow would be struck, that would resound from the
Athabasca to Montreal."[15]

The threat was not well-considered, for it released the pent-up
eagerness of the brûlés for war. Sutherland was aware of their keen-
ness, and Macdonell professed to be unable to restrain them. Grant
now had some sixty of his Young Fellows, the wilder brûlés of the
prairies and the northern rivers, under his command. He must use
them soon, or they would trickle away, back to their girls or out to
hunt on the plains. The first grass was springing and the ponies could
find enough to eat along the northern slopes of the valleys. He was
eager to be moving and, while Macdonell's story that it was the brûlés
who proposed the next move in the game need not be believed literally,
there can be no doubt that Grant and his men were keen to prevent
les anglais getting their pemmican away.

When Sutherland and Pambrun were seen loading their boats with
pemmican and embarking on May 6, Grant gave the word to his men

to saddle. The Hudson's Bay boats ran down the high water of the Qu'Appelle twisting tortuously in the broad bottom of its great valley flanked by the rounded slopes of its hills, their bare shoulders brown with the last summer's grass, the ravines dark with the poplar and oak. From headland to headland the *brûlé* scouts flitted on their ponies, watching the progress of the brigade. The main body under Grant moved quietly over the upper plain, out of sight of the boats in the depth of the valley.[16]

On May 8 Grant led his band down a ravine to the valley-bottom at a point where the river rounded a great bend and poured through the boulders and ledges of the Grand Rapids of the Qu'Appelle. There the channel required that the boats come round the bend and pass the rapids one by one. Grant left the ponies back in the trees and set his men in ambush along the willow-lined shore. As the boats came round one at a time, their crews were forced to put in to shore by the *brûlés'* levelled muskets and, unarmed, they marched into the willows. Sutherland and Pambrun with their whole party were taken neatly, boat-load by boat-load, by the politely smiling Grant. The smoothness of the operation was marred only by one boat grounding in the rapids. It was a coup of much distinction, simple and clever, which rejoiced the hearts of the *brûlés*.[17]

It was with many a joke, then, that they sent Sutherland and Pambrun and the men back to Qu'Appelle, and held the pemmican, except for one boat-load sent down the river to spare the colony the worst privations.[18] That done, they waited for Macdonell and the North West boats. Then while the North West boats and the Hudson's Bay boats went down the river laden with all the pemmican from the Qu'Appelle, the *brûlés* rode in two parties, one on either side of the river. The southern party of about thirty rode behind Macdonell, the northern one of over forty with Grant. They rode along the tops of the valley slopes, guarding the boats which wound slowly down the river loops below. At the head of Grant's party rode the guide bearing the blue flag. As Grant rode slowly through the warm May sun along the prairies of the valley crest and watched the river twisting far below and scanned the farther slope blue with haze, he must have felt that the life he had chosen was good.[19]

As they approached the forks of the Souris and the Assiniboine, Macdonell's party made for the North West Fort La Souris. Grant descended upon Brandon House, and captured it. The Nor'Westers were sweeping the Assiniboine as they descended, always alert for surprise by a party sent up the river from The Forks. Peter Fidler, the master of Brandon House, bitterly described the attack:

At 1/2 past noon about 48 Half Breeds, Canadians, Freemen & Indians came all riding on Horseback, with their Flag flying blue about 4 feet square & a figure of 8 horizontally in the middle, one Beating an Indian Drum, and many of them singing Indian Songs, they all rode directly to the usual crossing place over the river where they all stopped about two minutes, and instead of going down the Bank & riding across the River they all turned suddenly round and rode full speed into our Yard – some of them tyed their Horses, others loose & fixed their flag at our Door, which they soon afterwards hoisted over our East Gate next the Canadian House – Cuthbert Grant then came up to me in the Yard & demanded of me to deliver to him all the Keys of our Stores Warehouses & I of course would not deliver them up – they then rushed into the House and broke open the warehouse Door first, plundered the Warehouse of every article it contained, tore up part of the Cellar floor & cut out the Parchment windows without saying for what this was done for or by whose Authority – Alexr. McDonell, Serephim, Bostonais, & Allan Mc-Donell were at their House looking on the whole time – they broke open the store Door & Barn Door & carried away almost every thing there except the Packs of Furs & some empty Kegs – they also plundered every person in the House of part of their private property & took away every horse belonging to the Company & European Servants. Those Horses that McFynn [?] J. Favill Half Breeds had they let alone: all these men were armed with a Gunsack, a pike at the end of a pole, some bows & arrows swords . . . Bostonais told that it was Mr. Robertson's fault they had plundered our House – for taking their Fort at the Forks . . .[20]

After the pause to capture Brandon House and to do some drink-ing at La Souris, the descent was resumed. Once more the boats filed down the river by the Grand Rapids of the Assiniboine, leaving the Moosehead of the Blue Hills of Brandon behind, and into the narrow defile of the Sand Hills. Once more the *brûlés* rode in two parties on either bank. In the Sand Hills and the dense spruce woods north of the Assiniboine they could not keep the river in sight, and they pushed on towards the Portage des Prairies. Two days short of that point an Indian from The Forks met them to report that a strong body of men with a field-piece had set out from Fort Douglas to intercept the Nor'Westers at the Portage. But at that point they found only friends – some Nor'Westers under the clerk John Siveright. Macdonell and

Grant rode into the Portage on June 16, and on the next day the boats overtook them. So far the advance had been made in safety.[21]

Their recent precautions had not been baseless. In Red River Semple had heard of the approach of the Nor'Westers and his reaction was that he should endeavour to ambush and capture the Métis at the Portage. A party was called out, and this gave rise to the report Macdonell had received of an ambush at the Portage. But Semple had postponed the expedition on Robertson's advice, once more exhibiting himself as impulsive but indecisive.[22] Nothing more was done. Now the colony was on the verge of starvation and the settlers had to take to the fields to sow as much as possible to avert a worse danger in the coming winter. Robertson, believing his presence was only dividing the colony, made ready to leave. On June 10 an Indian had come to Fort Douglas to report that the Nor'Westers were coming down in force: eighty Métis, he declared, and forty Canadians. Robertson then advised Semple to pull down Gibraltar and use its logs to strengthen Fort Douglas. Semple agreed, but Robertson was still at odds with Semple's staff. That same day he was attacked by Bourke, the storeman at Fort Douglas, and on June 11 he left for York Factory.[23]

Between that date and June 19 two sets of actors moved slowly towards collision at Seven Oaks. On the Assiniboine the Nor'Westers with their pemmican were determined to open the river and supply their brigades. At The Forks Semple blocked the rivers, but encouraged his colonists to settle on their farms and to sow their crops for some two miles down the river from Fort Douglas. He thus challenged assault by the Nor'Westers and exposed to their attack the people whom he was bound to protect. In this discrepancy in Semple's actions lay the cause of the events of June 19. He had no desire for a conflict, and much reason to avoid one, but his actions and his position made one most likely.

For the moment, the danger did not appear imminent at The Forks. On June 12 the men from Fort Douglas began the destruction of Gibraltar. The great oak logs of the bastions were levered down, the palisades uprooted and flung flat. The logs were then rolled to the water's edge and rafted down to Point Douglas, where they were dragged up the banks to the fort. In the plots on the river lots the Highlanders were wielding the mattock, or driving the light ploughs the smith had made behind balky Métis ponies. Where the tough sod had been turned and chopped to a black loam, they were sowing broadcast the seed carried in a fold of the sower's cloak. The black-shawled women passed between the log cabins in the gentle June sunshine. From the river-side a lone cow bawled.

Up at the Prairie Portage the scene was less idyllic, the action brisker. There the Métis war band – it can scarcely be called otherwise – halted to organize for the advance on The Forks. The boats were beached when they arrived, and the pemmican piled in a square to make a simple defence-work. Macdonell and Grant had now to break Semple's blockade. Their plan was to send an advance party with provisions overland, since Fort Douglas barred movement by water. Their first purpose was to effect a junction with the Montreal partners below Fort Douglas "to prevent the canoes on Lake Winnipeg from starving." Once these were supplied, Grant could then, by blockading the lower Red, force the colony, now deprived of supplies from the Assiniboine, into submission and withdrawal. Accordingly Grant set out with a party of sixty-two, with Michel Bourassa and Antoine Houle as captains, and comprising four Indians, six Canadians, and fifty-two half breeds. They took with them two carts and fifteen bags of pemmican in a canoe. The pemmican – some 1,150 pounds of concentrated meat – was to feed the party and provision the Montreal canoes. They were to proceed to the Passage of the Assiniboine, a ford of the river about ten miles above The Forks, and to take the pemmican overland in the carts to Frog Plain on the Red.[24]

News of these preparations as carried to Semple at Fort Douglas by Indians who remained friendly to the colony, and by Moustouche Boutino, a half-breed who refused to join Grant and informed Louis Nolin, a Canadian in the service of the Hudson's Bay Company, that the Métis were coming down to capture the Governor and colony. This Boutino did because, when his own people had neglected him, his wounds had been dressed by Dr James White of the colony.[25]

On June 18 Grant left the Portage, and late in the afternoon of June 19 had reached the mouth of Catfish (now Omand's) Creek. This was considerably beyond the Passage of the Assiniboine, being only about three miles from The Forks. The reason for this departure from the plain is unrecorded. Probably the course of Sturgeon Creek was too swampy for passage. Whatever the reason for it, the change was to be significant. From there Grant led an advance party northeast across the plain to Frog Plain on the Red, his purpose still being to reach Frog Plain without being seen from Fort Douglas. To do this with a mounted party riding across a level plain against a sunlit skyline would have been difficult at best. It was in fact made impossible by the swampy ground back from the river from which Catfish Creek drained. The Métis had to ride up to their horses' bellies in water and mud, and were finally forced to swerve to the right towards the fort. The main party, following with the carts, had to do the same. The result was that the advance party came within an estimated mile and a half of the fort, which they could see directly to their right. They in turn were seen by the look-out at five o'clock.

At first they were seen indistinctly, but as they crossed some rising ground their silhouette came clearly into view. The look-out gave the alarm, and spyglasses were brought up to the tower of the fort.[26]

A look-out had been kept because Semple, forewarned, had expected the *brûlés*. He had even anticipated their goal, for he had been at Frog Plain at about four o'clock that afternoon with a paper which he proposed to read to the Métis.[27] This presumably was a warning not to commit acts of violence against the colony. But the Métis had not arrived at the expected time, and he had ridden back to Fort Douglas by the trail through the river lots.

Now, with Sheriff Macdonell, Semple scanned the party trotting slowly across the plain towards the northern end of the river lots. There some people were still working in the fields; he had seen them as he had ridden back to the fort. Semple at once decided to ride out with a party to cover the settlers and to find out what the Métis had in view. He called for fifteen or twenty men to come armed, for he had seen only Grant with his advance party of fifteen. Semple himself rushed down and fretted at the gate while Holte and Rogers, with fifteen or sixteen men from the colonial establishment – not settlers except John Pritchard, Grant's old bourgeois of 1812 turned colonist – were served out muskets, bayonets, ball and powder. When it was suggested that the three-pounder field-piece be taken, Semple impatiently brushed the suggestion aside, saying he was not going to fight but only to ask the fellows what they wanted.[28] The muskets were hastily loaded – two were to go off on the march and some failed to go off in the fight – and the party hurried out from Fort Douglas.

How long this took can only be conjectured. Meanwhile Grant and the advance party of the Métis had ridden on their way towards Frog Plain. As his route cut into the river lots, Grant saw the settlers at work in the fields. Fearing they would report his arrival to Semple, he ordered them, two men and a woman, taken prisoner, and went on.[29] The party passed round a point of trees along a ravine and jutting into the plain – these were known as the Seven Oaks – and rode towards Frog Plain, about two miles to the north.

The second party was not far in the rear. It was they who saw Semple's men on the march and galloped ahead to tell Grant that the English were coming. Grant's first concern was for the carts with the pemmican. He ordered his advance party to continue on to Frog Plain and make camp. Riding back to the main party, he ordered the carts to hurry on to the camp at Frog Plain. Then he collected the main party behind the point of Seven Oaks and rode back to meet Semple.[30]

Semple, on leaving Fort Douglas, marched on foot northwestward to the bend of the river at the north side of the base of Point Douglas. There was the farm of John McLean, the leading farmer and steadiest settler of all Selkirk's colonists. McLean joined the party. As they went on, they met Alexander McBeath, a veteran of the 73rd Regiment, coming in to the fort with his family. Behind were William and James Sutherland with their families. These were the only settlers going to the fort for refuge, all the others, except the prisoners, being there already. McBeath told Semple of the arrival of the main party of the Métis, and advised him that he would need two field-pieces if he was to deal with the numbers of the Nor'Westers. Semple again refused to listen to the suggestion that he would need artillery to impress the mounted Métis. He went on for a time, then changed his mind and sent Bourke back for one field-piece.[31]

The party waited on the plain for the gun to come. The trees along the river glistened in the level light from the sun sinking across the plain. The evening was quiet except for shouts from the fort. How long they waited is not recorded, but Semple became impatient. Back at the fort Sheriff Macdonell had made the gun ready, an ox was harnessed to it, and John Bourke[32] set out slowly along the trail. But Semple could no longer contain himself, and gave the order to advance without waiting for Bourke to come up. The party marched quickly and in excitement. Holte's hastily loaded gun went off, with nerve-wracking effect, and Semple turned on his lieutenant with asperity for his clumsiness. Yet there was to be another of these accidental discharges as the party hurried along.

On the other side Grant led his men forward and pushed into the scrub which grew around the Seven Oaks. As the party broke into the open, they saw before them Semple and his men approaching along the trail through the river lots.

Both sides halted at once. Then the *brûlés* fanned out on either side of Grant, who sat silent, watching Semple alertly. The ponies sidled and fretted. Semple by a gesture had his men deploy in line across the plain at wide intervals, as they sought to match the front of the *brûlés*. Then the two parties confronted one another, silent and motionless except for the snorting of a pony or the flash of a bayonet in the sunlight. In the west the sun was dropping quickly down the sky, and the shadows of man and horse lengthened darkly on the plain.

In the tense confrontation no one, not even Grant, could think of all the meeting might mean. But one thing is clear in retrospect. The meeting was not planned.[33] Because of the swampy ground, Grant's plan had failed. He had not passed Fort Douglas unobserved, and now he faced an armed and challenging foe. Anything could happen at any moment, and the confrontation become a collision. For if neither side had meant to attack that day, each was hostile and saw the other as an enemy ready to strike.

At the moment of meeting the opponents were not unequal. Grant had only twenty brûlés to some twenty-five men in Semple's party, but more and more of the Métis kept coming up through the Seven Oaks. Semple's only reinforcement was Bourke who with two or three companions and the field-piece was plodding slowly up the trail from the fort. If it came to a fight, Semple would be outnumbered and outflanked. Already the horns of the half-moon were edging forward as other brûlés rode up and the ponies stamped and fretted. Semple's men fell back slowly to keep their flanks clear, but the Métis pressed up persistently.[34]

What was to happen? Semple stood stiffly in front of his line but did nothing. Grant acted. Quietly he ordered the brûlé beside him, François Firmin Boucher, to "go to them, and tell them to ground their arms, and surrender, or we will fire upon them." As the brûlé kicked his pony forward, Grant unobtrusively covered the Governor with his gun.

"What do you want?" asked Boucher in broken English as he came up on Semple's right. "What do you want?" retorted the Governor, the question he had come out to ask. "We want our fort," returned Boucher curtly. "Well, go to your fort," snapped Semple, stung by the brûlé's tone.[35] "Why have you destroyed our fort, you damned rascal!" shouted Boucher. Semple then lost his temper and, seizing Boucher's rein and grabbing at his gun-stock, said, "Scoundrel, do you tell me so?"

The collision had occurred: the men who held The Forks had challenged the men from the provisions plains. Like a flash Boucher slid from his horse and ran for the Métis' line. A shot rang out. It was fired by Semple's men at an Indian who had kept edging forward when they warned him back.[36] A second shot came from the brûlés. It was fired by Grant and it hit Semple in the thigh.[37] A third brought down Holte.[38] The brûlés now slipped down behind their horses and levelled their guns over the ponies' backs. Semple's men began to crowd up to their leader to see how he was hurt. The Métis discharged a volley in their midst. Many of Semple's men fell. The rest turned to fight and returned the fire as best they could. Then the brûlés, as was the old French-Canadian custom in battle, threw themselves to the ground to reload. Semple's men, thinking their fire had taken effect, flung up their hats and cheered.[39]

Back on the trail, Bourke and his men saw the flashes and heard the reports of the guns. The field-piece would now be of no use, so Bourke sent it back with one man and came on bravely with the other.

The cheering of Semple's men was brief. The *brûlés* sprang to their feet and fired their second volley. Then they charged on foot. Grant, who had stood watching from beside his horse, ran towards Semple. At this moment the advance guard from Frog Plain swept around the Seven Oaks and charged in behind the survivors of Semple's party. These were now doomed. Some, like Rogers and John McLean, went at the Métis with the bayonet and died fighting savagely.[40] The rest broke and fled for the trees by the river, but most were ridden down and shot or speared. As Bourke approached, he was caught in a swirl of horsemen and wounded by a spear, but he and his companion fled into cover by the river. Only four others escaped, three by flight and one, John Pritchard, by shamming death and then begging mercy.

Meanwhile Grant had reached Semple, to find the Governor lying with a broken leg. Semple asked to be taken to the fort, where he said he might recover. Grant promised he would be, and then went out to restrain his men from further slaughter.[41] But as soon as he left, some-one – some said it was the Indian Machicabou, others the Canadian, old François Deschamps – shot the Governor in the breast and killed him.[42] This piece of savagery was matched elsewhere. The wounded were knifed and tomahawked, the dead stripped and ripped up after the Indian fashion. The wild blood of the *brûlés* was boiling, and it was some time before Grant could check their savagery.

The fight itself had lasted only fifteen minutes.[43] Semple and twenty of his officers and men were killed. One Indian of Grant's party had been killed, and one *brûlé*, young Trottier, wounded.[44] The victory was as complete as the fight was sudden.

The Métis now collected their ponies and, whooping and waving their plunder of blood-stained shirts and cloaks, galloped back through the bush to the camp-fires at Frog Plain. There Pierre Falcon,[45] the bard of the Métis and Grant's brother-in law, who had not fought but had seen the fight, was soon shaping the Nor'Wester view of the collision into the verses of his "La Grenouillère."

THE BATTLE OF SEVEN OAKS

Will you come and hear me sing
Of a true and recent thing?
On June nineteenth the *Bois-brûlés*
Arrived like warriors, brave and gay.

On coming to the Grenouillère
We took three Orkney prisoners there
Three men from across the sea
Who'd come to pillage our country.

As soon as we started to set out
Two of our comrades gave a shout,
Two of our men called out, "Alack!
There are the English, come to attack!"

At once we reined our horses in
And galloped back to meet them then,
Surrounding all their grenadiers
Who stood quite still, a prey to fears.

Like men of honour we did act,
Sent an ambassador, in fact,
Asking their governor to wait
And talk, before it was too late.

But the governor is full of ire
And forthwith tells his men to fire.
They fire the first – their muskets roar
And almost kill our ambassador!

The governor thinks he's an emperor,
A proud and arrogant seignior.
He tries to act like a lofty lord
– And, to his grief, gets his reward!

When he espied the *Bois-brûlés*
He tried to frighten them away.
He sallied out to drive them away,
And for this mistake with his life did pay.

Because he behaved so arrogantly
Most of his grenadiers did die.
Almost all of his men were slain;
Only four or five got home again.

Ah, would you had seen those Englishmen,
And the *Bois-brûlés* a-chasing them!
One by one we did them destroy
While our *Bois-brûlés* uttered shouts of joy!

Now who is the singer of this song?
'Tis the local poet, Pierre Falcon.
He wrote the song and it was sung
To mark the victory we had won.
He wrote the song, that very day
To sing the praise of the *Bois-brûlés*![46]

Wild was the talk that night, and long the singing by the fires. Seven Oaks passed at once into the balladry of the Métis, and into the heroic tradition of their race.

Grant, however, had to deal with more immediate consequences of the collision. He could win all by waiting, for the fight had driven the colonists from their fields into the fort, where they would soon face starvation. A blockade of the Red at Frog Plain would ensure the surrender of the colony. But Grant exploited his victory much more quickly. He talked during the early hours of the night with John Pritchard, who had succeeded in surrendering himself without being killed. Grant now played on the fears of his former *bourgeois*. "You see the little quarter we have shown you," Pritchard reported him to have said, "and now if any further resistance is made, neither man, woman nor child shall be spared." This message Pritchard was dispatched to bear to Sheriff Macdonell, acting-governor now Semple was dead. Macdonell received Pritchard in Fort Douglas where the colonists huddled with their families that terror-stricken night.

Macdonell could see no reason for immediate surrender; the *bois-brûlés* could not carry the fort by assault; he had still provisions to last until relief might come. He therefore refused to consider immediate surrender. Pritchard, however, went among the colonists, and his tale of the horrors of the massacre and his own unconcealed fear, whether by intent or not, so alarmed the colonists that they began to demand that Macdonell yield the fort on condition that they be allowed to leave Red River in safety.[47]

In the morning an act of kindness strengthened their resolve to surrender. Peguis and Louis Nolin, by Grant's permission, went to the field with some of his men and brought in the bodies of Semple and eight of his men in carts. Some of them were naked, some mutilated, all rent by spear or knife.[48] The spectacle completed the terror of the

colonists. Macdonell yielded to their clamour. He went down to Frog
Plain and concluded terms of surrender with Grant: a receipt for the
goods, and the safe conduct of the colonists. Late that afternoon Grant
and a band of his followers came riding up to accept the surrender,
some of them in the cloaks of yesterday's slain, a sight which added to
the horror of the colonists. What pity for man or woman could be
expected from these savages? But Grant was all firmness and kindness.
He was manifestly master of his men, and soon assured the colonists
that he meant them no harm and that none would come to them. He
himself would sleep in the fort to ensure it. Grant then accepted the
surrender, allowing the condition that the colonists be permitted to
leave unmolested and that inventory be made of the goods in store
in the colony.[49]

Grant's word, once given, was good, and his command of his men
absolute. No one was molested. The next day was spent in preparing
the boats for departure and in giving receipts for the colonial and
and Hudson's Bay Company goods surrendered. Hour after hour Grant
sat signing the inventory sheets as receipts till all was done, the educated clerk effortlessly succeeding the war chief.

On June 22nd all was ready for the departure of the colonists.
When Macdonell and Pritchard went to Grant to take their leave, they
found him perturbed at the receipt of an order from Alexander Macdonell at the Portage to detain the colonists. Macdonell had been told
of the clash at Seven Oaks by young Trottier, brother of the wounded
Métis and, wishing to arrest Bourke and Heyden of the colonial establishment, had sent the order. Sheriff Macdonell urged Grant not to
delay the departure and appealed to his pride in his word and his
sense of independence as chief of the Métis. Grant, caught between
his plighted word and the orders of his *bourgeois*, angrily decided to
stand by his promise and told Macdonell to go at once. He scribbled
a note giving the colonists protection from other Nor'Westers and
waved the sheriff and Pritchard away.[50] When the boats had dropped
down the Red, Grant and his men moved into Fort Douglas. Once again
they had "cleared the two rivers"; the pemmican would go down to
the Athabasca brigades and the *bois-brûlés* were masters of the soil in
Red River.

THE AFTERMATH OF SEVEN OAKS,

1817-1820

That the collision at Seven Oaks was an accident and the bloodshed that followed the result of accident, so far as the *bois-brûlés* themselves were concerned, was well understood on the morrow of the massacre. In after years it was also well understood that it was on those who had inspired the advance on the colony and dispatched Grant and his Métis from Qu'Appelle that the ultimate responsibility rested. In this knowledge lay the basis for reconciliation between *bois-brûlés* and colonists. In it lay the possibility that Cuthbert Grant would in the long run be remembered, not as the destroyer but as the guardian of the Red River colony.

After the colonists had embarked on June 22, Grant rode along the bank beside them until they were beyond danger of being molested, then returned to his band at Frog Plain. He was now no longer in charge of events. His commander, Alexander Macdonell, had followed close behind the orders he had sent to hold the colonists. He arrived on June 23 and, despite Grant's ignoring of his orders, heartily approved of the course events had taken. He took possession of Fort Douglas. He and Grant were thus masters of the river when on June 23 the Nor'Wester Archibald Norman MacLeod came up from Netley Creek where he had examined the colonists' effects and taken John Pritchard prisoner. MacLeod had led a party from Fort William and it was to make a junction with him that Grant had marched to Frog Plain on June 19. MacLeod and his companions, like Macdonell, warmly approved what had happened and praised Grant for the zeal with which he had defended the interests of the company. The young clerk must have felt a glow of satisfaction in having at once so decisively advanced the interests of his people and of his *bourgeois*.

The victory at Seven Oaks, however, and control of The Forks were but part of the campaign of 1816. That dangerous man Colin Robertson, bold of temper and fertile in expedients, was still at large in the northwest. Robertson had set out for England but had met the men of the Hudson's Bay Company's Athabasca expedition which, as Grant had written, had "gone to pot." With them Robertson might yet seek to retrieve that defeat by seizing the North West Company canoes at some place of ambush, such as the Grand Rapids of the Saskatchewan, or some place of assembly, such as Bas de la Rivière. By taking the latter, indeed, he would secure its provisions, some 400 to 500 bags of pemmican and its guns.[1] It was therefore necessary to safeguard Bas de la Rivière, and to that point at the beginning of July were sent some fifteen *bois-brûlés*, with three cannon, two wall guns and fifty muskets. It is not recorded that Grant went with the party then, but he was there at the beginning of August.[2]

His presence there is recorded because of his connection with the murder of Owen Keveny of the Hudson's Bay Company. Keveny,[3] the leader of the second party of Selkirk colonists in 1812, had been sent inland from Fort Albany in May 1816 to help restore the colony after the destruction of 1815 and to take some calves to the Red River colony by way of the Albany, English, and Winnipeg rivers. He had some trouble with his party and some deserted to the Bas de la Rivière in mid-August when the expedition reached that point. There Archibald Norman MacLeod, as a magistrate in the Indian Territory under the Canada Jurisdiction Act of 1803, examined the party which remained loyal to Keveny and issued a warrant for Keveny's arrest. Charles de Reinhard, a former colour-sergeant of the de Meuron regiment of mercenaries in British service in the War of 1812 and now a servant of the North West Company, and one of Keveny's deserters, Thomas Costello, were sent as constables to arrest Keveny on August 16. The next day he was sent under a guard of Métis to Fort William. The party was turned back, however, on the upper Winnipeg by Nor'-Westers bearing the news that Lord Selkirk, coming to the rescue of his colony with a band of discharged soldiers from Canada, had seized Fort William on August 13. Because of a quarrel in the party, caused by a shortage of provisions, sickness on the part of Keveny, and the anger of an Indian guide against the prisoner, Keveny was then left on an island in the river.[4]

When news of the capture by Selkirk of the depot of the North West trade at Fort William and of Keveny's being marooned reached Bas de la Rivière, Archibald McLellan, the master of the post, set out with a party in a light canoe to gain information of what Selkirk's movements might be and whether trade goods could be expected to come down from Fort William. He also intended to find out Keveny's whereabouts.

Cuthbert Grant was in McLellan's party. The first reaction of the Nor'Westers at Bas de la Rivière to the disaster at Fort William had been to try in a council to persuade the *bois-brûlés* to advance to Rainy Lake to hold that post against Selkirk. The *brûlés* declined, the majority "preferring to defend their lands in Red River."[5] Grant, therefore, was acting not as a leader of the Métis but as a clerk of the North West Company in accompanying McLellan and his party.

They found Keveny above the Dalles of the Winnipeg River, greeted him politely, but made him prisoner once more. He was put in the care of de Reinhard, an Indian called Joseph, or the White Partridge, and a Métis named Mainville. They set out for Rainy Lake ahead of McLellan, and shortly after, on September 11, Keveny was shot by Mainville and stabbed by de Reinhard.[6] It would seem that the murder was the result of some action by McLellan, to whose party Grant belonged and in whose confidence Grant evidently was. What McLellan may have done or said was never revealed. It is probable that McLellan hinted darkly that he would not inquire too closely if Keveny suffered an accident or were again marooned in the wilderness. If so, his hints were crudely interpreted and brutally carried out. It might still have been possible to make it appear that Keveny had been drowned in one of the many rapids of the Winnipeg and a cross might have been put up among the many crosses set by the waters of that savage stream. If the manner of Keveny's death can only be guessed, the reason for desiring it is equally difficult to fathom. One can only conclude that Keveny was a victim of the antagonisms and tensions of the growing conflict in a lawless wilderness. He was to be lost because he might be inconvenient, but he was murdered and one of the murderers, de Reinhard, insisted on talking, indeed, on turning King's evidence.

Grant as a member of McLellan's party was implicated, as the testimony of these witnesses make clear. He was implicated in the murder of Owen Keveny as he was in the whole web of events in the years 1815 and 1816. And those events were warfare carried on in the guise of defending lawful rights. It is of the nature of war to lead on from one brutality to another. In the circumstances it is perhaps best to be as reluctant to condemn Grant for his share in this crime as his contemporaries were to prove him a participant.

A reconnaissance of the Lake of the Woods discovered that Selkirk's de Meurons under Captain Protais D'Orsonnens had not yet advanced to the Rainy Lake post of the North West Company, but the brûlés in the party refused to go on to Fort William. Grant and his companions therefore returned to Bas de la Rivière and Red River, and arrived there on September 26. On October 1 Alexander Macdonell set out for Qu'Appelle with all the Métis but three,[7] and it is to be assumed that Grant went with them.

While Grant retired to the Qu'Appelle, other events were in the making at Fort William. Selkirk's bold advance from Canada and his capture of Fort William had, of course, cut off the Nor'Westers in Red River from help. Selkirk had also disrupted the Company's business for the year by arresting the partners at Fort William and seizing their goods. That he also tried to win their men away is suggested by a song of Grant's brother-in-law, Pierre Falcon, which records the drinking and feasting by which the fur companies tried to lure each other's men away.

LORD SELKIRK AT FORT WILLIAM

A Herald

Come quickly, come today,
Rats-musqués, Bois-Brûlés,
At Fort William Lord Selkirk gives a Ball.

Now hurry, don't delay,
You'll sing and dance and play,
The band strikes up; there's food and fun for all.

The Master of Ceremonies

McNab, now all should see,
Our friend McGillivray.
He'll add distinction to our famous ball.

And you beside him stay,
You'll sing and dance and play.
The band strikes up; there's fun and food for all.

McKenzie, now take care,
Your place is over there.
Come join us all in our gay little ball.

And if you think you dare,
You'll dance at our affair.
The band strikes up; there's fun and food for all.

Oh, Doctor, come draw near,
Your chair is over here,
Bring no gloom here, we want none at our ball.

So, Doctor, here this day,
We'll see you skip and play.
The band strikes up; there's fun and food for all.

Good Trader, join our dance.
There's Fraser's nose; one glance
Tells us that he will like our little ball.

There see the drink flow free,
You'll dance abandonedly.
The band strikes up; there's food and fun for all.

Meurons, without delay,
Please play us something gay.
A lively tune to start our happy ball.

Respected Bois-Brûlés
Just hop and jump and play.
The band strikes up; there's fun and food for all.

The Bois-Brûlés

My Lord, we now express
Our thanks for your kindness.
When can we traders give you such a ball?

Lord Selkirk

Now men, your joking stop,
Just dance and slide and hop,
The band strikes up; there's fun and food for all.

The Bois-Brûlés

Formalities away!
We'll join the dance today.
Milord, his feast – the devil takes it all!

And let *him* dance, we say.
While all his fiddles play,
A hundred years or more at such a ball![8]

As the festivities went on in Fort William, Grant was spending the early winter of 1816 at Qu'Appelle Post. This is known because in January and February of 1817 events at Red River provoked him into action which is recorded at some length. These events began with the winter march of the party of Selkirk's de Meurons under Captain D'Orsonnens[9] and Miles Macdonell from Rainy Lake to Red River. They employed as guide John Tanner, the young American reared as a Saulteaux in the Red River country, and set out on December 10, 1816, advancing by the Lake of the Woods, Savanne portage, and Roseau river route. They surprised and captured the North West fort at Pembina on December 3. From there they marched to Fort Douglas in bitter weather and attacked the fort in the darkness of the early morning of January 10. Archibald McLellan and his fifteen men surrendered without resistance. Fort Douglas was once more in the hands of its rightful owners, and in the morning the Hudson's Bay flag again floated over Point Douglas and Red River. McLellan was to be sent to Canada as an accessory to the murder of Owen Keveny. In the meantime, with the rest of his men, he was held prisoner.[10]

It is at this point that Grant came into the action again. In January he set out from Qu'Appelle with twenty Métis to reinforce the Nor'-Westers at Fort Douglas. He reached La Souris on January 22 and left on January 24.[11] On January 28 he was met by a messenger with a letter from Miles Macdonell. Grant had already been sent a letter by Macdonell. Macdonell had captured Joseph Cadotte at Pembina, and on January 4 sent him to Grant with a letter intended to lure the Métis chief away from the North West Company.[12] Macdonell was applying Robertson's policy of trying to win over the Métis when he wrote to their chief. The letter of January 4 seems not to have survived, but that of January 24 did:

Fort Douglas, 24th January, 1817.

Sir,

Having found here the Governor in Chief's proclamation of the 16th July, 1816, sent you by Mr. Johnston, one of his Majesty's justices of the peace, for the purpose of taking up and sending to justice all persons who have committed acts of violence in the country, I consider it my duty to send you now the said proclamation, being persuaded that you will, as a loyal subject, exert yourself to restore order and tranquility in the country.

Your humane conduct towards the people of the colony, after the unfortunate events of the 19th June last, confirms me in the good opinion I always entertained of you.

The Earl of Selkirk, who has a perfect knowledge of all that took place here this last year, harbours no enmity towards you, and I feel confident that he has no intention of commencing legal prosecution against you.

The partners of the North West Company, in their discomfiture, endeavor by the circulation of falsehood to conceal the truth. It is therefore your interest, as well as that of all those under your orders, to withdraw yourselves immediately from those who are certainly driving you to your ruin. If you will come here I shall give you a clear insight into all that has taken place until the present time, and I pledge myself you shall be well received, and freely permitted to return in safety, when you shall think proper.

> Your most obedient servant,
> (Signed) Miles Macdonell, Governor.

Mr. Cuthbert Grant.

I have a parcel containing some articles of clothing, sent by Mr. Daniel M'Kenzie for his son Roderick, I would like the young man himself to come here for them, he has nothing to fear.

> (Signed) Miles Macdonell.[13]

This was the letter that Grant received on January 28, together with copy of the Proclamation of the Prince Regent. This the Imperial Government had issued, ordering all parties to keep the peace in the Indian country. Frederick Damien Heurter, another de Meuron in the North West Company's service, reported that Grant threw the proclamation in the fire with the remark: "Voila encore une des Sacrés Proclamations!" Probably Macdonell's letter followed it into the Lames.[14]

The advance of the party certainly was not stayed by the letter. Grant advanced along the Assiniboine until he reached the house of the Canadian freeman, Jean-Baptiste Lagimonière. This was thirteen miles from Fort Douglas. On learning the strength of the opposition, he withdrew at once and retired to Qu'Appelle. On February 19 he reappeared at La Souris and urged the Métis there to join him. The Canadians refused. They had heard that the King's troops were coming to Red River, and they flatly refused to have anything to do with opposition to the forces of law and order. Grant tried to carry things with a high hand, and ordered the Canadian Marcelot to be courtmartialled for refusing to allow his half-breed son to join the Métis. This piece of military display – the forerunner of a more famous court martial under Louis Riel – was merely an attempt, and an unsuccessful one, at intimidation. One Amelin also refused to let his two sons go, but Grant forced one of them to follow him, leaving the other lest his father should need him. Grant and his Young Fellows were not to carry all before them from now on, as the old freemen asserted their respect for the law.[15]

His force, raised to between seventy and eighty men by such impressment, made its bitter winter march along the Assiniboine until on March 2 they reached Pointe au Chêne on the Assiniboine. At this point they halted and succeeded in killing some colony cattle for much-needed provisions. Grant then proposed to go to Frog Plain to repeat the tactics of the previous June, and reduce Fort Douglas by blockade and harassing. But first he had to be sure of provisions to maintain his force in this grim winter work.

He now dispatched a letter to Miles Macdonell who records on March 2 that Grant had "come with a parcel of Brûlés to the neighbourhood."[16] Grant demanded the release of the prisoners.

> Sir,
>
> The result of my voyage here is merely to request and demand of you Mr. McClellan and others who are in your possession whom we understand are most treacherously ill treated, especially Mr. McClellan whom I am positive is innocent of any crime. Such treatment Sir you cannot complain of when you were in our possession, you had your liberties and freely went out and in the Fort when you thought proper – neither was your prison a dark Dungeon. I feel very much for the poor innocent people. I have in company with me gentlemen from Montreal last summer who offer themselves to become bail for them and myself should I be acceptable. Should you not comply with this request the consequences that shall hereafter occur I shall not answer for.
>
> I am Sir, Your Humble Servant,
>
> (Signed) Cuthbert Grant.
>
> Please excuse this Ink and Scrawl![17]

So wrote the young Scots-Cree in his slightly Gallicized English. Macdonell replied denying that the prisoners were ill-treated. He ordered Grant and his people to disperse or to suffer arrest. He had, he said, already written Grant to that effect. Grant replied:

Sir, your threats you make use of we laught at them and you may come with your forces at any time you please. We shall be always ready to meet you with a good heart, you shall see me to-morrow morning under arms. I dare you to come out with your forces. Since you will not come to any reasonable terms you may do your worst and you may perhaps have cause to repent your expressions and folly. As for your General Order, I shall believe it when I see the original. I am Sir, Your Humble Servant

(Signed) Cuthbert Grant.[18]

Nothing, of course, would have pleased the young captain better than to have Macdonell with his inferior force come out from the walls of Fort Douglas. For while the de Meurons kept warm and well fed by its stoves and well-filled storehouses, his hardy men were sleeping in the snow, warming themselves in the houses of Canadian friends, and eating the last of the beef. When he threatened to invest the fort, Macdonell simply defied him, and the bluff failed. On March 4 the Métis began their retreat. Some ardent spirits wanted to go south and retake Pembina, but Grant quietly opposed this. "We are not barbarians," he said. All returned to La Souris and Qu'Appelle. There Grant remained during the spring. He spent much of his time explaining the Prince Regent's Proclamation to the Métis and Indians in terms favourable to the North West Company. The fears of the freemen had to be offset.[19]

In June, however, he once more appeared with a force of Métis on the Assiniboine above The Forks. He had come as in the previous year with provisions for the brigades to meet the bourgeois coming from Fort William. The pemmican was apparently in boats for what he sought was passage by water.

At Grant's approach Macdonell wrote to him on June 16 to propose that he and the brûlés should not approach nearer than the Passage of the Assiniboine River, some ten miles from The Forks. Grant replied that he would come himself on June 18 to arrange matters. Grant did not appear, however, and on the 18th Macdonell recorded the report that Grant and his men were determined to pass Fort Douglas by water.[20] Once more the strategy of the transcontinental fur trade was in play, with its accompanying set of local tactics at The Forks of the Red. Macdonell also noted with concern that the Indian chief Sonnant was in the Métis camp, wearing Cuthbert Grant's sword. Indians, except for individuals, had not yet been used in the traders' war. And for some days the camp was pitched, not at the Passage, but only two miles overland from Fort Douglas.

Macdonell was not disposed to prevent the Nor'Westers receiving their provisions. He did, however, fear that Grant, if allowed to encamp well supplied with provisions on the lower Red or the Winnipeg, would ambush and arrest Selkirk who was coming to Red River from Fort William. He therefore began to patrol the river and the plain to prevent Grant from passing. At night fires were kept burning on the river bank.

Impressed by Macdonell's resolution, the prisoner McLellan asked him on June 20 that the provisions should be allowed to pass. But Macdonell merely replied that Grant must make the request. No one else would do, for only Grant could perform such conditions as Macdonell might make.

Then on the next day came the message that Selkirk was at Bas de la Rivière.[21] Macdonell could now attempt to carry out his earlier threat to arrest Grant. He sent a party of twenty-five soldiers along with William Laidlaw of the colony establishment, F. D. Heurter,[22] who had been with Grant in the March expedition and had joined Macdonell, and Louis Nolin of the Hudson's Bay Company. They had with them a copy of the Prince Regent's Proclamation and warrants for the arrest of Grant and Cadotte.

When they entered the camp, they read the Proclamation to the silent *brûlés*. Then they served the warrants on Grant and Cadotte. But when Laidlaw attempted to take them prisoner, "they broke from them, and flew to arms." Their men did likewise. They would not allow their chiefs to be arrested. The two armed forces confronted one another, in a situation not unlike Seven Oaks, except that this was not a sudden collision but an attempt at a formally conducted arrest. A single gun-shot could have set off a furious fight. Then Grant averted a clash by saying that he and Cadotte would come in the day after tomorrow to answer all accusations. With this face-saving promise, Macdonell's men withdrew from their uncomfortable situation.[23]

Grant did not come, and it was impossible to attack his superior numbers without using artillery. This, too, was impossible because the Métis camp was under a high bank of the Assiniboine. So Macdonell had to content himself for the next few days with covering the approach of Selkirk.

The two parties thus remained at deadlock, Grant at his camp keeping up the pressure to obtain permission to send pemmican down the river, Macdonell safeguarding the advance of Selkirk. On June 21, at about 9 o'clock in the morning, Selkirk arrived at the site where his colonists had been endeavouring for the past five years to establish themselves in the anarchy of the fur-traders' war for control of The Forks of the Red. He had a bodyguard of seven soldiers of the 37th Regiment, the first redcoats to appear on Red River, and thirty-seven men of the de Meuron and de Wattville regiments. Even this reinforcement was not too great in face of the numbers and fighting quality of Grant's *brûlés*. Peguis, who had met with great satisfaction at Netley Creek the founder of the colony he believed would save his people, accompanied Selkirk with his warriors to Fort Douglas. The sturdy chief was anxious to drive the Métis away, but Selkirk refused to resort to force.[24] Grant indeed deployed his men, but they refused to attempt the contest. He had failed to deliver his company's urgently needed supplies. He had failed to force a passage of The Forks. From now on his fortunes were to waver, and doubts of the strength of his cause began to disturb his own mind.

He had still, however, to try somehow to get the provisions through to the Nor'Westers on the canoe route. On June 22 Macdonell proposed to Francis Heron,[25] a North West Company clerk sent by Grant to negotiate, that one canoe load of provisions might be allowed to pass, provided no wanted man came past the Passage of the Assiniboine.[26] Here was the nub of the situation. Selkirk and his officers were not seeking to starve the Nor'Westers or even to halt the passage of the brigades to the northwest. They were, however, resolved to bring to justice the culprits of 1815 and 1816.

There was another pause. As the days passed the presence of the great man, his personality, his armed force, his gifts of tobacco and rum, began to draw in the ever-curious and ever-needy Métis. The presence of the redcoats, soldiers of the King, underlined the warning of the Prince Regent's Proclamation and the refusal of the freemen to be found in arms against royal authority. Grant's force would soon begin to melt.

Then Angus Shaw, the North West *bourgeois*, came forward on July 3 and was arrested and granted bail. He asked Selkirk's permission to dispatch the provisions. Selkirk granted the request, but only on condition that no wanted man went with them.[27] This broke the deadlock. The pemmican passed down the Red under the guns of Fort Douglas, and Grant could break camp and retire up the Assiniboine.

He did not do so at once, for word was already circulating of the approach of W. B. Coltman, the Commissioner from Canada. It was brought by Richard Grant, a cousin of Cuthbert Grant, in the form of a proclamation. Coltman came as a royal commissioner, sent with Lieutenant-Colonel J. F. Fletcher to inquire into the deed of violence committed in the Indian territories. He would not, like Selkirk, be a reinforcement to the enemy, but an impartial investigator and perhaps a friend, for he came from Canada and the headquarters of the North West Company. Coltman reached The Forks on July 5. He studiously refrained from acknowledging the greeting of Selkirk at Fort Douglas and passed silently up the river. He landed near The Forks and pitched his camp with precision half-way between the two forces.[28] He then began his inquiry, preserving, to Selkirk's irritation, his deliberate impartiality, and taking depositions from all the principals he could reach.

Even Coltman's impartiality, however, was too much for Grant and the Nor'Westers. They ordered the uneasy Métis to move off up the river, and on July 9 the camp at the Passage was broken up. Coltman was alarmed at the prospect of so many witnesses fading off into the plains for the summer. After a hurried pursuit, he overtook the main body of the Métis, and persuaded them to return to the vicinity of The Forks. There he continued the taking of depositions throughout July, while after his colonists' return on July 19 Selkirk turned to the congenial task of re-establishing them on their lands.[29]

Grant did not return with the Métis. Their yielding to the authority of Coltman was a blow to his pride and to his hopes for the new nation. He rode up the Assiniboine with Joseph Cadotte, and lived near Brandon House, it is to be presumed with Bethsy, for the next month. While he passed this month of idleness and discouragement, he brooded over the breakup of the nation, and his position as an agent of the North West Company. He had acted boldly, gladly, confidently in the joint cause of his people and his *bourgeois*. Now the *brûlés* were at The Forks swearing depositions on the events of 1815 and 1816, in which he had led them, or wandering without him on the lonely plains. And the *bourgeois*, would they stand by him now that he was to be held responsible in his own person for deeds he had committed or approved in their cause? To Peter Fidler, busy at work restoring Brandon House for the Hudson's Bay Company, he confided his disillusionment with his nation.[30] His doubts about the *bourgeois* he kept to himself. But they were to increase.

Coltman was not content to deal only with the minor participants in the disturbances. He wanted Grant's desposition. He also wanted Grant. For Coltman, as his report was to reveal, did not regard his commission as merely one of inquiry. He regarded it also as a mission of pacification. For he, like the authorities in London and Canada, did not regard the troubles in the Indian territory as the crimes of individuals, as Selkirk did and as the Nor'Westers professed to do. The disturbances were in Coltman's view "private war," and common sense required not so much the prosecution of individuals as the restoration of order and the pacification of the parties.

The parties, however, were not only the two companies, but also the Métis. They too would have to be reconciled to ensure the peace, for already some of them had gone, and more were talking of going, to the Missouri, there to trade with the Americans. And they would not fail, one could be sure, to trade into British territory. The obvious man to quiet them and to hold them to their allegiance was their late leader, Cuthbert Grant. Coltman, like Selkirk and Macdonell, perceived that Grant was the man who more than any other in the Indian territory could made or destroy the peace the authorities were seeking to restore. If he were driven from Brandon House into exile on the Missouri, he would lead free traders back into British territory. If he were reconciled, he could persuade the Métis to live peacefully with the new order.[31]

But how was this to be done? Selkirk stood by, determined and able to lay charges of murder, arson and larceny against the destroyer of his colony in 1815 and 1816, the leader and accomplice of those who had murdered Semple and Keveny. Examples must indeed be made. Coltman argued that everything pointed to the conclusion that Grant's deeds and the repute in which even his opponents held him did not require that he be made an example. The problem, then, was how to clear him of the charges Selkirk would lay and preserve him as the leader and pacifier of the Métis. Here Coltman was following in the footsteps of Miles Macdonell and Robertson.

The first thing to do was to persuade Grant to come in and make his deposition. On July 31 Coltman wrote to Grant advising him that if he did not feel guilty of any great offence, to surrender as a prisoner and come to Montreal that his conduct might be investigated. He told him that he himself considered as great offenses the murders of Owen Keveny and of those who were dispatched in cold blood (as at Seven Oaks) and the robbing of the bodies after the battle. But he went on:

> . . . as for the battle itself, it is always understood that the Colony people pursued you, or came forward to meet you and fired the first shot while Boucher was speaking to them. I consider this affair, as well as the other violent deeds which took place, although as serious offences against the law, yet such as may be pardoned; all except perhaps those who were the first causes and instigators . . .
>
> I expect that I shall leave here on the 5th of next month and

I will take with me all the prisoners and shall probably return for a few more days at the end of the month if such time agrees with you better for your surrender. . . . Send someone to tell me which way you will be coming and if you wish I will send somebody to meet you lest you should be apprehended . . . and thus lose the honour of your voluntary surrender.[32]

Grant, doubtful as he was of his cause, but acute enough to catch Coltman's broad hint of pardon earned by submission to trial, took leave of Bethsy and their son, James, early in August and set out through the Sand Hills hot with summer. He rode quietly into Coltman's camp with Cadotte and gave himself up. There he made his deposition as to the events of 1815 and 1816,[33] and from there in September he left for Canada in Coltman's canoe. He did not travel as one under arrest, Selkirk's people complained, but as the friend and guest of the commissioner. Some time late in October or early in November he and Cadotte arrived in Montreal ahead of Coltman.[34]

It is not known whether Grant spent the winter of 1817-18 in Montreal at liberty or in jail. Certain it is that in February 1818 a true bill was returned against him at Montreal for the murder of Owen Keveny as well as five bills on other charges.[35] It is also a matter of record that in March he was held in the common gaol of that city. There he made his will out of concern for his wife and son left without support in the Indian country.

Last Will & Testament
of
Mr. Cuthbert Grant
17 March 1818

Before the Undersigned Public Notaries duly Commissioned & Sworn in & for the province of Lower Canada residing in the City of Montreal.

Personally Appeared Mr. Cuthbert Grant Late of the Indian Country at present of the City of Montreal aforesaid Gentleman who being in perfect sound health memory & understanding as appears to us the said Notaries by his Words and actions But considering the Certainty of death and the Uncertainty of the time thereof and Being desirous to dispose of all his property by Will did Make publish & declare Unto us the said Notaries this his Last Will & Testament in Manner following, that is to say.

First, the said Testator doth Will & require that all his just

& lawful debts his funeral & testamentary expenses be first fully paid and discharged.

The said Testator doth give and bequeath unto his Natural son James Grant (Now in the Indian Country) by a Maitiss woman named Elizabeth McKay, the sum of Three thousand pounds Currency of the province to & for his Use & Benefit.

The said Testator doth give & Bequeath Unto the said Elizabeth McKay living with him while in the Indian Country as his Wife the sum of Five hundred pounds said currency to & for her own Use & Benefit & at her own disposal.

And with regard to the rest residue and remainder of all & singular his the said Testator's Estates property & effects both personal & real whereof or Wherein he now is or shall or May be in any Wise possessed or Interested at the time of his decease he the said Testator doth hereby Will bequeath and devise the same to be paid and divided to and between his Nephews now living & being in the Indian Territory or Indian Country aforesaid, to Wit John Wills Junior son of John Wills a partner in the North-West Company, and Francois Morin Junior son of Francois Morin Senior residing in the Indian Country aforesaid the said Testator hereby Constituting them his said Nephews John Wills Junior and Francois Morin Junior his residuing divisers & legatees.

And for the Execution of the present Testament the said Testator hath & doth hereby Constitute & appoint The Honorable William McGillivray of the said City of Montreal Merchant and Mr. John Stewart of the Indian Country aforesaid Merchant executors thereof with power & authority Unto them to hold and exercise their trust Jointly or severally in that Capacity over & beyond the year and day limited by Law and in as full and ample a Manner as executors or an executor Can or May hold & Exercise the same by the Laws of England any Law usage or Custom of this province to the Contrary Notwithstanding. Hereby revoking and Making Void all former or other Will & Wills or Codicils by him at any time heretofore made or Executed Willing & desirous that these presents shall take place and be executed as being his Intention and last Will & Testament, for thus it hath been made dictated and Named Unto us the said Notaries and by one of us read & read over the other being present which said Testator hath persisted therein at Montreal aforesaid in the Common Gaol of the District of Montreal, in the appartments of Gwyn Owen . . . [illegible] the Gaoler the Seventeenth day of March in the year of our Lord one thousand Eight hundred and Eighteen in the forenoon and signed by the said Testator in the presence of us the said Notaries who have hereunto also Subscribed our Names in his presence & in the presence of each other these presents being twice read to him according to the law.

(Signed) Cuthbert Grant

Thos. Barron, N.P.   H. Griffin

Not. pub.[36]

Having put his private affairs in order, Grant awaited trial with de Reinhard, McLellan, and others for the murder of Keveny. It proved impossible to find impartial jurors in Montreal, and the case was adjourned to Quebec and the session of the Court of King's Bench. There the Grand Jury in March found true bills against de Reinhard and McLellan, but not against the others.[37] Grant ought then to have gone to the sessions of the Court of Oyer and Terminer in Sandwich, Upper Canada, to which the North West cases had been transferred, to stand trial for the murder of Semple. But he was released in Quebec on a slight recognizance and left at once for Montreal.

He did not go to Upper Canada at all. As early as May 12 Selkirk had protested against the transfer of the case from Lower to Upper Canada. The Solicitor-General for Lower Canada replied that he had orders not to proceed further against Grant, but that he was sure Selkirk would be able to do so in the courts of Upper Canada. This Selkirk expressed his determination to do,[38] and a true bill was later returned against Grant and others at York for murder of Semple. But word soon came to Selkirk in June that Grant had left Quebec for the Indian country and that his recognizance was likely to be forfeited, as apparently it was.[39] Selkirk at once wrote to the Solicitor-General, urging that Grant be arrested before his departure from Montreal, and a warrant seems to have been issued for the purpose. But before it could be served, Grant had left for Fort William in a light canoe.[40] Grant was thus not brought to trial on any of the six charges against him in the courts of Upper Canada, and he was to remain in the northwest until the trials had ended and the troubles in the Indian country subsided.

What conclusion is to be attempted as this chapter in Grant's life ended? Was he, as Selkirk bitterly wrote, a "notorious criminal" allowed to jump bail and to go untried and unpunished? The considered answer, made here in the face of much evidence is, no. Two views may be taken of the violence in the Indian country in 1815 and 1816. The events may be regarded as the incidents of a private war among two great corporations, each in effect claiming to exercise sovereignty at least in its own defence. The agents of such contestants might be held to be agents only and not principals. This was Coltman's view, exhibited when he repeated Grant's claim that he had orders for all he did.[41] The other view is that the deeds of violence were crimes for which individuals might be responsible before the law as principals. It was on this view that the arrests were made, the charges laid and the trials held, and it was to make this view prevail that Selkirk pushed the prosecution in the courts of Canada. It was in deference to this view that Coltman thought examples should be made.

To explain how Grant emerged from the trials unscathed and why it was possible in his after life for bygones to be treated as bygones, it is necessary to look at his part in the violence of 1815 and 1816 from both points of view. Grant was an agent of the North West Company, loyally carrying out orders. But he was also a private individual implicated in the crimes of murder, arson and larceny. On the first view much might be excused, especially as he was a man of great and perhaps decisive influence in the Indian country. But justice required that he stand trial in person for the crimes imputed to him. This Grant did, but apparently by arrangement. He faced trial for the murder of Owen Keveny, as an accomplice in the second degree, but in the preliminary hearing at Quebec, no bill was found against him. This verdict seems to have been in accordance with the facts. He was then tried by implication and by proxy, as it were, when Boucher was tried at York in Upper Canada, and acquitted, for the murder of Semple. This undoubtedly was arranged, as the handling of the transfer of the cases to the Upper Canadian courts suggests. It is also to be noted, as testimony to the thoroughness with which the legal friends of the Nor'Westers proceeded, that the case of Boucher was "one of the least aggravated."[42] But it created at least the presumption that if Boucher was innocent, Grant and the other participants were also.

Grant was thus by implication cleared of the charges of murder. However reprehensible the connivance of the law officers of Lower Canada may have been, and it was reprehensible,[43] it seems clear after a study of the events which led to the deaths of Semple and Keveny, that Grant cannot be held to have been guilty of murder in either case. He did not seek the encounter of June 19; he did not fire the first shot; he did not kill Semple. He did not order the death of Keveny, did not kill him, and was not present at his death.

For the other less serious crimes it may be sufficient to regard them as being in fact incidents of private warfare, reprehensible in them selves but not acts for which individuals might justly be held account able.

Finally, there was the ground of policy to be urged, that Grant, if purged of the charges against him, might in fact be an influence for peace in the Indian country.

These views and the argument are in fact those of Coltman, the pacifier and friend of the North West Company. He had sought Grant out; he had pointed out to him how necessary it was to clear himself He had indicated the future he might have in the service of the North West Company, and of the Métis, perhaps even of the government He must have assured Grant that the clearing could be arranged, not without risk, but with a fair certainty of success. And Grant had followed his lead and gone with him to trial.

Coltman on the eve of Grant's trial proceeded to develop his theme. In his report the Commissioner had argued that the events of June 19 were more akin to war than to ordinary homicide. What was required was not so much to make the punishment of every individual concerned in the troubles as severe as the letter of the law required as to ensure that of those guilty of atrocities or unusual and unnecessary violence, as old Deschamps and his sons seem to have been, should be made examples. He had then proceeded to discuss those of whom an example might be made. Alexander Fraser he had exempted, for humanity shown and testified to. And he had specially singled Grant out for his restraint and his humanity after the collision, and had given credence to his claim that he had tried to stop the barbarities.[44]

This view of Grant's role Coltman now repeated in his letter of May 14, 1818, written at the request of Lieutenant-Governor Sir John Sherbrooke for Coltman's individual view of the disturbances. He stated his opinion that in the meeting of June 19 "the two parties seem to have met accidentally, and with arms in their hands, and with mutually irritated feelings"; that the meeting was unintended; and that the first shot, "next to a certainty," was fired by Semple's party. Coltman then proceeded to point out that Grant had tried to check the outburst of savagery that followed the exchange of shots. He added that "the total absence of any accusation against Grant on this score [of savagery] and the numerous testimonies to his general humanity, leave little doubt of the truth of this assertion."[45] Grant's conduct, however, only seemed to him to underline the dangerous policy the North West Company had been pursuing in using the Métis for its own ends.

On May 20, 1818, Coltman wrote again to the Lieutenant-Governor elaborating his views of how the disturbances in the Indian country might be pacified. There was nothing, he wrote, to fear from the Indians in the Red River country. Most of the half-breeds, however, had retreated to American territory and might be used by Americans to capture the fur trade. Plans for such a capture might already be in agitation. But should Cuthbert Grant clear himself "as to be at all considered a fit instrument for Government to make use of, that may be wished for with the other half-breeds, amongst whom his influence appears very great, as I believe it also to be with the Cree Indians, from a considerable family belonging to which tribe he is understood to be descended on his mother's side."[46]

Here was the full development of the plan Coltman had begun to make at The Forks of Red River on July 31, 1817. Grant by his influence over his people might be the pacifier of the northwest.

It was therefore desirable to bring Grant and the others to an early trial for the murder of Owen Keveny. It was desirable to clear Grant for the great work. Grant himself, Coltman went on, was not unworthy of such consideration. His "general appearance" bespoke "frankness and generosity." There was (now) no other instance of atrocity against him except the charge of implication in Keveny's murder. But there were "many" instances "quite the reverse." The violence Grant had used "must be allowed to be greatly palliated by the sincere opinion he seems to have entertained that the half-breeds and the North West Company were the attacked and injured parties."

Coltman then referred to Grant's having been orphaned at seven years of age, and to his being raised and educated by the company, which had been as a father to him. He also urged that the other charges against Grant could not be tried until further witnesses were brought from the Indian country.[47] This last point was of course meant particularly to affect the treatment of Grant by the authorities.

The whole was a persuasive brief for letting Grant go free immediately and indefinitely, and of seeking redemptive services from him once he had been cleared of the charge of complicity in Keveny's murder. The Grand Jury freed him shortly after Coltman wrote, as has been seen, and by mid-June he was on his way back to the Red River country. His Nor'Wester friends had used their influence to serve him well. Justice was not formally done. Grant should have stood trial at Sandwich. But there is little reason to suppose that he would not have been acquitted there.

The above is offered, not so much as a conclusive explanation of Grant's trial and acquittal, but as the only partially coherent explanation of what happened that it is possible to draw from the surviving evidence. Grant was brought to trial by Coltman's persuasion, and his trial and that of others were so conducted as to be tantamount to an acquittal of Grant from the capital charges against him. As an explanation it is defective in detail, but it does square with the whole conduct of Coltman's commission and with the tenor of the trials in the courts of Canada. The charges against Grant were tried in his person by the Grand Jury of Quebec and by proxy in the Courts of Upper Canada, and he was cleared, directly or by implication, of all the indictments. And his subsequent career in the northwest was to demonstrate his virtual innocence even more clearly than any sifting of the facts of the past.

CHAPTER VI

THE YEARS OF UNCERTAINTY,

1818-1823

By mid-summer 1818, Grant was once more back in the Red River country and on his way to Qu'Appelle. He came back, it may be supposed, older and graver. He had returned from the prisons and courts of Canada unharmed. The North West Company and its friends had stood by him in Canada, if they had left him to appear the man responsible for Seven Oaks in 1817. They had in effect cleared him of the charges laid by Selkirk. But the old exuberant loyalty to the company had been damped. Grant had seen that the cause of the Nor'Westers was not the clear case he had thought. He had sensed the fine distinctions of the law, and had seen that law might be the defence of his enemies. He had reflected on the consequences of violence. And he had not freed his mind of the suspicion that the Nor'Westers had used him and the Métis for their own ends, and had left them exposed to the law when Selkirk and Coltman had held The Forks of the Red in 1817. Henceforth he would serve the company with a growing reserve. To the cause of the Métis, his Young Fellows, however, he was now more than ever attached.

He had returned to the northwest also full of thoughts of Bethsy and their child. He had had many long thoughts of them during their extended separation when he was in Montreal and Quebec. As he had sat in the gaoler's quarters in Montreal making the will which provided for their future from his father's estate, he knew it would make Bethsy a woman of means and importance in the Red River country and that perhaps his son might have a better life than he had had.

But he found on his arrival that the one happiness which he had thought remained to him was gone. Bethsy had disappeared and had taken their child with her. It seemed the end of everything, and the happy dreams that had helped to sustain him in his troubles were ended.

Bethsy never again appeared in his life, and shortly afterwards Grant entered into a second *mariage du pays* with a girl named Madeline Desmarais, daughter of a well-known Métis family. This union seems to have been short lived, and ended in 1820 with the birth of a girl whom Grant named Maria. He placed the child in the care of his sister Mrs John Wills, who afterwards brought her to live with Grant when he had settled.

The changes in Grant's life were matched by a change in Red River. Selkirk's colony was now re-established and in fact would not again be disturbed. The de Meurons had remained in the colony as soldier settlers. In them the colony had a defence that Grant and the *bois-brûlés* were not to choose to challenge. It was not fear of the de Meurons alone that stayed them; it was as well fear of the law which in 1817 had extended its arm into the Indian Territory. The warnings of the freemen were remembered, and for the future their half-breed sons would be as cautious as themselves about coming into conflict with the law.

For this reason many of the freemen and *brûlés had* remained away from The Forks since the summer of 1817. They had no wish to be drawn again into the fur-traders' war. That war, however, had not been quenched either by the Prince Regent's Proclamation or the trials in the courts of Canada. The Nor'Westers still hoped to harry their rivals from the northwest, and the Hudson's Bay Company, strengthened by the re-establishment of the Red River Colony, was becoming ever more bold. The Nor'Westers now sought to use Grant and the *brûlés* once more, this time by playing desperately on their fear of the law. On Grant they urged the necessity of his continuing to lead his people. The need was greater than ever, they declared, for the colonial authorities proposed to arrest more of the *brûlés* for trial in Canada. (Warrants were indeed promised by the Canadian authorities for the arrest of various Nor'Westers.)[1] These arrests, they affirmed, would certainly result in conviction despite the acquittals of 1818. Among the *brûlés* they spread the same rumours and misrepresentations. Greatly alarmed, many of the *brûlés* drew together in the Pembina hills, where they formed a menace overhanging the colony all the winter of 1818-19 and summer of 1819.[2] That Grant was with them at least part of the time may be supposed, but no account remains.

The year 1819, though an important one for Grant, has left little record of his life. No word from him, and scant word of him, has been found, but it is evident that he continued as a clerk of the North West Company at Qu'Appelle where his sister, the widowed Mrs Wills, may have shared his home and his difficulties.

Grant's personal life was pushed into the background by the bold offensive begun by the Hudson's Bay Company in the summer of 1819. The fur-traders' war then flared up with its old fierceness. Colin Robertson, returned from England, had led an expedition into the Athabasca in the summer of 1818.[3] During the winter he was opposed with every variety of North West violence and finally arrested. But the Hudson's Bay Company was now governed in Rupert's Land by a man of spirit akin to that of the Nor'Westers. He was William Williams, who had been appointed Governor-in-Chief and sent to Red River in 1818. Williams was a pugnacious old soldier, a rough-and-ready martinet who would not knuckle under to North West bullying. At the news of Robertson's arrest he gathered warrants for the arrest of the Athabasca partners and "battlers" of the North West Company. On June 8 he left Red River with a party of twenty de Meurons and sailed in a decked and armed schooner (not the *Cuchillon* which the Nor'-Westers had burned in 1817) to the Grand Rapids of the Saskatchewan. At the foot of the rapids, he ambushed the Athabasca brigades, the partners and their strongly armed men, and put them under arrest. Only one small party escaped by way of Lake Winnipegosis. The arrested men were sent by way of York Factory to England for trial. One of them, Benjamin Frobisher, escaped and died of starvation.[4]

This humiliating stroke aroused the now weakening North West Company to make one last blow in the old style. It was not directed at the Red River colony. It was explicit retaliation − an ambush of Colin Robertson's Athabasca brigade at the Grand Rapids in the summer of 1820. Once more the *bois-brûlés* were used, because they as natives of the country could hope to escape arrest and trial more easily than the partners. During the winter of 1819-20 all the old work of rousing and cajoling the Métis went on. The buffalo were driven away from Pembina and Governor Alexander Macdonell issued a proclamation against running the herds; the de Meurons were tempted with drink to desert and the older inhabitants of the colony were inflamed against its officers.[5]

It seemed a repetition of the harrying of 1815. It is to be supposed that Grant played his part in this, for when the *brûlés* mustered at Bas de la Rivière at the end of May Grant was with them, as one of the "clerks and interpreters" among the partners of the company. With him were many of the men of Seven Oaks. A party of sixty men left in five canoes for the mouth of the Saskatchewan. There they laid in ambush at the foot of the falls and waited for Robertson's canoes. On June 28 Robertson, having failed to find a guide to lead him around the ambush of which he had been warned, ran the rapids and was captured. Among his captors were William Shaw and Cuthbert Grant, "half-breed clerks of the North-West Company," who, as Robertson noted, had been concerned in the destruction of the Red River colony in 1815 and 1816.[6]

In an altercation which followed over the warrant for arrest, Robertson observed that it was strange that in the execution of a lawful warrant the "murderers of Red River should be employed." At this

Grant drew his pistol, exclaiming, "Don't insult the half-breeds or I'll shoot you!"[7] Robertson was then sent off to Canada for trial on a charge of murder. But Grant's exclamation stands out. He threatened the contemptuous and probably derisive Robertson, not in his own defence or that of the North West Company, but on behalf of the Métis. Henceforth their cause alone was to be his cause. The North West Company was crumbling. The blow at Grand Rapids was its last. The fur-traders' war was about to be ended. But the Métis would remain in the northwest, and Grant with them.

The renewal of the war in 1819 and 1820 could not, indeed, be further tolerated by the Imperial Government or in any case continued by the North West Company. The Imperial Government now insisted that the rivalry of the companies be ended by union; and in union the influential men of the two companies saw the only hope of preserving the fur trade. In 1821 the two united as the Hudson's Bay Company, in what was in effect the wedding of the name, the charter, and the stability of the British company with the experience and hard-driving skill of the North West wintering partners. In the negotiations in London the latter obtained the key positions and a preponderance of power in the new company. John George Mactavish, a leading *bourgeois*, was moved at once to take charge of the new company at York Factory on Hudson Bay. In the union those who had lately been engaged in bitter and violent competition had to learn to work together at counter and council. Old Nor'Westers, *bourgeois* and clerks, now found themselves factors and traders, clerks and interpreters of the new company. And with the new order peace came at last to the northwest.

Grant, however, was not among the Nor'Westers who were taken into the service of the new company. In the whole fur country only two North West men of significance were excluded from the new company, and of these Grant was one. It was a bitter blow to him. At first sight the passing over of Grant seems strange. But his patron, William McGillivray, was not one of the makers of the union. Grant's was an old Nor'Wester name. No one had served the Company more loyally. No one had more influence over the Indians and Métis of the Red River country. He had been ignored.

The reasons are not apparent.[8] Perhaps the issues which were worked out in London in 1820-21 were too big for the fate of a young half-breed clerk to be taken into account. Perhaps the memories of Seven Oaks and Grand Rapids among the Hudson's Bay Company were too lively and too bitter. Whatever the reason, Grant found himself in the fall of 1821 adrift and without employment. And Mc-

Gillivray still controlled and had not transferred his father's legacy to him. Cuthbert Grant was in an anxious and humiliating position.

The winter of 1821-22 was to prove the season of his severest trial, from which he was to emerge with his course clear before him. If Grant was discontented, there were many opportunities to express his discontent in a way the new Hudson's Bay Company might have long regretted. There was, for example, distress in the Red River colony. The crops of 1821 had been very short and, although the provident Scots settlers were not in want, the Canadians and the de Meurons were again dependent on the plains for provisions. They had to hunt the buffalo. In the autumn the plains Indians had deliberately kept the herds away from Red River "by obstructing them at their usual passes to the North-West, setting fire to the plains," to show their resentment at the union of the companies. They feared that the monopoly would mean higher prices for the goods they had to buy. But when the winter came, Indians and colonists were alike threatened with starvation, for deep snow followed the Indians' fires to keep the buffalo far away from the Red River valley.[9]

In this time of distress and resentment, Grant heard that three Canadian traders – Nolin, Larante, and Forrest, the last an old North West name – had appeared at Pembina. And he knew that his old friend of 1817, Joseph Cadotte, was at Rainy Lake. Both the Indians and the Métis would welcome this re-appearance of competition, and the union of the old companies might be undone by a new opposition.[10]

Grant soon heard that the Canadian freemen and the Métis were plotting to revenge the defeat and loss they had suffered from the merger by attacking and plundering the new company's posts at The Forks and at Pembina. Their anger at the monopoly was overcoming their newly acquired respect for law. They only needed a leader to wave them on, to put on war paint and ride down on Red River as they had done in the early summer of 1816. Grant listened to the reports of their grumblings and plottings but held his own counsel. But they knew his resentment at being left out of the new arrangements, and the knowledge fed their own resentment. They counted on him to lead them again as in 1815 and 1816. They sent a deputation to him at Fort Hibernia (on the upper Assiniboine near the source of the Swan River, just five miles upstream from the site of his boyhood home, Fort Tremblante) where Nicholas Garry, a member of the governing committee of the new company sent to supervise the union in Rupert's Land in 1821, had allowed Grant to winter.[11] The freemen and the Métis came to Grant privately there, told him of the plans, and asked him to lead them against the company's establishments.

Grant "declined that honor."[12] He had made up his mind. He woul
not again lead the Métis in lawless violence. The old North West caus
held him no longer. The careless loyalty of his youth was ended. Gran
had put himself squarely and firmly on the side of law and order. B
doing so he made it possible to bring the Métis over to the side of lav
under the new regime. It was the most critical decision of Grant's life
and it was crucial for the history of the northwest. There was to b
no renewal of the old North West opposition, no guerrilla trade of th
plains waged by Grant's Métis.

How dangerous an opposite decision by Grant might have been i
illustrated by what was happening at Pembina. That settlement, ar
other "forks" of the Red, had rivalled Selkirk's colony at The Fork
since 1812. It had the great advantage of proximity to the buffal
herds, which were kept away from The Forks by the marshes of th
Rivière aux Ilets de Bois. There some of the freemen and Métis wer
settling (as they thought) on British soil, and the Reverend S. S. Du
moulin[13] had begun a mission of Saint-François-Xavier among them
shortly after he and the Reverend J. N. Provencher had begun th
Red River mission in 1818. But Peter Fidler, the Hudson's Bay Com
pany's surveyor, had declared that Pembina was south of the nev
boundary laid down at the 49th parallel in 1818, and Major Stephei
Long of the United States Army proved him right in 1823.[14] Thus th
Métis settlement at Pembina would be outside the jurisdiction of th
Hudson's Bay Company. When the Canadian traders came there in
1821, it was clear that a new opposition might shelter there beyon
the reach of the Hudson's Bay Company. Had Grant chosen to lea
such an opposition, a new North West Company might well hav
sprung up. American traders would come north from St Peter's on
the Mississippi, and Canadians from Prairie du Chien in Wisconsin
Small wonder that John Halkett,[15] executor of the Selkirk estate, wa
to resolve in 1822 that the settlement must be moved north to The
Forks. Or that George Simpson, Governor-in-Chief of the Hudson'
Bay Company's Northern Department, would decide that Grant wa
a man who could not be ignored and must be brought into the com
pany's service.

Grant and Simpson had met at Fort Hibernia at the end of February
1822. Simpson may indeed have been in time to help Grant make hi
decision not to lead the Métis against the company's post. Certainl
it is difficult to believe that their meeting was casual. Grant seems to
have responded to the direct approach and brisk warmth of the
calculating young Scots governor. What Simpson thought of "the

elebrated Cuthbert Grant," he recorded in his journal of this journey
f February 28:

> Cuthbert Grant is not on the books altho allowed to remain at
> the post: he appears a very steady good tempered well behaved
> man possessing strong natural parts and some Education about
> 25 years of age Stout & active; he seems to have been entirely
> made a party tool of & in the late unfortunate business more
> activated by the impulse to irritation of the moment than design
> and I am convinced regrets it as much as any one; he might be
> made a most useful man of by good management as he possesses
> much influence among the Servants halfbreeds & Indians but if
> treated w[it]h. harshness a most dangerous enemy and on the
> Score of policy I think it might be judicious to allow him to re-
> main in the Service; he is not satisfied wh. the Messrs McGillivrays
> as they have given him no statement of his Fathers affairs &
> seems to suspect that he is not justly treated. I have recom-
> mended his being allowed to remain about the place & hope to
> be enabled to get him into the Service again.[16]

This was Simpson's first impression of Grant. Their acquaintance
was to ripen quickly. Simpson's next destination was Brandon House
and, as there were on the track some thirty tents of Indians who were
ikely to give trouble, Grant volunteered to act as guide. He went
ahead to the "Hunters Tent," where Simpson overtook him on March 4.
Riding on in company, they stalked and wounded three buffalo, a
failure which Grant later redeemed by killing a bull. They reached
Brandon House on March 6, where they found Colin Robertson and
John Richards McKay in charge.

The intimacy which had developed on the trip now led Grant to
take Simpson into his confidence. Simpson records:

> Grant showed me a letter from Mr. Wm. McGillivray recommend-
> ing his going down to Canada to get clear of the Bills of Indict-
> ment which he is determined on doing in Spring; he also proposes
> going to England to make some Enquiry after his private affairs.
> Mr. McGillivray acknowledges that he has from (£)4 or (£)5000
> in his hands but Grant has pretty good information that it should
> be (£)13 or (£)14000 & suspects that they are inclined to impose
> on him; his object seems to be [to] deposit his money in safe
> hands & re-enter the Service but if not admitted I suspect he will
> be inclined to form an opposition & if he does so he will be a

very dangerous man as he has many followers & great controul over half breeds & Indians, he gave me a full statement of the Red River unfortunate affair from which it would appear that he did little more than defend himself party & property and altho dissatisfied w[it]h the N.W. Coy. disclaims any instructions or previous arrangement for destroying the Colony; he is a manly spirited fellow & I should hope that the Committee will not object to his being again admitted into the Service.[17]

Simpson then ends his record by noting how Grant chastised a Canadian who grew troublesome at a dance that night.

Grant remained at Brandon House, while Simpson went on to The Forks. Grant, Simpson had resolved, must be won and kept for the company. But how could he persuade the committee in London to admit the outlaw of Seven Oaks into the service? He turned to Andrew Colvile, one of the most influential men in the Company, and brother of Lady Selkirk. Grant, he wrote, had been convinced that Semple had meant to attack his party at Seven Oaks. If there were more to tell, his dissatisfaction with McGillivray would have led him to tell it. Grant, however, did admit that Alexander Macdonell made a tool of him; his only desire had been to obey. Grant was now "about 25 years of age, an active clean made fellow, possessing strong natural parts and a great deal of cool determination: His manners are mild and rather pleasing than otherways." He wished to be in the service again and his appointment would gratify "all the North West party in the country." Simpson thought Grant had no wish to be troublesome, but was sure he could be. Might he not be "smuggled into the Service," or made leader of the proposed expedition to the South Branch of the Saskatchewan?[18]

Meantime, Simpson would win Grant to the company's side by every means he commanded. On May 29 Grant came down to The Forks from Brandon House. On June 1 he and Simpson talked at length, although neither seems to have recorded what passed. But surely Simpson told Grant the substance and intent of what he had written to Colvile. And surely he promised him aid in going to England to settle his affairs with McGillivray. Certainly, Grant lent Simpson what service he could. When two of Simpson's canoe-men deserted, Grant pursued one of them to Pembina. In three days he was back with his man, a Canadian. After this demonstration of his mastery of the people of the country, Grant embarked on June 7 in the Governor's canoe for Montreal. He was no more an overlooked and disregarded clerk. He rode beside the most powerful man in the fur trade, whose chief concern it was to keep him out of the country, or content within it.[19]

Nothing is known of what Grant did in Canada, except that he made a new will. This was necessary, as his will of 1818 was made pointless by Bethsy's desertion or death. In the new bequests he remembered his relatives, Peter Stuart in Scotland, who had perhaps arranged for his education, and, despite the loss of Bethsy and her child and the strain of the fur-traders' war, his one time brother-in-law and constant friend, John Richards McKay. The residue he left to his infant daughter Maria, born in 1820 of his union with Madeline Desmarais. This second will is one of the fullest remaining documents of his life:

> On the thirteenth day of November in the year of our Lord one thousand eight hundred & twenty two; Before the undersigned Public Notaries duly Commissioned and Sworn in & for the province of Lower Canada residing in the City of Montreal in the said province.
>
> Personally appeared Mr. Cuthbert Grant late of the Indian Country now in the said City of Montreal, Who being in perfect health, sound Mind Memory and understanding as appears to us the said Notaries by his words and actions, and who considering the uncertainty of this Transitory life is desirous of disposing of all his property by Will and therefore did make publish and declare unto us the said Notaries his Last Will & Testament in manner and form following that is to say: —
>
> First — The said testator doth Will & require that all his just & Lawful debts his funeral & testamentary expenses be first fully paid and discharged.
>
> The said testator doth give & bequeath unto his Cousin Peter ————— Stuart whom he supposes to be residing in that part of the United Kingdom of Great Britain & Ireland called Scotland brother of John Stuart one of the partners in the Honorable the Hudson's Bay Company the sum of Five hundred pounds Current Money of the said province of Lower Canada.
>
> The said testator doth give and bequeath to his brother-in-law John Richards McKay now of Red River Clerk in the Honorable The Hudsons Bay Company's service, a like sum of Five hundred pounds Current Money aforesaid.
>
> And with regard to all the rest Residue and remainder of his the said testator's Estate property & Effects as well personal as real whereof or wherein he now is or shall or May be in any

wise possessed or Interested at the time of his decease he the said testator doth hereby Will bequeath and devise the same – unto his natural daughter, Maria now in the Indian Country, a Minor, to & for her own use & benefit and at her own disposal hereby appointing his said daughter Maria his sole residuary deviser & legatee.

And for the Execution of the present Last Will & Testament the said testator hath & doth hereby name and appoint Henry ———— McKenzie of the said City of Montreal Esquire and the above-Named Peter Stuart Executors thereof with full power unto them to hold and exercise their & his trust in that Capacity either jointly or separately over and beyond the year & day limited by Law and in as full & ample a manner as Executors or an Executor can or May hold and Exercise the same by the Laws of England any Law usage or Custom to the Contrary therefor notwithstanding hereby revoking & Making void all former or other Will & Wills or Codicils by him at any time heretofore Made or executed willing & desirous that these presents shall take place and be executed as being his intention and last Will & Testament; for thus it hath been made dictated & named unto us the said Notaries and by one of us read & read over the other being present which said testator hath persisted therein at Montreal aforesaid in the Office of Henry Griffin one of the said Notaries of the day Month & year first before Written in the afternoon and signed by the said testator in presence of us the ———— said Notaries who have hereunto subscribed our names in his ———— presence of each other these presents being first, twice read to him according to law.

(Signed) Cuthbert Grant

P. E. Daveluy, N.P.   H. Griffin, N.P.[2]

Whether his presence in Canada and especially in Montreal stirred the authorities to bring him to trial for the old indictments of 1818 is unknown. It is more than likely that everyone was content to forget them, and that McGillivray had mentioned them to keep Grant in the northwest, not to bring him to Canada. Whatever the reason, it is clear that Grant did not become involved in the courts on this visit but came and went freely.

Neither is anything known of his journey to England nor of his visit there. (He did not succeed in settling his financial affairs; McGillivray was not to give satisfaction until 1825, when Simpson finally arranged matters.)[21]

In the spring of 1823 Grant sailed for Canada and the fur country. e evidently travelled westward from Montreal with his cousin hief Factor John Stuart. As they neared one of the Rainy Lake sts, they were hailed by John Tanner, who was lying wounded on e shore of a small island. He had been shot by an Indian escaping ith one of the white man's daughters. Tanner had heard a trader's noe was coming, and had waited for the help it might bring. The port that Grant produced a lancet to help remove the bullet from nner's chest,[22] hints that he may have spent part of the previous inter (1822-23) in England studying medicine.

Other than this story, supported as it is by knowledge of his later edical practice among his people,[23] there is no indication of how rant passed his winter in the Old Country. In any event he seems ly to have acquired a skill any ship's captain or experienced traveller the time possessed.

But preparations were being completed for taking Cuthbert Grant to the service of the Hudson's Bay Company. Obviously the London mmittee had agreed to Simpson's proposal of 1822. On July 5 the uncil of the Northern Department of Rupert's Land appointed rant, along with Cuthbert Cummings, James Hargrave, and Andrew cDermot, to be a clerk in Lower Red River for three years at a salary ' not more than £120.[24] Simpson wrote a formal letter at York Fac-ry, addressed to "Mr. Cuthbert Grant, En Route," informing him of s appointment, and directing him to proceed to Fort Garry at the rliest opportunity, and place himself under the charge of Chief actor Donald McKenzie.[25]

In early August Grant travelled from Fort Alexander to Norway ouse. On his arrival on August 5, he found Governor Simpson's letter waiting him. Grant replied:

> Sir
> Your polite note of the 14th July I only received yesterday on my arrival here, and have to acquaint you that I am agreeably willing to accept of the offers made to me and for the time specified in your note, for which allow me to return you and Council my sincere thanks — I shall avail myself of the first opportunity that shall offer to proceed to Red River without loss of time, and remain
>
> > Sir
> > With respect, your Most Obedient
> > and very humble servant
> > (Signed) Cuthbert Grant[26]

Thus rather oddly and, as it was to prove, mistakenly, Grant set to work in the heart of the colony he had twice harried out of existence. At first all seemed well. The Records of Clerk's Services for 1823 noted that he was "a tolerable clerk good Trader active and steady will be extremely useful in Red River on account of his influence with the Half breeds."[27] All this was true. Grant's presence did begin to draw the suspicious and still resentful Métis to Fort Garry. The de Meurons, remembering his fame as a warrior, respected him. And Grant gave to his new master that steady loyalty he had given so staunchly to the old.

In his new position he found himself in congenial company among the other young clerks. There were his cousin Cuthbert Cummings, a genial Irishman named Andrew McDermot, and a young Scot, James Hargrave, all appointed with him.[28]

Grant's surroundings at the Fort were probably much the same as those described by later clerks. The walls of the counting-room were gay with colour, painted for three feet upward in bright blue. This gave way to a band of flashing red, above which an expanse of yellow was topped by a strong orange ceiling. This room was an office by day, furnished with "two large desks and several very tall stools, besides sundry ink bottles, rulers, books and sheets of blotting paper." But at night the place was transformed, for here the clerks gathered for their fun around the huge corner fireplace piled with blazing logs. The clerks' three bedrooms, with doors always open in winter for warmth, lent to this room a background of colour, with bright-hued Hudson's Bay blankets on the beds and gaily-beaded garments and shot-belts hanging on pegs driven into the walls.

The life to which Grant had come meant writing hour after hour each day, which the clerks suffered as best they could. A Scottish clerk who came to the Fort Garry a little later described his method of relieving these endless hours. "When I begin to nod in the midst of calculations," he wrote, "I have recourse to my old antidote, the Blue Bonnets over the Border. Turning round from the desk . . . I advance . . . bawling out as lustily as I can 'March, March, Etterick and Teviotdale etc. etc.' "[29]

In late summer when Grant joined them the clerks, once work was over, relieved the tedium by mounting their horses and galloping over the prairies, frequently taking their guns along to snipe at small game.

In winter the main sport was on the frozen river where all the settlement, clerks included, raced their horses or, wrapped in fur robes, drove in their carrioles for miles along the smooth windswept pathway on the river ice.

Grant visited in the family of Angus McGillis whom he knew and
who had recently retired to Red River. Late that autumn of 1823 he
married Marie, oldest daughter in the household.[30] From her descendants one gathers that she was a buxom lass, and in addition she brought
her husband a dowry of £500. The marriage ceremony took place in
t Boniface Cathedral. No doubt it was a festive occasion and, such
was their status, the young couple may even have been given quarters
in the Fort.

Simpson congratulated himself that Grant's admission to the new
company had given much satisfaction, but the Governor had not yet
acquired all the astuteness which characterized his management in
later years. He might better have assigned Grant to any other post
than that of the colony which he had twice wiped out. Furthermore,
Simpson had immediately brought him into further prominence by
swearing him in as a special constable in some current friction between
the colony and the company caused by the desire of some colonists
to go into business as traders.

Though Grant, no doubt, was happy in being settled and regularly
married, he was soon aware of a certain undercurrent against him.
His appointment had inflamed Alexander Macdonell, Governor for a
time and now a member of the Council of Assiniboia. Grant sensed
that he was still his enemy, and before long Macdonell showed his
hand as such, using several settlers who had not forgotten that it was
Grant who in 1816 had taken their fort and sent them off homeless in
the boats. They made a "premeditated and unprovoked attack" upon
him when he was on duty. Grant preferred a charge against them,
which Governors Simpson and Pelly brought before the Council.[31]

Simpson reported on the proceedings to Andrew Colvile:

> After a long and impartial investigation Grant's charge was fully
> and clearly substantiated and the aggressors were punished by
> a light fine, but at the close of the proceedings Macdonell could
> not conceal with all his duplicity and cunning the highly im-
> proper and indecorous part he took in the affair, and nearly
> suffocated with rage which he could not suppress . . . asserting
> that Grant was brought to Fort Garry merely to alarm and hurt
> the feelings of the Settlers and that *he* would represent the matter
> at home![32]

But in spite of Grant's vindication, Simpson decided that it would
be best for him to retire from the service, and Grant's resignation was
accepted in 1824.[33] It may be that in coming to this decision the

Governor was influenced by an urgent need he had for Grant elsewhere in a problem that for some time had been calling for a solution.

In 1822 John Halkett visited the colony in the interests of Lord Selkirk. After the amalgamation of the companies in 1821, the Métis at Pembina were considerably increased in number by people from discontinued posts. Mr Halkett considered settlement there undesirable. Its situation on the border increased the danger of a Métis alliance with the American traders. There was also danger from the Sioux. Governor Simpson admitted that Pembina was "much exposed to the hostile visits of the neighboring Indians (the Sioux)."[34] It had been attacked that season several times, and fourteen people had been either killed or wounded. The Company had withdrawn the post in an endeavour to concentrate settlement at The Forks. They relied on Bishop Provencher's influence with the Métis to effect their removal.

Provencher wrote on September 1, 1822, "I will try to enter into the views of Mr Halkett and induce the people [the Métis at Pembina] to settle at The Forks or its vicinity."[35] The following July he commented further, "Mr. Halkett who moved Heaven and earth to destroy Pembina neglected to tell the Governor what to do with these people. We moved nearly all of them this Spring [1823] and they are at the Forks. They are camping along the river."[36]

Upon Grant's retirement in the spring of 1824 they were still there and still presenting a serious problem to the Governor. These displaced people must be settled, and the idea of a new nation which they still held must if possible be quenched. Who could so well establish them as their former leader, Cuthbert Grant, now so loyal to the new Company? Who could better win the Indians than this man who had "more influence with them than anyone in the country"? After the attacks of the Sioux at Pembina, Grant had offered to lead reprisals against them but the Governor had a different idea. Grant could found a settlement with these Métis to guard the colony against further attacks. As early as January 27, 1824, Simpson reported, "Grant has some idea of turning Settler with his Father-in-law next season."[37] On May 31, Simpson wrote to A. Colvile of the Company in London:

I have made it my business to secure Grant's attachment and good offices . . . and by management I have got him to retire from the Service, and turn settler. I have got an order on McGillivrays to transfer his money into the hands of the Company, in which he has made me his trustee and executor, and put his affairs principally under my management. He is regularly married to a half-breed daughter of McGillis (who is a settler

with from £2,000 to £3,000) and related to or connected with
the principal freemen or half-breeds who look up to him as their
chief and great man. As I formerly remarked he this spring
became a settler and has got a grant of land on the White Horse
Plain, about 12 miles above this place (Fort Garry) on the Assiniboine where he is joined by McGillis and about 80 or 100 families
of half-breeds all steady married men. Grant is turned very
serious (religious) and by management will become a useful
man to the Colony and Company . . .[38]

The land grant was only part of Simpson's policy of using Grant to
serve the purposes of the Hudson's Bay Company. On January 4, 1824,
he wrote to J. G. McTavish at York Factory: "Mr. Cuthbert Grant I consider to be a fit person to conduct this transport business [between
Norway House and Red River] and for that purpose he will be dispatched with the craft from hence at the opening of navigation."[39]
Grant now became a private freighter, transporting goods in 1824 and
1825 from York to Red River both for the company and on his
own account. For the role Simpson had planned for Grant was not
merely that of settler, but also of a free, or private trader who would
purchase the furs the Métis might otherwise take over the border to
sell to the American traders from St Peter's or from the Missouri. Grant
was to be his agent in solving the whole problem of the place of the
Métis in the new order. If they were not to be a menace, they must be
brought to settle in the colony and they must be induced not to sell
furs to the Americans. They must also be restrained from provoking
the Sioux Indians to attack the colony. Grant, with his unequalled
influence over the Métis and his deep concern for them, could more
than anyone else bring them to settle and accept the Company's rule
and monopoly. Of this undertaking, Grant's projected settlement
would be the centre-piece. Simpson, surveying the whole enterprise,
wrote in June:

The Half-breed population is by far the most extended about the
Settlement and appear to require great good management otherwise they will become in my opinion dangerous to its peace;
hitherto they have lived almost entirely by the chase, and in
consequence of the great demand for provisions have been
enabled to indulge in their rage for Dress, extravagance, and
dissipation; but domestic Cattle are now getting so numerous
that in the course of two years hence there will be no market
for the produce of their hunts, and those people if not brought

gradually from their present vagrant mode of life will then become worse and more destitute than Indians being un accustomed to the privations & hardships to which the latter are frequently exposed, & ignorant of the mode of hunting fur bearing Animals; – their notions of pride and independence are such that they will not enter the service moreover they are no the Class of people that would be desirable on any terms as the are indolent and unsteady merely fit for voyaging. – Under thos circumstances it is necessary to watch and manage them wit great care, otherways they may become the most formidabl enemy to which the Settlement is exposed. – Cuthbert Gran whom your Honors were last years [sic] pleased to admit as Clerk in the service, is warmly attached to this race of peopl & has much influence over them which he seems desirous t use in furtherance of your views: for these last two years th Sioux have committed several murders in the neighbourhoo of Pembina; this in my opinion did not arise from any hosti feeling towards the Whites but in consequence of the intrusio of the Half-breeds on their lands, and with a view to get po session of their Horses & Women, and if the latter could b drawn from those hunting Grounds I think the Settlement woul experience no further annoyance from that Tribe. – Grant, wit a desire to avenge those murders and deter the Sioux from repetition of such outrages, offered to lead the Half-bree against them this spring, but as such a measure was likely t involve very serious consequences we could not sanction encourage it. Under all those circumstances we consider it high! necessary and proper to withdraw the half-breeds from Pembir and encourage them to adopt a more settled mode of life, i furtherance of which I have released Mr. Grant at his own reque from his Engagement to the Company, and he has this sprir established himself as a regular Settler at the White Horse Plai on the East bank of the Assiniboine River about 14 miles fro hence, and has got upwards of Fifty families of Half-breeds Freemen to join him already: they have commenced their Ag cultural operations on a small scale and received every facili we could render, & if the season is at all favorable it will indu others to join them: the few who are still at Pembina do n consider themselves safe there and will remove in the cour of the summer. – The Catholic Mission enters warmly into th plan; they have much influence over those people & Monr. Pica the priest is to be established among them this summer so th

I trust the plan will be attended with beneficial effects and meet your honors' approbation.[40]

Grant was thus vindicated by Simpson in the trouble at Fort Garry, and turned by the governor to fields of enterprise much more likely to reconcile the Métis to the new order than Grant's serving as a clerk at Fort Garry. The Governor's plans also fitted Grant's own disposition well. With his patrimony which Simpson had obtained for him from McGillivray he was now prepared to settle down on the land Simpson had given him. The Governor's plans were his plans, and the two men moved in harmony towards the same end. Simpson watched and noted with approval Grant's first preparations for his new life.

Though he felt Grant was useless in the company's service because of the old feeling over Seven Oaks, the Governor now felt satisfied that he had found a place where Grant could be of real service. His marriage to Marie, daughter of Angus McGillis, seemed to be a turning point in his life. Bethsy and her child had long since vanished. Of his liaison with Madeline Desmarais, only his infant daughter Maria remained. These unions of his young and unsettled days were now replaced, as befitted a gentleman of the fur trade, by the formal wedding in the church of St Boniface. Grant's marriage into a devout Roman Catholic family not only made him a settled married man but also began the conversion of the one who had been baptized in the Presbyterian Church to membership in the Roman Catholic Church. This settling of his domestic life was part of the beginning of the settlement of Grant's people with him at Grantown on the Assiniboine.

CHAPTER VII

THE FOUNDATION OF GRANTOWN,

1824-1830

The site of Grant's settlement lay some eighteen miles westward from the Forks, up the Assiniboine River. Its western boundary was at an old Indian encampment in the lee of a slight, almost imperceptible ridge which made a dry camping-place in the surrounding plain. It was known as the *coteau des festins*, because the local Indians from time immemorial had held dog feasts on the site. From the loop of the river-ridge, a wide view opened southward over the plains towards the lands of the Sioux. On the points and bays of the winding course of the Assiniboine were the hardwood groves which would furnish wood for fuel and building, lumber for carts and maples for sugar.

Here where the Canadian prairies begin we find an area which has left us a legend. This was the Legend of the White Horse. The story was as follows.

In an early period of the seventeenth century, when only Indians roamed the western plains, the most northerly nation, the Crees, were being pushed farther and farther towards Hudson Bay by their traditional enemies, their fierce neighbours to the south, the Sioux.

Finally the Sioux gained a foothold in the wealthy Cree country as far north as Lake Winnipeg and the point north of the tip of Lake Superior now known as Sioux Lookout. It was a serious situation for the Crees. They were desperate. In this barren land they faced near starvation and possible extinction.

Then came their salvation, the arrival of the white men at Hudson Bay with whom they soon began to trade. Before long they had the white man's guns and were making effective war with them against the bows and arrows of the Sioux. So the invaders in turn were pushed farther and farther back into their own territory, and the Crees became the great warriors, more invincible than ever the Sioux had been.

As a consequence of this, the Crees' nearest neighbours to the south, the Assiniboines, a branch of the Sioux who formerly had protected the Sioux from the incursions of the Crees, were glad not only to make peace but later to ally themselves with this powerful and and irresistible nation which fought their enemies with fire. Against this alliance the Sioux, though flaming inwardly, could do nothing. Nevertheless they kept a jealous eye on the movements of both.

Early one summer in the 1690's, a large band of Assiniboines was camped on the banks of the Assiniboine River about ten miles west of present-day Winnipeg, near the place where St Charles Church stands today.

The chief of these Assiniboines had a beautiful daughter, and to his lodge came two suitors for her hand – a Cree chief from Lake Winnipegosis and a Sioux chief from Devil's Lake in North Dakota.

The Cree was the favoured suitor for he had to offer in exchange for a bride that rarity, that coveted prize of the prairies, a horse as white as the winter snows, a Blanco Diablo, which came from that famed breed in Mexico. Nimble of foot, swift as the wind, strong and sturdy, a "white devil" could outrun and outlast any other horse, and go three or four days longer than any other without food or water. The prospect of such a gift was irresistible, and the father succumbed.

But not all the Assiniboines in the camp, notably a powerful medicine man, favoured the alliance with the Crees. The memory of Cree war-parties with Assiniboine scalps flying in the wind was ever before his eyes and he nursed in his heart the old bitterness. He protested fiercely against the making of peace with their hereditary enemies. He protested especially against the mingling of blood with that of the hated foes of the past.

But his protests were in vain. So he sought by his magic and exhortations to strengthen in the camp the hatred against the Crees.

The marriage was planned for a time when the Sioux chief was to be on a war expedition, but they counted without the medicine man. Secretly he sent the young Sioux word of his rival's success.

On the day appointed for the ceremonies, the Cree bridegroom, gorgeous in the trappings of his chiefdom, arrived from Lake Winnipegosis mounted on a fine grey steed, and leading the white horse loaded with additional presents for his prospective father-in-law.

The gifts were presented and the Cree claimed his bride. Then, with the feasting and merry-making scarce begun, suddenly there was an alarm, a cloud of dust in the distance. The flouted and vengeful suitor with an escort of Sioux warriors was fast approaching over the prairie.

All was confusion in the camp. Cries of Sioux and Cree sympathizers alike filled the air. "Up, up! Away! It is your only chance!" cried the father to the Cree. "Take your horses and flee!"

The bridegroom ran with his bride to the tethered horses, helped her mount the white steed, jumped to the grey in a flash and they were off. Westward they flew, but not unobserved. The Sioux with his party was quickly in pursuit.

But even the time gained at the start and the swift pace of their fleeing ponies did not save the bridal couple. Though they doubled back on their tracks to mislead their pursuers and at times were hidden by patches of bush, once out on the open plain the white horse was the mark that betrayed them.

On, on they sped over the prairie. The frightened girl held back the pace of her horse to that of her husband's grey, and the Sioux were gaining on them. Finally at a point just east of the present day village of Saint François-Xavier the avenging arrows of the Sioux sped to the hearts of the fleeing couple and killed them both.

The grey horse was caught, but the white steed escaped into the deep woods. For years it roamed the plain, thus giving its name to the region, and the Indians, believing that the soul of the girl had passed into its body, feared to approach it. As time passed the belief grew that, in ghostly form, the white horse continued its wild wanderings.

Such was the legend that gave its name to the plain adjoining the *coteau des festins*, the White Horse Plain.[1]

Here then on the north bank of the Assiniboine, beginning twelve miles west of Fort Garry, and extending for six miles westward along the river to the *coteau* and six miles in depth back from the river front, was the tract of land which Governor Simpson gave to Cuthbert Grant for a settlement. It was his land, his seigniory, as he thought and claimed for many years. He remembered those grand gentlemen on the streets of Montreal, who came in from their estates along the St Lawrence, to transact the business of their small realms; and he resolved that he, Cuthbert Grant, would be a good seignior, a father to his people, on the banks of the Assiniboine.

To Grant, who had been rescued from despair through his Hudson's Bay Company appointment only to have his hopes for a life of respect in the service ruined by an outburst of the smouldering resentment which still existed against him in the settlement at The Forks, this was a new hope indeed.

One may still see the spot as Grant saw it. Standing there, on the site he had chosen, he gazed out over this land of his, where no craft going up or down the river could escape his eye, and made plans that went far into the future. As he stood on the point that day, he must have pictured the settlement much as it came to be – with his own big white house, the parish church, the school, and the neat white-washed houses along the river-bank.

He well knew the difficult task that faced him, for these Métis had never had a settled home. The fur-trader John Siveright, in a letter to his colleague, James Hargrave, dated May 2, 1825, wrote:

How does Cuthbert Grant get on with his settlement at the White Horse Plain? I fear he has a turbulent set, and not very steady or easily satisfied to deal with. I sincerely wish him every success.[2]

Grant's task as an English-speaking Scot with Cree blood from his mother, was to found a French settlement under the auspices of the Roman Catholic mission at St Boniface. He was aware of his people's limitations. They had only the skills of the huntsman to bring to the building of a settlement, yet Cuthbert Grant had no fear for the outcome. The houses would be primitive at first, he knew, but like a true founder, he had bright visions of his enterprise.

He gathered together the Métis displaced from Pembina and some from the northwest. Each settler was given one of the river lots twelve chains wide, which ran two miles back from the river.

The new settlement had its centre at Grant's house on the *coteau des festins* at the northeast corner of the loop of the river turning to flow at that point. There on the western limit of his seigniory, Cuthbert Grant built the great log house, in the Red River frame style, which was to be his home for the rest of his life.

The foundation logs still mark the site of Grant's house and, from the vantage-point their mouldering remains afford, one can see across the brown Assiniboine, running between its steep clay banks, to the wide open plain that stretches treeless to the southern horizon. It was this view that explained Grant's choice of the site for his house. From it he could keep perpetual watch for the approach of the Sioux, the deadly and inveterate enemies of the Métis as they had been of their Cree and Saulteaux mothers' people. This watch and ward was part of Simpson's design, for to be a bulwark of the Red River colony against the Sioux was one of the chief purposes in the foundation of Grantown. And the Red River people were to testify that they slept easier in their beds in the knowledge that Grant's warriors were at Grantown.

From the river Grant's great, double river-lot ran back into the plain. On either side of him he placed his friends and relatives, the leaders, the bravest men and most successful hunters among his people. Next him to the east lay Angus McGillis's lot, and beyond it those of McGillis's sons. Next lay that of François Paul, then that of Pierre Falcon, and next Alexandre Bréland's. To the west lay the lots reserved for the mission that Rev. Picard Destroismaisons first began with services in Grant's uncompleted house. Beyond the mission land lay the lot of Urbain Delorme, next to Grant the greatest of the plains hunters and traders. Thus, as a nucleus for the new community, Grant had settled on either side of himself the leadership and aristocracy of the Métis, the captains and the soldiers of the buffalo hunt.

Around him Grant drew the members of his own family: Mrs Wills and his daughter Maria came down from the Qu'Appelle to join him; and his other sisters, Mme Falcon and Mme Morin, were in their new homes close by. Grant's new settlement was a family home as well as a settlement of his wandering people.[3]

From eighty to one hundred families settled at the White Horse Plain, now to be called Grantown, in that spring of 1824.[4] Not only did Grant and the McGillises, the Falcons and the Brélands begin building their houses but they also broke land and began farming in the new settlement.[5] Nothing could have been more dramatic. The Métis had hitherto been *voyageurs* and hunters who only occasionally planted a patch of potatoes as a safeguard against famine in the winter. Now under Grant's leadership they were turning away from the wandering life of the *voyageur* and the hunter to the settled life of the farmer, with all that meant for their families, for religion, and for their own comfort and safety. It is true they found the work of the field and the barn a drudgery which they all too readily shirked.[6] But how earnest the more stable of them were is shown by the fact that three years later, in 1827, Cuthbert Grant had thirty-four acres under the plough, Angus McGillis twenty acres, and Alexandre Poitras four acres.[7] In the days of the walking-plough and in those early years of the Red River colony, these were large and impressive acreages. Through the years Grant's fields remained the largest.

Grantown was not only of interest as the first farming settlement formed by natives of the northwest. One significant and picturesque claim to distinction was that it was the first westward extension of the Red River colony along the Assiniboine. By reason of its distance from The Forks, it was almost an independent colony, and so remained for years until the growth of settlement along the Assiniboine in St James, St Charles, and St Margaret's (Headingley) formed a continuous line of settlement between The Forks and Grantown. The little Scotland of Kildonan was matched by the little Canada of Grantown.

Another and even more noteworthy fact was that Grant and his people were not to be farmers only. Their farms were intended only to give their families a winter home and winter food. Few farmers in Red River at that time could live by farming alone, and certainly Métis just removed from the fur posts and the life of the plains could not. The men of Grantown were to keep up the buffalo hunt, on the returns from which they, and indeed the Red River colony, still depended for survival. Some of them were to serve as *voyageurs* in the

THE FOUNDATION OF GRANTOWN-95

boat brigades to Norway House and York Factory; others became voyageurs with the cart brigades as the movement of freight by Red River cart developed.

Cuthbert Grant became a freighter at once, and his people followed his example. Grant, however, became a trader in furs as well as a freighter, and this was a privilege only a man of his standing could have enjoyed. After laying out his settlement in the spring of 1824, he spent the summer on the voyage to Norway House and returned to Red River on August 13. On August 18 he removed his outfit of goods to Grantown.[8] The new settlement was to be not only a home for his people but also both a trading-post itself and the base for trading in Grant's old country of Upper Red River.

That first winter of 1824-25 probably found all with housing of some sort, but Governor Simpson had no idea of leaving Grant idle at home for the winter. He would use this skilled plainsman against the American traders who were making incursions on Hudson's Bay Company territory. The company could not afford to lose the returns from the rich southwestern buffalo plains, and under Simpson's sponsorship Grant was established in an independent trading-post on the Souris River.

That autumn he went up to Brandon House "to trade on his own account."[9] Under the monopoly and in his circumstances, he could trade only with the special licence of Governor Simpson. He went west to the area beyond Brandon House and ranged north and south from Turtle Mountain to the Qu'Appelle under such a licence. Similarly, young Andrew McDermot, later to be a famous trader and merchant in Red River, went to Pembina. Both were to win furs away from American traders who had come north from the Minnesota River and from the Missouri.[10] The furs once obtained were to be sold by McDermot and Grant to the Hudson's Bay Company, whose monopoly was thus maintained.

Grant had other difficulties than the competition of the American traders to face during his first winter as a licensed trader. The Fort Garry Journal noted in 1825 that "a general scarcity of Buffaloe has prevailed this season all over the country; and we are informed by Mr. Grant who arrived this day from Brandon House (where he went last autumn to trade on his own account) that he was from mere necessity and want of other food obliged to kill his horses and dogs, on which he himself and his people subsisted as long as they lasted and were then forced to abandon the place."[11]

Grant's attempts to establish himself as trader and his position of leadership in the great buffalo hunting expedition to the plains no

doubt kept him away from home a good deal. At any rate we know
that he was away from Grantown during the last few days of May
1825. At this time Governor Simpson was approaching Fort Garry
across the plains to the west, and found himself in a destitute condition at this stage of an incredibly arduous return journey from the
Pacific coast. He appealed to Grant for assistance on the last lap of
his journey. In an entry in his journal for May 26 Simpson wrote:

> Put up at the old Pine Fort. The Settlement is still three long days
> march distant, considering our worn out condition and finding
> that we could not all get that length without assistance
> despatched the two best men of our party, Burassa and Cadotte
> with a note to Cuthbert Grant at the White Horse Plain, begging
> that he would immediately send us relief in provisions and
> horses.

No help came. After he had succeeded in reaching Grantown by
Saturday, May 28, Simpson wrote:

> May 28 . . . we however persevered and got to the White Horse
> Plain at Dusk. Grant was not at home otherwise we should have
> had earlier assistance, but our Messengers being unable to pro-
> ceed themselves hired an Indian to go to Fort Garry with my
> note, which by a few hurried lines from Governor Pelly and
> Mr. McKenzie astonished them beyond measure, they instantly
> despatched men, horses, eatables, drinkables and dry clothes
> for our relief but I was so anxious to get once more among my
> much valued Red River friends that without looking at the con-
> tents of their saddlebags (altho furnished with an excellent
> appetite) I got across my old charger "Jonathan," gave him the
> rein with a smart cut across the haunches and commenced a
> furious attack on the gates of Fort Garry at 12 P.M.[12]

Although Grant had been absent on this occasion, his home was to be
a haven for travellers many times in the future.

The failure of his first winter as a licensed trader did not put an
end to Grant's new activities. In the summer of 1825 he went with
two boats to York, and returned with a cargo mainly of company
goods.[13] If Grant went trading in the following winter of 1825-26 he
must have suffered from the rigours of that terrible season. The cold
was intense and prolonged; the snow came early and fell to record
depths. Buffalo and other game were snow-bound, and Indians and

étis alike suffered and starved in their buried winter encampments.
is certain that Grant was in Grantown late in the winter, for Chief
actor Donald McKenzie sent him out with a party to rescue a group
Métis known to be starving on the plains. Supplies were taken by
nowshoe and toboggan, and the dazed and frost-bitten survivors
ought back to the settlement.[14]

The early freeze-up and deep snows of the winter were a prelude
the great flood of the spring of 1826. Nor was this all. After a winter
privation, food was short. By April 8 a state of famine existed in
ue Red River settlement and the Métis, the surly de Meuron settlers,
nd the disappointed Swiss colonists were in a state of near-mutiny.
ut the Métis of Grantown did not encourage their distressed and
ngry relatives at The Forks, because Grant set his face against any
uch proceeding.[15] Once more Grant had cast his decisive authority
n the side of order, and the flood confirmed his stand by driving all
efore it. The Red River settlements were flooded many feet deep in
arly April, and the colonists driven to seek refuge on Silver Heights,
tony Mountain and Bird's Hill. But the grey waters of the Assini-
oine, although they spread for miles over White Horse Plain to the
outhwest, did not cover Grantown.

For Red River the summer of 1826 was one of slow recovery from
ne spring's disaster, the worst flood in the history of the Red River
alley. Grant, busy sowing his new and dry fields at Grantown, was
oon given another subject for thought. Just as Pembina and the
ouris valley were regions where American penetration was to be
eared, so was the Snake River country, by which American traders
rom the Missouri could penetrate the Columbia River territory. The
vhole area beyond the mountains was jointly occupied by Great
ritain and the United States, but the Hudson's Bay Company was
ending every effort to keep the Americans from penetrating it by
rapping out the border country. In the Snake River country Alex-
nder Ross, the future historian, had come to grief because he had
ot dealt rigorously enough with his American rivals, and was soon
o be retired to Red River.[16] Now Simpson was planning an expedi-
ion from Red River to the Snake River country. He had already
ecided who was to lead it. On July 10, 1826, he wrote to Chief
actor John McLoughlin at Fort Vancouver that Cuthbert Grant was
n nominal charge of the party but his second-in-command, Chief
rader Simon McGillivray,[17] was to have the principal direction of
he enterprise. Grant, that is, was to control the Métis, but Mc-
Gillivray was to be in charge of the business of the expedition. "Mr.
McGillivray's spirit, activity and business like arrangements," Simpson

went on, "renders [sic] him well qualified for the conduct of the enterprise. Mr. Grant's courage and firmness are undoubted, the people who are all hunters and accustomed to the use of arms are from their habits and character well adapted for the dangerous service to which they will be put. . . ."[18]

After the matter had been discussed in the Council of the Northern Department, Simpson wrote to Grant. First he reviewed Grant's relations with the Company during the past three years:

> I was favored with your Letter by Joseph Cook. . . . Your conduct both as far as regards the Company and Colony has since my first acquaintance with you afforded me most perfect satisfaction and the treatment you have experienced at my hands should convince you that we duly appreciate your merits, and that we have every desire to be useful to you, and you may rest assured that while you continue the line of conduct you have hitherto pursued you will find that we have your interest at heart. When you retired from the service it was not at my suggestion, nor was it with my approbation, on the contrary it was my wish that you should have remained, but as it was considered you would be enabled to mend your own circumstances by going free, I fell in with your views and rendered you every assistance in my power, at the same time considering you as much attached to the Company and their interests as if you had continued on the Establishment; in this I have not been mistaken having always found you equally at our disposal as when a member of the concern; we still regard you in the same light, and I trust we shall not have occasion at any future period to do otherwise.

Simpson then proceeded to discuss arrangements for the expedition:

> . . . The readiness with which you have fallen in with my views in regard to the Expedition is very pleasing to me and I have submitted a plan to the consideration of Council connected with that object which has been approved. – The Party is to consist of 50 in all not one white man to be unattached thereto, and Mr. Simon McGillivray and yourself the Leaders – 20 or 30 women without families may accompany the Expedition and none of the men should be under the age of 25 years – I am anxious that Memisis should be of the party, and have to request that you

and he meet me at Bas de la Rivière about the 1st. to the 5th. Septr.; my stay there shall not exceed one night, you should therefore be there on or before the 1st. and wait my arrival. – The whole plan will then be submitted to your consideration and I have no doubt we shall come to a satisfactory arrangement on the subject; every preparatory step in regard to Horses, Traps, Supplies &c &c &c has been already settled, and if you enter into my views with the determination of succeeding I am convinced that the benefits to arise both to yourself and the Company will be very great likewise to all who may be attached to the Expedition. – all I have now said is for your own private information and it is desirable that the business should be kept secret until you see me, letting Memisis merely know that I have something particular to communicate to him at Fort Alexander.[19]

In obedience to Simpson's summons, Grant went to Fort Alexander in a company light canoe on August 26.[20] There Simpson made a provisional agreement with him to raise a party for a trapping expedition to the Snake River country. In October, however, Simpson was obliged by a dispatch from the Governor of the company to order Grant to suspend his preparations until further orders. The Governor and Committee feared such an expedition might lead to collision with the Americans.[21] No more was heard of an expedition led by Grant.

In consequence Grant resumed his trading by special licence in the region of Brandon House, where Simpson soon found good use for him. He was in fact both maintaining a camp at Brandon House and trading on the Souris towards the international boundary. There he established a fort, to be known as "Fort Mr Grant," north of the 49th parallel and situated near the present town of Hartney.[22] It remained on the map until recent times. In January 1827 he returned to Fort Garry and reported that, while provisions were scarce on the Souris, furs were reasonably plentiful. Two American trading companies had established themselves near the unmarked boundary. Though in opposition to one another, they united to oppose Grant and threatened to seize his property on the pretext that he was situated within American territory.[23]

This challenge by the American traders was answered by Governor Simpson. He renewed Grant's licence, and gave orders to Chief Factor Donald McKenzie, Governor of Assiniboia, that immediately on his arrival at Fort Grant, George Taylor, sloopmaster at York Factory, should be dispatched to run a line along the 49th parallel of latitude from Pembina on the Red as far as he might conveniently go. The line was to be marked, and Americans who crossed it were to be warned off. One Louis Giboche was licensed to trade along with Grant "along the boundary line from Turtle Mountain to Qu'Appelle."[24] Here, Simpson wrote, Grant and his partner had a number of Indian and Métis relations and were intimately acquainted with all the Indian tribes of the region. Thus they could compete more effectively with the Americans than the company could by establishing a fort.[25]

That summer of 1827 Grant went again to York Factory and returned at the end of August with a cargo of goods for his own trade.[26] When George Taylor visited him in October 1827, Grant was unwilling to accompany him at that season and was indeed planning to spend the winter of 1827-28 at Grantown.[27] Taylor had accordingly to proceed without him to Brandon House. There he ascended the Souris, and found that Grant's house was in latitude 49° 28' 45" north latitude or about thirty-three and one-half miles north of the 49th parallel, well within the British boundary. From Grant's fort, Taylor proceeded to Turtle Mountain to mark the line of the 49th parallel.[28]

But Grant was not allowed to spend a peaceful winter at home, busied among his neighbours with the affairs of the new settlement as he had planned. The Assiniboine Indians made trouble for his people at Brandon House and on the Souris. Late in December Grant had to go up to Brandon House to pacify the Assiniboines and to take charge of the trade.[29] By March he had succeeded in quelling the Indians and made "an excellent trade."[30] By May he was back at Grantown. The keeper of the journal at Fort Garry commented on May 5, 1828:

> Mr. Grant has arrived at his establishment at the White Horse Plain, from his trading station near Brandon House, with his returns in three bateaux, amounting to 50,000 Musquash (it is said) and other furs, besides a considerable quantity of provisions, robes & leather – Mr. G's trade in furs at the White Horse Plain, is also reported to be little inferior to that above stated, but most of the latter are disposed of in the settlement, to all such as have goods to give in exchange – and deal in that line.[31]

The fixing of the boundary line by George Taylor raised the possibility of proceeding against American interlopers by legal process as well as by competition. Simpson had given Grant authority in this regard and had written to the Governor and Council in 1827 referring to this possibility. "If it be considered expedient to seize persons and property it had better be done in the spring when full handed than earlier in the season, and I have prepared Grant for this part of the duty who is prudent firm and efficient either among whites or Indians and will act up to the letter of any instructions he may receive."[32] There is no record of Grant making any seizures, and he seems not to have been an officer of the company at that date.

In July 1828, the Council of the Northern Department regularized his position by creating for him an office, the title of which was unprecedented in the records of the company, but which was wholly appropriate to Grant's career and the responsibility imposed on him. The Council resolved "That Mr. Cuthbert Grant be appointed Warden of the Plains of Red River at a salary of £200 p. Annum and that the Duties of his Office be the prevention of illicit Trade in Furs within that District under the direction of Chief Factor McKenzie."[33]

Grant's services under special licence had given Simpson the idea of creating a unique post for him on the Council which would place him among the governors of the country. Grant, always influential among his people, now became a figure of dignity. Over the whole area of the vast plains of Red River, in policing the fur trade, the business of the country, his word would be law. He was now in a position of authority, a position that carried prestige. He was an appointee of the supreme governing body of the country, the Council of the Northern Department of Rupert's Land. After years of struggle and humiliation he had at last achieved recognition, and the salary attached would, with his own fortune, make him a man of means in Red River.

Thus Grant once more found himself in the service of the great company, but in a role which recognized his peculiar capacities – his knowledge of the country and his ties with the Métis and Indians. Simpson had finally solved the problem of how to keep Grant loyal and to use him to defeat the threat of American encroachment and the rise of a new race of free traders.

That year Grant went again to York and returned with goods for both the company and himself.[34] Once more he traded on the Souris in the winter.[35] But the American danger had ended, and Grant's trading on the Souris ceased. Late in 1828 the company began the rebuilding of Brandon House, which meant that the Indians and Métis could turn to that post for goods.[36] In consequence Grant's licence to trade on the Souris seems not to have been renewed. Thus his interests began to centre more and more on his settlement. As

Warden of the Plains he became, not a police officer patrolling the frontier against American intrusion, but an influence in the background of the plains trade and an envoy who could be dispatched to deal with any outburst of trouble. His salary as Warden relieved him of the need to trade or freight. Henceforth he could stay at home, save when he led the buffalo hunt. The still young and active Grant was already beginning to show the lineaments of the patriarch and elder chieftain.

Caring for the health of his people was always Grant's particular concern. There is little doubt that he had some regular medical training, probably acquired in England or Scotland in 1822-23. His grandchildren have attested to the fact that it was recognized in the family that he had had medical training. People visiting the Old Country in that period had to remain for the winter, as there were no winter sailings for Canada. During Grant's first recorded trip after the amalgamation of the fur companies, he would have much leisure. It seems only natural that he would try to get what knowledge of medicine he could, when he was going back to a country where it was sorely needed. At that time being apprenticed to a doctor and working with him was a usual practice, and this would seem the only possible way Grant's medical knowledge might have been gained.

Grant's care for the health of his people is illustrated by the following letter from his friend James Hargrave at York:

5 Sept. /43.

My Dear Sir:

I duly received your kind note of 9th ultimo the other day and in reply have to assure you that our Doctor, Mr. Gillespie has done his utmost to complete your order for medicines out of the slender stock which now remains in our Depot after the outfits have been completed. Had it reached me in spring we could have met it better. It is forwarded in a case containing a variety of other matters for Fort Garry.

Mrs. H. feels much gratified by the kind wishes & enquiries of such an old friend of her husbands. She is now in excellent health, although for a long time very delicate last winter ailing some months after the death of our second boy. She unites with me in best regards to Mrs. Grant and yourself whose kind hospitality at Grantown I shall long remember & with sincere esteem. Believe me – Dear Grant –

Yours faithfully
J. H.[37]

Clearly, a man who could write ordering drugs from the British Pharmacopœia by their scientific names must have known something of scientific medicine. Dr Gillespie was the medical officer at York Factory and he received the drugs for the whole country. It would seem that Cuthbert Grant was probably the first man in his settlement to practise regular medicine. Two of his medicine-chests are still extant. The first is a crude one made in the country, and no doubt Grant used this for some time before he acquired the second fine brass-bound one. But it was the country-made box that Grant always took with him on the buffalo hunt.

When epidemic swept the country Grant travelled far and near treating those who needed him, and old settlers recalled times when he did not lose one patient, while in the mother settlement where medical care was available there were a number of deaths.

The Desjardin family of Grantown was one group known to have been rescued by Grant in a severe snow-storm in which many perished on the plains – perhaps that of 1826. The story of this rescue has been cherished in this family and is still told by the descendants. Buried beneath the snow and without food for some time, Desjardin and his family faced certain death. When they heard dogs barking they could hardly believe their ears. What could it mean? They were far out on the plain and near no habitation. But the dogs were soon followed by their master Cuthbert Grant, who with a couple of men was out looking for victims of the storm. He sent back to his camp for supplies, including his medical chest, and administered the medicine needed to revive those of the party who had almost perished. The Desjardin story always ends with the statement that it is certain that they would all have been lost but for "Mr Grant."

Grant's eldest daughter Maria, the child of his marriage to Madeline Desmarais, grew up to be his devoted assistant. He imparted to her much of his knowledge, and after his death she carried on his medical work. A third generation grew up in Cuthbert Grant's big white house, for one of Maria Bréland's sons remained at home after his marriage, and his family was brought up there. Her grandson Alex Bréland has recalled much of the historic home in which he grew up. Maria though not tall had grown to be a very stout old lady (not an uncommon thing in that age of hearty fare), and Bréland recollects that as a boy his special duty was to lift up on to a chair whichever medicine box his grandmother needed when she was dispensing medicines. Two old ladies also remember Mme Bréland's work as a medical practitioner. Mme Delorme of Ste Agathe has told how she measured out powder onto little squares of white paper and then folded them in the conventional manner used by regular physicians in those days.

That Grant should be not only the chief, as he was, but the seignior and even the patriarch of his people, was more and more likely as his settlement at Grantown on the White Horse Plain grew strong and developed. It was becoming a river front village, a côte, modelled on and reminiscent of those of the St Lawrence, with the seignior's house in the centre marked by the parish church and spire. It is true that there was as yet no church at Grantown, but Bishop Provencher, from his see at St Boniface, saw to it that the people of Grantown did not lack the ministrations of the church. When the Reverend Picard Destroismaisons returned to Quebec in 1828, the mission at Grantown was taken up by the Reverend Jean Harper. The mission was entitled Saint-François-Xavier, which had been the name of the mission at Pembina. Earnest Jean Harper first joined the people at Grantown when he went with the hunters to the plains in the summer of 1828. In the fall of that year he first held chapel at Grantown, and by the following summer was living most of his time there. The chapel was a pitifully crude little building of poles. Harper later opened a school for boys, which was run by a former clerk of one of the fur companies. The latter is described as not knowing very much but persistent in trying to carry on the school. At any rate the services of religion were from henceforth usually available to the people of Grantown, at home or on the summer hunts, and a beginning had been made towards providing education for the children.[38]

In the summer of 1829 Grant once more went to York Factory for freight and arrived back in Red River at the end of August.[39] Although not legally obliged to do so in Red River, he now determined to discharge one of the principal obligations of a seignior, that of providing his people with a flour-mill. Grant decided not to build a windmill, such as had already been erected in Red River, but a water-mill. The flat plains of the Red River valley were poorly drained and in most years acted as great sponges from which water made its way down creeks to the Red and Assiniboine. This seemed to promise a steady head of water for a water-mill, particularly in a large creek such as Sturgeon Creek which rose on the plains behind Grantown and made its way eastward to run into the Assiniboine about two-thirds of the way down to The Forks. At some point on this creek, now unknown, Grant began to build a dam in September 1829 and put a number of men to work on the operation.[40] His mill was not wholly successful. According to the satirical account of Alexander Ross, the enterprise was neither well conceived nor well executed. The dam broke repeatedly and the mill did not grind efficiently. Grant was reported to have lost £800 in this venture.[41] Nevertheless, he persisted in his endeavour to supply his people with the services of a mill and, after the failure of his water-mill, built a windmill at Grantown which served the village for the remainder of his life.[42]

When Grant had succeeded, as he did, by the early 30's, in providing his people with a windmill, as well as with land on which to raise their crops, and with employment as freighters for the Hudson's Bay Company and for himself, he had given his settlement the means of livelihood. Because he succeeded in doing these things, the settlement was confirmed. In 1831 Bishop Provencher remarked that there were more than fifty families living at Grantown.[43] At Grantown and at St Boniface and along the Red River, Provencher and Grant had succeeded in collecting nearly all the Métis people of the northwest. Some, it is true, still clung to the settlement at Pembina; some still remained scattered along the Saskatchewan and other rivers. But they had made Red River the centre of their life, and in Red River Grantown was the most characteristically Métis community. There were few people living there who were not of mixed blood.

The success of Grantown, however, meant that Grant's life became merged with that of his settlement. Hitherto he had been an individual figure of note, and the records which remain of his life are surprisingly numerous. After 1830, however, there are few references to Grant as an individual. He merges with Grantown. Henceforth the story is the story of Grantown rather than of Grant — of the buffalo hunt rather than its captain, of the Métis rather than their chief.

Once planted, the little settlement of Grantown grew steadily in importance through its two functions of providing protection and of supplying food and other items from the plains for the mother settlement at The Forks. Also travellers going across the country, after outfitting with what was usually obtained at Fort Garry for trips to the west, counted on supplying their further needs at Grantown.

The hamlet became a mart continually surrounded by encampments of travellers and, a little farther away, Indians who came to trade horses and other articles. Grant usually saw that the village had on hand what was needed to supply the travellers' demands:

buffalo sinews for thread, knives made from sharpened bones, large needles made from roots of trees, maple sugar in season, dried meat and bags of pemmican, and tallow – the bladder of the buffalo often being used as the container into which this latter was packed. Another important item was buffalo-skins or robes, as they were called. The buffalo-robe had its great importance from the fact that the animal grew wool on its skin, not hair, as was to be found on the other large animals of the plains. For his bed on the ground, nothing could keep the traveller so warm on a frigid night as buffalo-hides with their thick growth of wool, both under and over his blankets.

Governor Simpson usually directed travellers going long distances to Grant to make their arrangements, if he were available. Titled travellers from the Old Country, on their way west to hunt big game or to cross the continent, were graciously received at Grant's home, and in one case, that of Lords Caledon and Mulgrave, Grant accompanied them for a considerable part of their journey.

On all expeditions to the sugar-lots or buffalo-plains, to cross the plains or to hunt for sport, Red River carts made up part of the caravan. Grantown soon became noted for making of the great "dished" wheels used on Red River carts, the only wheel that would stand up for travel over the rough country. Not only travellers, but the Scottish settlers on the lower Red came to Grantown to get these wheels for their carts.

From the first years of the settlement, the annual sugar-making was a regular part of the year's varied tasks. The trek to the sugar-lots began each year before the snow had left the ground, and this meant that the women would have to slosh about, half-way up to their knees in deep snow and slush gathering the sap from the trees which the men had tapped. The sugar season was a time of much merry-making also, and it was a wonderful time for the children.

Though the events recounted happened years after the people of Grantown first began to go to their sugar-lots, the free trader, Peter Garrioch, in his unpublished diary gives an interesting account of a trip to the sugar bush. Leaving his home at St Andrew's on the Red River, he travelled the usual route to White Horse Plain. He writes:

April 10 – Started with an ox and cart to meet the sugar-makers with some goods to trade sugar. Spent the evening with Mr. Pascal Breland.

April 11 – With the kindness and assistance of my good host

I got my ox and cart over the river (Assiniboine), which was
getting very bad, and after getting into my cart I went on my
way thinking of sugar and Isabella.[44]

It was not easy to get around the country to the sugar camps,
even if one was not in love, as Garrioch was with his Isabella. There
were spring freshets and much water on the ground. Garrioch had
difficulty in getting his cart-load of trading-goods over some streams,
and some he could not attempt so had to change his course. At times,
though it was raw cold weather, he had to strip and swim across
streams to reconnoitre the road ahead.

By the evening of April 14 he had arrived within a mile or so
of the Ilets de Bois camps, but he was unable to get across the swampy
ground in the dark, and so had to make his solitary and uncomfortable camp within sight of the flickering fires of the merry-makers.
The next day he reached the camps and, his woes forgotten, wrote
of April 15 and 16: "Spent these two days among the sugar-makers
feasting on the grateful sap of the saccarine maple." On continuing
his sugar-trading journey farther south he reported finding other
sugar-makers with "little else to live upon but sugar."

Thus while Grant was wintering on the Souris as trader in the
first years of the settlement, the people at Grantown would be getting
ready each spring for the trip to Rivière aux Ilets de Bois some thirty
miles to the south and west. Many of them had lived at Pembina
where the river's wide, low, maple-covered banks had long been
known as a source of sugar. As early as the beginning of the 19th century, Alexander Henry the Younger, a fur trader for the North West
Company at Pembina, recorded rich returns in maple sugar from
that area.[45]

As the people became established they were better able to make
more elaborate preparations for the sugar-making season. Each year
birch bark was harvested from the trees in the spring and piled to
the ceiling in sheds to await the work of the women in winter, and
making vessels (called rogans) of all sizes and shapes became one of
their principal activities.

Grantown was not only a new agricultural settlement; it was also
the focus of the old way of life of the western plains. In this life the
buffalo hunt was the chief annual event.

CHAPTER VIII

GRANT'S SOLDIERS OF THE BUFFALO HUNT

If Grant was increasingly to be identified with Grantown, in no way was he more so identified than as leader of the summer buffalo hunt of the people of White Horse Plain. For although his people had settled with him along the tree-fringed banks of the Assiniboine, and although they had loyally followed his lead in taking up farming, they still continued to go out to the plains every June to hunt the buffalo. They did so partly because they loved the movement and excitement of the hunt; but they did so also because neither their crops nor their wages as *voyageurs* would maintain their families all year. Pemmican and dried meat were needed to fill their own larders and for sale to the Hudson's Bay Company and to the Scots settlers at Red River. The hunt perforce remained an essential part of the life of the people of Grantown.

Grant led the hunt from White Horse Plain for many summers.[1] While for most years there is no definite record of his being on the hunt, the tradition of the people of Saint-François-Xavier was that he customarily led them, and that in fact he played a large part in shaping the organization of the hunt. There is no reason to doubt this and every reason to believe it. Grant could not have been the leader of his people that he was if he had not led them in what was their great corporate activity of the year, the buffalo hunt. In it they became a people, the new nation, as they boasted, in a way they could never have become had they settled down completely as farmers along the river-fronts. Thus the buffalo hunt continued the work the Nor'Westers had begun for their own purposes.

From time to time we catch a glimpse of Grant as the leader of the hunt. On December 19, 1831, Thomas Simpson, later an Arctic explorer, wrote from Fort Garry to Chief Factor Donald Ross at Norway House: "The plains hunters have had a very successful season and the quantity of provisions they have brought home is immense. Grant, Nolin, Bourke, all the old hunters were out with the hunt."[2] By that date, then, Grant was already an "old hunter," to be named with the Canadian Nolin of St Boniface and John Bourke of what was to be St James as a leader. We may see him as such, as well as Warden of the Plains, and assume that in most years he led his people out on the summer hunt at least, if not on the fall one also.

The buffalo hunt had its origins in the provisions trade of the fur companies. As a clerk at Qu'Appelle Grant had dealt with the hunters, and probably had taken part in the hunt. Then Selkirk's colonists from 1812 to 1818 had gone each winter to Pembina to live on the hunt, and had stimulated its growth from there.

The heavier hunting of the herds soon drove them away from the Red River. No longer did the itchy beasts rub at night on the stockades of the forts or trample the banks of the river, as the younger Henry tells us they had done in the early years of the century.[3] As a result the hunters began to go out in bands, not singly, partly to make a common approach to the herds, and partly for defence against the jealous and hostile Sioux who claimed the hunting-grounds west of the Red. Out on the plains of the valley or in the Hair, or Pembina hills, the hunters would run the buffalo: they would charge the herd on horseback, and shoot down from the saddle the beasts they chose, reloading at the gallop and riding on to kill again, sometimes up to a dozen animals.

Each would mark his own beasts by dropping a glove, or other article, and when the run was finished would return to dress the kill. Only the best cuts were taken, but the transport of even these became a matter of difficulty as the hunts moved farther out from the river. The toboggan in winter, the *travois* in summer, served at first, but as early as 1803 there is mention of a rude cart being used for this purpose at Pembina.[4] From the need to bring back the produce of the hunt the Red River cart developed, a reproduction of the wooden peasant cart of Quebec and of the Scottish Highlands. As made in Red River, it was all of wood, with no metal or any other material used at all, except sometimes a bit of raw leather, or *shag-a-nappi*. Made from the trees that fringed the prairie streams, light, buoyant, and difficult to upset when its wheels were "dished," the cart made possible the longer and longer range of the hunt over the plains.[5]

Actually the Red River hunt had always three sources and was made up of three parties. One was Pembina. The Red River hunt began there, and not all the Pembina people had joined Grant at White Horse Plain when he founded Grantown. Very few remained there between 1824 and 1840, but by the later date their numbers were growing again. Their most famous hunter and customary captain was Baptiste Wilkie.[6]

The second source was The Forks, mostly St Boniface, from which came the "main river party." They crossed to Fort Garry, outfitted at the fort and then proceeded westward to the Passage, some eleven miles west of The Forks on the Assiniboine. There they might join the White Horse Plain group, before crossing the river.

The White Horse Plain's hunt would come down to the Passage, and proceed southward along the same trail as the main river party to the rendezvous. Their start would be slow, confused, and noisy, as the whole settlement, except for the very old and very young — men, women, dogs, horses and carts — moved out, with shouting and barking, along the Assiniboine to the Passage. And night by night the campfires would punctuate their progress across the plains of the Red River valley.

All three parties normally met at a rendezvous to proceed to the buffalo plains together. If the Sioux were at all aroused, this was necessary. Normally the rendezvous was somewhere on the Pembina River, more and more to westward as the buffalo-herds retreated. The Pembina party moved up that river. The others proceeded from the Passage south-west to the Rivière aux Ilets de Bois (now the Boyne) and then moved southward along the great terraces at the foot of the Pembina hills until they reached the Pembina.

Once the rendezvous was reached some days were spent in visiting and waiting for late-comers and stragglers to draw in. If a Sunday were passed in this way, Mass was celebrated by the priest (normally the Reverend Jean Harper or, after 1831, the Reverend M. Boucher) as it would be regularly each Sunday thereafter while the hunt encamped for the day.[7] When the parties were in, the organization of the hunt would begin. First a captain of the whole hunt was elected, and it was this office Grant held. It may indeed have grown out of his leadership of the Métis in 1815 and 1816. The captain then chose from among the men ten other captains, the old hunters. Each captain then chose ten soldiers, who served under him as camp guards and as scouts on the march during their captain's day of duty. The ten captains formed the council of the hunt on whose advice the captain of the hunt acted.[8]

When the hunt was organized, the march from the rendezvous to the buffalo plains began. It was now a controlled and orderly march, for at any moment either buffalo or Sioux might be encountered. At the head of the column rode the guide, carrying the flag of the buffalo hunt. He gave direction, and when he halted, the columns of carts halted too. Ahead and on either flank rode scouts, who kept watch for herds and for Sioux, and rode in with their intelligence. This they delivered to the captain as he rode between the two or four columns of carts, proceeding in formation over the prairies so that any moment they could halt sharply, or wheel into formation to corral horses and oxen, and stand off the Sioux. Grant, as he rode behind the flag man, or between the columns, must often have felt like Joshua leading the children of Israel in the wilderness, or like a general leading his forces towards contact with the enemy.

The conduct of the march was determined by the need for instant reaction to news of the buffalo or the Sioux. When it was reported that the herds were just over the next swell of the plain, camp was struck. The women formed the carts in a circle, inside which they put the stock. Then they reared the tepees outside. The men mounted their buffalo-running horses and, Grant leading, rode out with the scouts towards the herd. The approach was made as close as the ground would permit; then the hunters fanned out to right and left and, at a gesture from Grant, rode in line over the covering ridge and charged the herd. Each singled out his beast as the herd turned to run, shot it down from the saddle, dropped a glove, poured a handful of the powder kept loose in his pockets down the gun barrel, spat a bullet from his mouth into the muzzle, struck the gun-stock on his saddle and, as his experienced runner brought him alongside another lumbering cow, brought his gun down across the saddle and fired from the waist. That kill was marked with a second glove, and without pause or check the hunters drove on, loading, firing, drunk with the fury of the hunt. And so buffaloes, horses and men swept away across the plain, with bellow and gun-shot, the dust whipping away from the knolls in the prairie wind, and the long lines of slaughtered beasts stretching out behind.[9]

When the run died down, the hunters turned back to bleed and skin their kills. Meanwhile, the women had come up from the camp with the carts; and the hasty and heavy work of butchering began. The tongues and *depouillé* or hump meat were delicacies to be eaten at once or, in the case of the former, to be pickled in brine. The beef of rib and flank was cut in long strips for drying. The fat and sinew were carefully separated and preserved. Then the carts rolled back to camp with the spoils, and the work of drying the meat and making pemmican commenced. It was women's work,[10] and the men loafed around the camp in the intervals of sentry or scouting duties. It was no doubt on occasions such as this, as well as during long visits to his house in winter, that Grant began the heavy drinking on which his friends have commented.[11] For the Métis, like the Indian, kept his door open to any visitor, and whatever he had he would give in hospitality. On no one was this rule so binding as on the chief.

If his friends remarked on his drinking at the time, his people did not remember it later. They remembered him as the ever-patient counsellor, the constant and kindly overseer. And it seems in accord with all we know of Grant that he himself preferred, not the drinking in the tepee, but the stroll down among the women to see how their work was getting on. He took care that they did not lack for wood when fire had to be used to aid the sun in drying the meat, that the boys did not fail to keep the dogs away, and that the men were there to load the dark slabs of dried meat and the ninety-pound leathern bags of pemmican on the carts.

After the returns from the hunt were preserved, the march was resumed. The whole procedure was repeated, until the carts were filled. By 1834 some 700 carts went out, and each cart could carry between 500 and 1,000 pounds.[12] So much dried and concentrated meat and tallow was a great store of food and of considerable value. It was the staple which kept the western fur trade going and maintained the Red River colony.

It was not always the buffalo-herds that were encountered; sometimes it was the Sioux. Usually these encounters were mere brushes, an exchange of shots and arrows, a night raid to steal horses. Sometimes, however, the Sioux would cut off and shoot down a scout, and then picked men would ride out for revenge and to discourage the Indians by some stern act of retaliation. On a few occasions the Sioux would attack in force. Then the hunt would go into lager. The carts would be formed into a circle, surrounding the stock and the women. The barricade would be strengthened with poles and ropes, to prevent the stock stampeding, for without them the party was lost. Then some picked men would ride out to skirmish, and others would lie out from the cart-circle behind rocks or in gun-pits to hold the enemy out of range, so that they could not shoot the horses in the lager. The Métis marksmen could usually pick off enough Indians to discourage any bold advance on the camp. And after the foe had withdrawn, the march would continue in four columns, ready instantly to wheel into square to stand off a return of the Sioux.

The one encounter of this nature which is recorded both in the memory of the people of Saint-François-Xavier and in writing is that which took place at the Grand Coteau in 1851. Grant was not then present, but his people fought with the discipline he had taught them, and their story will be told later.[13]

Although he was absent from the most heroic of his people's battles on the plains, Grant nevertheless was their war leader, the man who had made the buffalo-hunters the formidable military force they were, both on the plains and in Red River. He was their leader in the formative years of the hunt, and its organization and discipline took shape under his personal leadership. The regularity of the procedure in the annual election of captain and council, the laws governing the hunt, the stern discipline of the march and the run, all these bear the impress of a single personality and a directing mind. That mind must have been Grant's. No one else among his people had the education, the experience, or the prestige to know how to shape Indian custom and tradition into a coherent and intelligent mode of government and manœuvre. In particular, no one else could have been acceptable from the first to the parties from St Boniface and Pembina as well as to the hunters of White Horse Plain.

Thus the buffalo hunt and the hunters of White Horse Plain had emerged by 1830 as the suppliers year by year of those "plains provisions" on which the operations of the fur trade and the larders of Red River were dependent. Red River was fed by its crops, the buffalo hunts, and the fisheries; and if any one of these failed, there was a shortage. In this fact lay the explanation of why Grant and his people never severed their ties with the wild life of the plains. The pemmican and dried meat they provided were a necessity. At the same time the Métis remained the bulwark of the colony against the Sioux. Grant's authority may be seen in the fact that on the hunts they were careful never to annoy the Sioux needlessly. But they could always deal with the Sioux, whether the prowlers and thieves who frequently hung about the colony, or the occasional band which came to Red River.

This dual role as hunters and soldiers made Grant's people, with those of St Boniface, an ever ready and efficient military force. Year by year the Métis became ever more French as the Scots were assimilated, yet ever a more distinct people. They were a nation in arms, whose annual organization in the buffalo hunt gave them a primitive but effective government, and a military formation admirably adapted to the plains. Their mounted marksmen could fight from either the saddle or the ground, were dashing in attack and resilient in defence. In this organization lay the strength which was to make them the decisive element in Red River in the rebellions of 1849 and 1869, under the elder and the younger Riel. But this development Grant did not plan, and he was to be its first victim. What he had done was to shape, for the livelihood and defence of his people and Red River, the instrument the Riels were to use to win self-government for the Métis and for Manitoba.[14]

Grant influenced the growth of his people in another and equally decisive way. One object of settlement was to ensure that the ministrations of the missionaries should be available. Bishop Provencher had used all his influence to ensure the removal from Pembina to White Horse Plain. He did his best thereafter to keep a missionary priest at Grantown. In 1830 the Reverend Jean Harper left for Quebec and was succeeded by the Reverend M. Boucher. The new missionary kept up the services in that first rude chapel built close to Grant's house, and endeavoured to teach the children, for the first schoolmaster had proved a failure. But when most of his flock went to the hunt, what was the pastor to do? Boucher went with his flock, and thereafter the hunt was normally accompanied by a priest. Thus the work of the mission was kept up summer and winter, and the good people of White Horse Plain were not without the consolations of religion during their wanderings on the plains. What dangers were attendant on these ministrations are revealed by the following adventure of Father Boucher in 1831. "The Priest, Bouche [r]," wrote Thomas Simpson, "joined the band and had some singular adventures, having separated from one party to go to another; lost his way on the plains and continued wandering about without food for days, almost terrified to death by the howling of wolves on his track. When he at length fell in with Cuthbert Grant's party, he looked more like a spectre than a man. . . ."[15] And the Reverend Louis Laflêche was to cheer his people in 1851 during the battle of the Grand Coteau.

It is perhaps not surprising that Boucher retired to Quebec in 1833 and was succeeded by the Reverend Charles Edouard Poiré.[16] The new curé found that the mission was one of 424 people, and that a new, larger and more durable chapel was being built to replace the flimsy first one built by the inexpert settlers of Grantown.[17] Grant had begun the building of this first church in the early years of the settlement, but the builders were inexperienced and substantial timbers were not obtainable. Of the building of the second church which was started in 1832, the story is told of how the strong man of Grantown, Toussaint Lussier, exhibited a feat of strength. One day when his ox was pulling a huge building log up from the river he unhitched it, and hauled the great oak timber which was forty feet long and ten inches in diameter, up the river bank himself, amid the applause of his fellow workers.

The first service, which was held in this church on Christmas Eve 1833, must have been a great satisfaction to Grant.[18] Some original chairs and part of the altar furnishings and woodwork are still used in the present church. The interior work and furnishings of the church, the grille work of the altar (made by auger holes in oak), the burning of the pascal candlestick, the fretwork of the altar — all this was accomplished over the next few years by the Reverend Georges Belcourt and the Reverend J. B. Thibault. The former, especially, became

ert as a turner. The benches were all hand made with wooden
s, and were taken over from the first chapel. Three chairs, placed
the gallery for the lay sisters who came after 1844, were made by
d also, and their seats were of laced buffalo-hide.

The expert joining and turning which which went into the chapel's
niture was presumably helped by the skill and tools of the cart-
lders who were beginning to emerge as a distinct craft at Grantown.
ree of them, François Richard, Michel Chalifaux, and Michel Pate-
ude, were to become the most expert in the colony. Their specialty
s in the making of the wheels, and the best Red River carts rolled
wheels made in Grantown.

Hitherto the missionary had lived in Grant's house. In 1834
presbytery was built at the end of the chapel, and Father Poiré
ved into it on his return from the summer hunt. He found that
ther Belcourt or Father Thibault had cared for the mission during
absence.

It was in the next year, 1834, that the registry of births, marriages
d deaths was first kept at Saint-François-Xavier. Hitherto this had
en done at St Boniface. The records relating to Grant's family are
at his daughter Nancy, aged two years and five months, died that
ar on August 21, and that on August 22 a son, Cuthbert Louis Marie
orge, was born.[19] This quick balancing of the scales of life and death
as common in those days of primitive medicine and unchecked
idemics. One can only hope that young Cuthbert's coming softened
e loss of little Nancy.

There was perhaps other reason for sorrow in Grant's home at this
ne. Grant's friends made frequent and saddened references to his
inking. By this they meant drinking beyond what was usual in an
e and place in which men used liquor freely. It does seem that in
e middle 'thirties Grant drank enough by the standards of his time
excite some comment. Moreover, in an incident much commented
at the time, his drinking may have impaired his judgement in a
here peculiarly his own. In the spring of 1834 a party of Sioux
sited Fort Garry under the chief La Terre qui Brûle. They came in
ace, to urge the Hudson's Bay Company to open a trading-post at
ke Traverse to afford some competition to the American traders
ere. Chief Factor Alexander Christie explained that the Company
uld not operate on American territory, and this satisfied the Sioux.

The Saulteaux Indians of the colony, however, many of whom
e Reverend Georges Belcourt had persuaded to settle at his mission
Baie St Paul west of Grantown on the Assiniboine, were excited
y the presence of their hereditary enemies, and combined to cut

them off. Christie and his officers resolved to protect the Sioux and to escort them out of the Settlement. They were leading the Sioux across the Assiniboine at Fort Garry, when Grant galloped up to the fort at the head of a party of Saulteaux. Both Sioux and Saulteaux bristled at once. Guns were pointed, and a fight seemed unavoidable. But Christie and his men, supported by some Scots settlers and half-breeds, intervened and got the Sioux away before there was violence. Thomas Simpson, Alexander Christie, and Governor Simpson were all extremely critical of Grant's action. Simpson, who must have got his information from Christie, reported that Grant was inebriated.[20]

He also pointed out that it was only with difficulty that Christie had kept the Scots from attacking Grant's party. They were resentful of many insults they had received from the Saulteaux from time to time, and "it was evident that the Scotch had neither forgotten nor forgiven Cuthbert Grant for the part he acted in the lamentable occurences of the year 1816."[21]

These accounts of the reawakening of the memories of Seven Oaks and the belief of the Hudson's Bay people that Grant had acted in headstrong and even drunken folly have no offsetting records. In the existing sources Grant appears in a bad light. He indeed failed to keep his friends informed of his thoughts and doings. John Siveright had written of him: "I corresponded with Cuthbert Grant, but his letters gave little information and he writes but occasionally and with funny reluctance. Grant is a good fellow. I have met with none who possessed more personal bravery and determined resolution in time of danger, but that is the best that can be said. Friendship or real regard for anyone beyond the moment, I don't think is in his nature or in that of many of his countrymen."[22] But it is evident that Christie had endeavoured to deal with the Sioux alone, without informing Grant. Grant, left without information may well have thought that it was for him to ride with all possible help against the traditional enemy. Thus what appeared to Christie as a foolhardy intervention in a carefully conducted negotiation was most likely meant as a dash to the rescue. And if Grant had been drinking, it clearly was not to such an extent as to affect his seat in the saddle, or his judgement when the situation became clear. For the fact is that there was no fight, which means that Grant abstained from battle, as he need not have done had he chosen to follow the Sioux southward.

Moreover, the episode obviously did not affect his status in Red River colony, and in later years there was little further comment on his private habits. In 1834 the Selkirk family sold Assiniboia back to the Hudson's Bay Company. Thus the company became responsible for the government of Assiniboia, or Red River. The government was reorganized by Governor Simpson in 1835. The Council of Assiniboia was enlarged and made more representative. Grant was made a member of the Council and attended a meeting for the first time on April 30, 1835.[23] The colony was also organized into four judicial districts and on February 12, 1835, Grant was made a Justice of the Peace for the Fourth District, of which White Horse Plain was the main settlement.[24] Thus Grant was made a Councillor and a Magistrate, in some sense the only representative of the half-breed people on the Council and the Bench at that time. These offices of trust showed the respect and esteem in which he was held. On both the Council and the Bench he was to serve successfully and to rise in rank. On June 16, 1837, he was made Magistrate for the Upper District with Captain George M. Cary, Superintendent of the Experimental Farm.[25] On May 20, 1839, he was reappointed Councillor of Assiniboia and one of the two sheriffs of Assiniboia, the other being Alexander Ross, the historian.[26] Grant was thus one of the chief men of the Red River colony, a legislator and an officer of the law. The gay young war leader of 1816 had come far.

Yet Grant's reputation as a warrior and the reputation of his men as fighters had spread far beyond the limits of Red River. Their fame was to lead to their services being sought by the American adventurer and freebooter, General Dickson.[27]

One of the most intriguing episodes in the history of the Canadian West was the invasion attempted by James Dickson, self-styled "Liberator of the Indian Nations," and a picturesque character. In 1837 Dickson arrived in Red River from Washington and New York, hoping to recruit the Métis as soldiers in his army of liberation. His ambitious plan was to march from Red River to Sante Fe, "free" the Indians there, and found a kingdom in California of which he was to be the head.[28]

He had introduced himself in Washington and New York as General James Dickson, and said he had lived for several years in Mexico. He also called himself "Montezuma II, Liberator of the Indian Nations." He caused quite a stir as he proceeded to recruit officers for his army. He had all the stage trappings: fine English tailoring executed with imagination, plenty of gold lace and gold braid, a handsome sabre-scarred face with beard and moustache. He wore small arms and a British general's gold-inlaid sword. Dickson also had in his extensive military luggage a coat of mail for which he never found a use. He was well-bred, a convincing talker, and had command of money. The officers and aides whom he recruited were lavishly equipped, and some carried with them extra beards and moustaches. The major of artillery wore silver epaulets, gold lace on his chest, and silver lace down the sides of his pantaloons.

His preparatory organization complete, Dickson proceeded to Montreal where he recruited, as additional officers, some half-breed sons of Hudson's Bay Company officials who he felt would be useful in Red River when mobilizing his Métis soldiers.

In August 1836, Dickson with his officers and attendants, numbering in all about sixty, embarked at Buffalo in a chartered vessel. They planned to traverse the Great Lakes on their way to recruit the soldiers of the liberating army at Red River, and thence proceed to Sante Fe – a trek of 5,000 miles or so.

Before they reached Sault Ste Marie the party was shipwrecked. On arriving there, they were arrested on a trivial charge (the sailors had stolen a cow) so that American authorities could investigate the party. The Liberator had been talking too freely of his plans. Finally released, a much-diminished army proceeded to a certain point on the Mississippi. They arrived there in boats and canoes, having lived on barrels of sour apples procured on the way.

Meanwhile Governor Simpson was travelling east from Red River. He was in Detroit when he learned of this newest threat to the settlement which he had nursed through so many vicissitudes. There he was startled by a newspaper account headed "Pirates on the Lakes," which gave a highly-coloured version of the incident at the Sault, and of the invaders bound for Red River. The thing had ugly possibilities. Without the Métis of White Horse Plain the settlement could not survive. It might even be wiped out, or added to the Liberator's empire. An ominous note was that Dickson's "Secretary of War" was a son of the Hudson's Bay Company's dire enemy, Kenneth McKenzie, called the "Emperor of the American Fur Trade." Simpson quickly dispatched messages to company headquarters in London and to the War Office and instructions to Governor Alexander Christie at Red River.[29]

When winter descended, Dickson with his party still further reduced started off by dog-sled and foot for Red River, and the frozen prairies took their toll. Guides deserted, men wandered and perished, and the remnants became separated. Finally, in December 1836, four months after starting off from Buffalo, the survivors (Dickson and eleven officers) straggled into the Red River settlement in a pitiable state.

Simpson's plans to defeat the invaders, though supremely simple, were an example of his superb strategy. The Hudson's Bay Company on his orders refused to honour Dickson's drafts, and no army could be raised. Red River was saved. Also under Simpson's orders, the Hudson's Bay Company absorbed some of Dickson's half-breed officers by offering them good positions. The others dispersed and Dickson, a defeated, deserted and deflated man, was stranded in Red River for the rest of the winter. Thus rendered harmless, he cut a gay figure in the settlement; for evidently, Dickson managed to bring considerable equipment with him. The Reverend G. H. Gunn's mother used to tell of the various and resplendent uniforms in which he appeared. He spent much time with Cuthbert Grant at White Horse Plain, and when spring came Grant outfitted him and gave him guides to start south to Santa Fe.

In character to the end, Dickson staged his last scene at Red River with care. On that spring day in 1837, guides, horses, drivers, and carts were waiting beside the church at Grantown for him to begin his journey, and a crowd gathered to say goodbye. He made a last laudatory speech of thanks to Cuthbert Grant. Then he removed his ornate military hat, bowed ceremoniously to him and — according to family tradition — said: "You are the great soldier and leader; I am a failure. These belong to you, not to me." In grandiose manner he removed his epaulets, fastened them on Grant's shoulders, handed him his sword, mounted and rode away. Thus ended the great invasion.

For many years Dickson's sword had an honoured place in Cuthbert Grant's home; and the epaulets were valued ornaments on the altar of the church at White Horse Plain. Unfortunately they were destroyed by fire.[30]

The final scene in this drama, where Dickson bids a sad farewell to the Métis, seemed to Pierre Falcon a fit subject for a folk-song. A characteristic of his songs is their spontaneity, for they seemed to take shape in his mind in the enthusiasm of the moment. On this occasion we can imagine him leaving the group around the church, mounting his horse, starting for home, and composing his verses to the rhythm of his horse's hoof-beats.

Le Général Dickson

C'est à la Rivière-Rouge,
Nouvelles sont arrivées, } bis
Un général d'armée
Qui vient pour engager.

Il vient pour engager
Beaucoup de Bois-Brûlés } bis
Il vient pour engager
Et n'a point d'quoi payer.

Dit qu'il veut emmener
Beaucoup de Bois-Brûlés. } bis
Ils sont en renommée
Pour de braves guerriers.

Vous, Monsieur Cuthbert Grant,
Maître de régiment, } bis
Mes épaulettes d'argent
Je vous en fais présent.

Moi, Général Dickson,
Je cherche ma couronne } bis
Je cherche ma couronne
Chez Messieurs les Espagnols.

Ville de Mexico
Beaucoup de Généraux } bis
Aussi des cannoniers
Qui vont vous couronner.

Adieu, mes officiers,
Vous m'avez tous laissé } bis
On marqu'ra sur la le papier
Dickson, pauvre guerrier.

Bourgeois de compagnie
Je dois vous remercier } bis
De te faire ramener
Au fort de Mackenzie.

Je dois vous remercier
Puisque avec vos deniers } bis
J'ai pu me faire guider
Par deux des Bois-Brûlés.

Qui en a fait la chanson?
Un poète de canton: } bis
Au bout de la chanson,
Nous vous le nommerons.

Un jour étant à table
A boire et à chanter } bis
A chanter tout au long
La nouvelle chanson.

Amis, buvons, trinquons, ⎱
Saluons la chanson   ⎰ bis
De Pierre Falcon,
Le faiseur de chansons.[31]

CHAPTER IX

THE SIOUX WARS AND FREE TRADE

By 1840 the career of Cuthbert Grant was at its apex. Still the "chief of the half-breeds" by right of their devotion to his person, he was by appointment of the company Warden of the Plains, Councillor of Assiniboia, Sheriff and Magistrate. For nine years more he was to enjoy these honours and fulfil the duties attached to them, then, after the Sayer trial his unchallenged position as leader of the Métis was lost to him and his importance in the Red River colony ended.

Of this nothing was evident in 1840. Indeed, Grant was now about to render his people as great a service as any he had done in the past. He was to lead them in war with the Sioux and to make peace after victory with those proud warriors.

The Sioux war of 1840-44 was an intensification of the old hostility, active since the days of La Vérendrye, between the Sioux and the Saulteaux. The people of Grantown and the Red River half-breeds were usually of Saulteaux, or Cree, descent, as Grant himself probably was Now the formation of the Saulteaux village at Baie St Paul west of Grantown was tending to renew the old ties between the people of Grantown and the Saulteaux. It was this old enmity, inflamed by Sioux killings of Saulteaux, and this old tie, which had led to the intervention by Grant and the Saulteaux in the Sioux visit to Fort Garry in 1834.

Now, six years later, the enmity was to be inflamed by further clashes on the plains. The growth of the hunt was driving the buffalo farther and farther to the southwest. The hunts ranged deeper and deeper into Sioux territory. The Sioux became more and more resentful and hung on the flanks of the hunts watching for chances to strike Alexander Ross, Sheriff of Assiniboia and historian of Red River, tell how he accompanied the hunt in 1840. (Grant was not at the hunt that year, for the captain was Jean Baptiste Wilkie of Pembina.)

Ross first tells how the hunt had grown from 500 Red River carts in 1820 to over 1,200 in 1840. Clearly an expedition so large mean a very considerable number of buffalo would have to be slaughtered to load so many carts. The historian then proceeds to give his classi account of the organization and conduct of the hunt which has bee drawn on by so many later writers.[1] But Ross also describes the danger from the Sioux, and relates how a Métis, Louison Vallé, was killed b dozen Sioux who caught him and his son working at cutting up their buffalo on the plain alone. The father's warning enabled the son to get away, and ten half-breeds rode in pursuit of the Indians. Four of the Sioux escaped, but eight were shot down from the saddle like buffalo by the angry Métis.[2]

This kind of crushing vengeance was, of course, the half-breed's chief defence against attack by the Sioux. But the half-breeds aggravated the danger from the Sioux by allowing bands of Saulteaux to accompany them to the plains. Ross does not make it clear that Vallé was killed in 1840, although he probably was, because the matter was settled that year by negotiation with the Sioux chief La Terre qui rûle. But he does describe as an eyewitness a skirmish between a party of Sioux and forty or fifty Saulteaux from Red River. The encounter took place on the banks of the Cheyenne on the return of the hunt to Pembina. The Saulteaux attacked, as they probably would not have done had they not had the presence of the Métis camp to encourage them. Six Métis watched the exchange of fire. Ten Sioux and seven Saulteaux were killed or wounded. It was later learned that a half-breed, one Parisien, was with the Saulteaux and actually fired the first shot.[3]

It was as the outcome of this affair that the encounters between the Métis and the Sioux multiplied in the "war" which was ended in 1844.

Grant, however, did not immediately take part in the war. As Ross does not mention him, and as Wilkie was captain of the hunt, it is to be assumed that Grant that year remained in Grantown. This he now began increasingly to do, if not for the summer hunt, then for the fall hunt. The chief responsibility of those who stayed at home was to tend the crops, to put up hay for the buffalo-runners and the cart-ponies, and to support themselves. To accomplish the last, Grant now often undertook to care for the old men and others who were unable to accompany the hunters. They would go to camp at a nearby lake which is still named Grant's Lake, although very few people today now the origin of the name. There his guns supplied them with game for food, the best the land could furnish, and feathers to fatten pillows and warm comforters for winter, until the hunters returned with the "plains provisions," for the season of the hunt was always one of shortage for those who were forced to remain at home.

Grant did not go to the hunt in 1841 either. In June of that year when the hunters were preparing to leave for the plains, Grant, with a party of his people, acted as guide at the request of Governor Simpson to Lords Caledon and Mulgrave. Simpson reported: "On the 19th

I despatched my noble fellow-travellers . . . under the escort of Mr. Grant, who holds the office of Warden of the Plains, and a party of half-breeds. . . ."[4] Grant, that is, took these sportsmen out on the plains to hunt buffalo. In this he was acting in a role in which another great plainsman, the Honourable James Mackay, was later to win fame. But although Grant was eager to oblige Simpson, and always gave the Governor of the Hudson's Bay Company the same loyalty that he had given to the Nor'Westers of old, this expedition surely indicates that the war with the Sioux was not serious that year.

In 1842, however, Grant was called to the plains. On July 30 of that year Chief Factor Nicol Finlayson wrote to Hargrave that "Grant has not yet returned from the War. I daresay you will hear the result before I can."[5] The result no one now can learn, apparently, for no record of it for that year or the next has been found. But, as Ross recounts the events, "for the last four years up to 1844 the half-breeds . . . suffered considerably." In the last year, however, they apparently struck out and killed eight Sioux, four Sisitons and four Yanktons. Grant must have been with the hunt that year, for he writes of the event as an eyewitness. The Sioux sought compensation in the following communication.

> White Bear's Lodge, 14th November, 1844
> Friends, – We hang down our heads; our wives mourn, and our children cry.
>
> Friends, – The pipe of peace has not been in our council for the last six days.
>
> Friends, – We are now strangers. The whites are our enemies.
>
> Friends, – The whites have often been in our power; but we always conveyed them on their journey with glad hearts, and something to eat.
>
> Friends, – Our young men have been killed. They were good warriors: their friends cry.
>
> Friends, – Our hearts are no longer glad. Our faces are not painted.
>
> Friends, – You owe the Sisitons four loaded carts, they were our relations; the half-breeds are white men: the whites always pay well.
>
> Friends, – The four Yanktons did not belong to us: but they are dead also.
>
> Friends, – Tell us if we are to be friends or enemies? Is it to be peace or war? Till now our hands have always been white, and our hearts good.

Friends, – We are not frightened; we are yet many and strong. Our bows are good; but we love peace: we are fond of our families.

Friends, – Our hearts were not glad when we left you last; our shot pouches were light, our pipes cold; but yet we love peace. Let your answer make our wives happy, and our children smile.

Friends, – Send Langé with your message, his ears are open; he is wise.

Friends, – We smoke the pipe of peace, and send our hearts to you.

Friends, – Tell Langé to run, he will eat and rest here. He will be safe, and we will not send him off hungry, or barefooted.

Signed by the chiefs.

Wa Nen De Ne Ko Ton Money	X	La Terre qui Brule
In Yag Money	X	The Thunder that Rings
Etai Wake Yon	X	The Black Bull
Pin E Hon Tane	X	The Sun.

Grant replied refusing compensation, but offering peace in the following letter.

Grantown, 8th December, 1844.

Friends, – The messenger which you sent to us, found us all sad as yourselves, and from a similar cause: a cause which may give a momentary interruption to the pipe of peace; but should not, we hope, wholly extinguish it.

Friends, – You know that for half a century or more, you and we have smoked the pipe of peace together; that during all that time, no individual in your nation could say, that the half-breeds of Red River lifted up their hands in anger against him, until the late fatal occurrence compelled them in self-defence to do so; although you well know, that year after year, your young men have killed, and, what we regard worse than death, scalped many belonging to us. Not that we were afraid to retaliate; but because we are Christians, and never indulge in revenge. And this declaration, which may not be denied, brings us more immediately to notice and to answer the several points in your message to us.

Friends, – You say your people have been killed: we believe what you say, and sincerely regret it; but at the same time, you forget to express your regret that our people were killed also: the one fact is as well known to you as the other; and they were killed first. You forget to notice, that whilst La Terre qui Brule and party were in the midst of our friendly camp, smoking the calumet of peace in all confidence and security, your people at that moment were treacherously murdering our friends within sight of that very camp! You forget to mention that our dead were brought into the camp, the bodies yet warm, and laid before your eyes! Till then, never did it enter into the head or the heart of a Red River half-breed to seek in revenge the blood of a Sioux.

Friends, – You state that our people have often been in your power: we acknowledge what you say; but you must likewise acknowledge, that your people have often been in our power, and we sent them off with glad hearts also. Even on the late fatal occurrence, when our dead were before your eyes, and when a hundred guns pointed with deadly aim threatened La Terre qui Brule and party with instant death, yet more were for you than against you; so you were safe; La Terre qui Brule and party were safe in the camp of the half-breeds. The brave are always generous.

Friends, – You state that when you last left us, "your shot pouches were light and your pipes cold." There is a time for everything; was it a time to show you special kindness when murdering our relations? You demand from us four loaded carts for the four Sisitons: we never refuse paying a just debt, never consent to pay an unjust one. Let us see how far we are liable. In the first place, then, you know your people were the first aggressors. You, La Terre qui Brule, saw with your own eyes our dead, and you knew that none of your people were then killed, and we gave up all thoughts of retaliation, still clinging with fond hopes to that peace and friendship which had so long cheered our intercourse together; but the very next day after you left our camp, a party of your people were discovered rushing upon one of our hunters who happened to be a little on one side and alone; the alarm was given, when the first at hand scampered off at full speed to the rescue of their brother, and in the onset your people were killed. Four, you say, were Yanktons. The demand you make we cannot comply with, either for Sisitons or Yanktons, be the consequences what they may, because we consider it unjust. We may give a pipe of tobacco, or a load of ammunition voluntarily; but we will submit to no unjust demand.

Friends, – You put the question, "Shall we be friends or enemies, or shall there be peace or war?" We leave yourselves to answer the question. They who would have friends must show themselves friendly. We have violated no faith, we have broken no peace. We will break none. We will not go to find you to do you harm. We will always respect the laws of humanity. But we will never forget the first law of nature: we will defend ourselves, should you be numerous as the stars, and powerful as the sun. You say you are not frightened: we know you are a brave and generous people; but there are bad people among you.

Friends, – We are fond of you, because you have often showed yourselves generous and kind to the whites: we are fond of you from a long and friendly intercourse, and from habits of intimacy. To sum up all in few words, we are for peace, peace is our motto; but on the contrary, if you are for war, and you raise the tomahawk in anger, we warn you not to approach our camp either by day or night, or you will be answerable for the consequences.

Friends, – You have now our answer; we hope you will take the same view of things, and come to the same conclusion we have done. Langé will lay this before the great chiefs; may your answer be the sacred pipe of peace. Put your decision on white man's paper. And may that peace and friendship, which has so long knit our hearts together heretofore, still continue to do so hereafter.

> (Signed) Cuthbert Grant,
> Chief of the half-breeds,
> and Warden of the Plains.

To Wa Nen De Ne Ko Ton Money.
    In Yag Money.
    Etai Wake Yon.
    Pin E Hon Tane.

The chiefs replied as follows:

To Cuthbert Grant, Chief of all the half-breeds, and Warden of the Plains.

> White Bear's Lodge, 12th Feb. 1845.

Friends, – Langé is here, and your message is now spread before us in council. Ne-tai-ope called for the pipe; but Wa-nen-de-ne-ko-ton-money said no: all the men were then silent; but the women set up a noisy howl out-doors. Nothing was done till they got quiet. The council then broke up. Next day it was the same. The third day the council received your message as one of peace. We now send you our answer. Langé promises to run

Friends, – I, the afflicted father of one of the young men killed
by you, wish that he who killed my son should be my son in hi
stead. He had two feathers in his head.

Ne tai Ope.

Friends, – Among the young men killed by you, I had a
nephew. He who killed him I wish to be my nephew. He was the
smallest of all the unfortunates.

Friends, – You killed my son, he was brave, San-be-ge-ai-too
tan. He who pointed the gun at him, I wish to be my son. He ha
a feathered wand in his hand. I send it by Langé to my adopte
son.

Tah Wah Chan Can.

Friends, – I wish the brave who killed my brother, should b
my brother. He had a gun and many feathers in his head. He wa
young.

Hai To Ke Yan.

Friends, – I am old and bowed down with sorrow. You kille
my brother-in-law. He was braver than the bear. Had thre
wounds, and a scar on the face. Whoever killed him, I wish him
to be my brother-in-law for ever. He was bareheaded. Hai
painted red. Many bells and beads on his leggings. He was tal
and strong.

Tah Tan Yon Wah Ma De Yon

Friends, – My cousin never returned. He is dead. Whoeve
deprived me of his friendship, I wish him to be my friend an
cousin. He had been wounded before, and had a crooked hand
His feathers were red. He had garnished shoes.

Wah Ma De Oke Yon.

Friends, – You killed my father last summer. I wish him wh
made me fatherless, should be my father. He was a chief,
Sisiton warrior, had a gun and a bow, had been scalped young
His feathers reached the ground. Whoever will wear thos
feathers, I will give him a horse. I will be proud of him.

Friends, – You killed my uncle, Thon-gan-en-de-na-ge. I ar
sad. The man who was so brave, I wish to be my uncle. He wa
a Yankton. My face is always painted black. He had on clot
and leather leggings, and one feather.

Kan Tan Kee.

Signed by the chiefs.

Wa Nen De Ne Ko Ton Money.	X	La Terre qui Brule.
In Yag Money	X	The Thunder that Rings.
Etai Wake Yon	X	The Black Bull.
Pin E Hon Tane	X	The Sun.[6]

This terminated the negotiations in what was considered a peace. The hunt went out in 1845, and a Sioux party visited Fort Garry. Once more the enmity of the Saulteaux led to violence. A Sioux and a Saulteaux were killed by a Saulteaux. The slayer was, however, convicted and hanged, and the peace Grant had made was maintained for the next few years.

Since it is no longer possible to separate Grant's career from the various aspects of the community with which he had become so completely identified, it is desirable to look once again at life in Grantown itself. Grant's own affairs were still in good order. His house was the centre of the village, the ever open source of hospitality where every neighbour was welcome and every traveller called. His family continued to grow. To Sophie Caroline, born in 1839, was added Julie Rose born in 1841. And the same year saw his eldest daughter Eliza married to Henry Pagée of Grantown. Next, in 1843, his son Charles married Euphrosme Gladu, also of Grantown.[7] Grant was in process of becoming a patriarch in fact as well as in role. The census of 1843 showed that he still cultivated 50 acres of land, a very large area for Red River, and that his windmill still ground the grists of the people of Grantown. He was, in short, still the chief man of the settlement.[8]

The settlement itself was growing steadily. There were, in 1848, 146 families resident at White Horse Plain. These were mostly the original fifty families and their children, but others had joined them, and in 1840 a considerable number of settlers had come down from the northwest to take up lots at Grantown.

The parish continued to be a worry to Bishop Provencher, not because its people and their leader were not devout, but because few priests could stand the rigours of life on the plains in the northwest winter. In 1839 the Reverend Charles Poiré followed Harper back to Quebec. He was succeeded by the Reverend J. A. Mayrand, but Mayrand's health soon gave out, and the mission relied again on the intermittent services of the Reverend Georges Belcourt and the Reverend B. Thibault, both busied in the main with Indian missionary work.

Grant knew the value of christianizing the Indians and realized the necessity for educating his people. He aided Bishop Provencher St Boniface by providing accommodation for any priests who could come to Grantown to minister to the needs of the parishioners. The priests who came held school for the boys in Grant's home; and he looked to Bishop Provencher to find young women with some education who would be willing to come for short periods and hold classes for the girls. Grant's zeal for the church he was helping to found is also evidenced in the parish records where his name appears as godfather for many of the Indians he was trying to christianize.

As early as 1838 Bishop Provencher was anxious to replace the church of 1833 by a more substantial structure. Unfortunately workmen could not be procured and for years the building could not go forward as planned. Though progress was slow, the new church was finally completed in the early 1840's, and the finishing touch to this new church proved to be a bell for its steeple. In 1820 Lord Selkirk had sent out a bell weighting 180 pounds for St Boniface Cathedral and, after the cathedral received a chime of three bells in 1840, Lord Selkirk's bell was passed on to the Saint-François mission. This church was in use for many years, though as time went on it too proved insubstantial and had to be buttressed. The bell hung there until 1868 when it was blown down in a storm. Its subsequent history is worth noting. For long years it lay forgotten in the long grass of the church yard, and with new generations all knowledge of its existence and significance was lost. For ninety years it rusted in obscurity, but it was rescued and now rests in the museum in the St Boniface city hall. Cuthbert Grant knew of the significance of that bell, and must have felt gratified when it was hung in the church at Grantown. How the sound of that bell would break the silence of the empty prairie, ringing joyfully for weddings and in slow, solemn tones for funerals. It was an acquisition of which the Métis were very proud.[9]

The priest's house also was in poor condition, and the Governor had not yet given the Bishop title to the land on which it stood; nor had a schoolmaster yet been found to maintain a school at the church.[10] It was for these reasons, the poverty of his mission and the unreliability of secular priests with no special vocation for mission work, that Bishop Provencher was to seek and find in 1844 the help of two orders especially devoted to missionary work. The Oblates of Mary Immaculate, of whom Father Taché was one, came to the northwest in 1844, and the Sisters of Charity, or the Grey Nuns, arrived at St Boniface in the same year.[11]

The war with the Sioux, and problems arising in the home community were not, however, to be the only troubles in which Cuthbert Grant was engaged in 1844. Trouble had broken out within the colony itself, and it was such as to call for Grant's exertions both as Warden of the Plains and as a Sheriff of Assiniboia. That year saw an outburst of free trading which was to lead up to the Sayer trial of 1849, with all that was to mean to Grant.

The origins of this new trouble were both immediate and remote. The remote origins lay back in the twenties, when Grant himself had traded under a special licence given by Simpson. He had bought furs free traders might have bought, and traded them to the company. Thus the monopoly was preserved and the free trade damped down. But at least one other trader, Andrew McDermot, a former clerk of the Hudson's Bay Company, had been given a special licence in 1823. Thereafter he continued as a storekeeper in the colony, and it may be as a trader in furs who sold to the company also. During the thirties the free trade was tolerably under control. But private traders, notably Andrew McDermot and a younger man and a half-breed, James Sinclair, continued to deal in groceries and dry goods, which were sold for currency or country produce. These men also became engaged, as Grant has done, in freighting supplies for the company. Both as traders and freighters they served the company's interests by performing functions the company was glad to leave to them, and as long as they sold any furs they traded to the company little was feared.[12]

In 1843, however, the Chief Factor at Fort Garry, Duncan Finlayson, refused to renew McDermot and Sinclair's contracts as freighters.[13] Difficulties followed over the forwarding from York Factory of an experimental shipment of tallow which they had made. The reasons given were that their services as freighters had not been satisfactory, and that there was no room in the ship of the year for the tallow. McDermot and Sinclair chose to regard Finlayson's action as a punitive measure directed at their trading in furs, and one cannot escape the impression that the Chief Factor's interest was to put two able and ambitious traders in their places.[14]

If such was his purpose, he must have regretted his action. For two things immediately happened. One was a visit of Norman W. Kittson to Red River in December of 1843. It is difficult to believe that the visit was not inspired by the angry Red River traders, although the breakup of the American Fur Company was causing the traders on the Mississippi to cast their eyes northward again. In the summer of 1844 Kittson opened a trading-post at Pembina, and the danger Simpson had feared and avoided in the 1820's, of a trading-post beyond the reach of the company to which the Métis might resort, had been realized.[15]

The second consequence of Finlayson's action followed immediately. The young half-breeds of Red River rushed into the fur trade.

A new generation was coming, that of the mixed-blood sons of the fur-trade officers and servants who had settled in Red River, as Grant's people had done. There their children had grown up and, after a fashion, had been educated. But the company rarely employed half-breeds in posts of trust, whether clerical or higher. Red River farming had little to offer, for want of a market for farm produce. The market for the "plains provisions" of the buffalo-hunt was soon glutted in a year of good hunts. So many a bright young man had little enough to stir his ambitions or engage his energies in Red River.

But the free trade gave entrance to the one really rewarding enter-prise of the country, the fur trade. Furs produced profitable returns, certainly in goods from St Peter's on the Mississippi, and sometimes in gold or dollars. Numbers of them now rushed into the fur trade. All round Red River, at Lake Manitoba, at Portage la Prairie, on the Winnipeg River and the Roseau, they trapped or traded. The furs they concealed in their houses, in the stables, in the woods along the rivers, in the bluffs of oak on the prairies. Some ran their furs to Kittson at Pembina. Some went to St Peter's itself, such as that band whose adven-tures Peter Garrioch recorded in his unpublished journal, and which cut the trail through the woods east of Red River to avoid the warring Sioux, the trail thereafter known as the Crow Wing Trail.[16]

This was not tame free trading, in which the company ultimately received the furs. This was real free trading in which the furs went to other buyers. It was entirely illegal, and of course highly dangerous, both because the practice would spread if not checked, and also because the high prices it caused would encourage the Indians to bring their furs for hundreds of miles.

Nothing could have been more distressing to Grant than this out-burst of free trading. As Warden of the Plains, as Sheriff and Magis-trate, he was bound to try to suppress it. But his own people were tempted by the profits of the free trade, by their manner of life and their past, to take part in it. If Grant did his duy, he might forfeit the affection of his people. If he did not, he would lose his offices and his income.

Thus Grant faced years of trouble after 1844, for the fur-trade dispute was to run until the Sayer trial of 1849, and indeed beyond. But at first there was no doubt of where he stood. The first reaction of the company and of the Council of Assiniboia was to endeavour to suppress the free trade by all public and private means. Houses and premises were searched for furs. When furs were found, they were confiscated. Cart-trains were stopped and searched for furs, and the furs confiscated.[17] In all this Grant took part as an officer of the law.

The Council of Assiniboia imposed new and higher duties on goods coming in from the United States, particularly on the stoves which the free traders needed to heat their trading cabins.[18] The wording of land titles was tightened, in order to make effective the clause providing for forfeiture of lands on conviction of trading in furs. This apparently raised the question of by what title lands were held in Grantown. The mail of private traders was made subject to inspection by officers of the Hudson's Bay Company, although in this Grant had no part. But clearly Grant was the company's man; he was on the side of the law and against the free traders who had sprung up in Red River. Fortunately few of his own Grantown people seem to have been involved at this time.[19] The open and defiant free traders came from the lower Red, in the parishes of St John's, Middlechurch, and St Andrews. When in August 1845 a number of half-breeds, led by James Sinclair, wrote to Chief Factor Alexander Christie, who had succeeded Finlayson at Fort Garry, to ask a series of questions relating to the rights of the native-born people of Rupert's Land, no Grantown name appeared among them.[20]

By that date the free traders were openly challenging the monopoly of the Hudson's Bay Company and were seeking to undermine its political authority. A petition for help was sent to the Congress of the United States, another to the Government of the United Kingdom. The peace of Red River was seriously threatened, and Grant and his people might well have had serious work to do, if the dispute with the United States over the Oregon territory had not led to the dispatch of a detachment of British troops to Red River in 1846.[21]

The troops were to remain for two years. Their presence both quieted the turbulent half-breeds and soothed the discontented free traders by affording them an unaccustomed market.[22] Public life in Red River once more became sedate and unruffled. So also was Grant's private life. Peace with the Sioux left the hunts untroubled; the suppression of the free trade gave no further occasion for raiding homes or searching the oak islands of the plains for furs. An epidemic of measles imported from Missouri in 1846 must have caused him concern as a father and a physician, for the disease was severe upon a population not at all immunized to it.[23] But Grant's family escaped the deaths the disease brought to some households. In 1848 his daughter Marie Rose was married to one of the Grantown boys, Pierre Gariepy.[24]

One change had come over the parish of Saint-François-Xavier. While Bishop Provencher still hoped to establish a school in the parish, he had given up his endeavours to maintain a secular priest there. The services were performed by Oblates sent out from St Boniface, or by the Reverend M. Belcourt from Baie-Saint-Paul. That stout missionary was soon to fall foul of Governor Simpson, however, for he supported the half-breeds in their demand for self-government in the spring of 1846. The good priest was promptly accused of trading in furs – he may have accepted some as gifts from his Indian converts – and was sent packing to Quebec. Governor Simpson erred in this, for Father Belcourt returned to Pembina in 1848, and in 1852 led his flock up the Pembina River to St Joseph's in the United States territory of Dakota, which thereafter became a second home to the Red River Métis and a haven to free traders and any one else in trouble with the authorities in Rupert's Land.[25] (All Simpson's careful work of the 1820's, in which Grant had been his indispensable ally, was beginning to crumble away.) By the fall of 1848 Grantown was again served by a secular priest of their own, for in that year the Reverend Louis Laflêche, who had served in the mission at Lac la Ronge in the northwest, was sent to Saint-François-Xavier to recuperate after the strain of northern service, and for the next few years served his people in the parish and on the hunt.[26]

The uneasy truce in the free trade struggle which had existed since 1846 ended abruptly in the spring of 1849. The peace and progress of the three preceding years came to an end shortly after Chief Factor John Ballenden took over from Chief Factor Alexander Christie the trying job of suppressing free trade without challenging the half-breeds to a trial of strength. The task was much more difficult now, for the withdrawal of the troops in 1848 had left the free traders again at liberty to defy the law. The troops, it is true, had been replaced in 1848 by a small band of Chelsea out-pensioners. These last, if resolutely commanded, might have strengthened the forces of law and order in Red River, but their commander, Major W. B. Caldwell, was a slow-witted and irresolute man. He was also Governor of Assiniboia, an office held by the Chief Factor at Fort Garry since 1835, but this additional authority only aggravated the effect of his want of intelligence and resolution. Moreover, he was soon at odds with his second-in-command, Captain V. C. Foss, and suspended him from discharging the duties of his office. The result was that the pensioners could scarcely be counted on to support the civil power in Red River.[27]

There was in consequence considerable free trading during the winter, and Ballenden determined to take legal action in an endeavour to check it. He laid charges against four Métis: Guillaume Sayer, McGillis, Laronde and Goulet. Sayer and McGillis were from Grantown, McGillis being a brother-in-law of Grant. The cases came up for trial on May 17, 1849, with Sayer the first of the four to enter the dock.

On the bench sat the Magistrates of Assiniboia, beside Recorder Adam Thom of the Quarterly Court of Assiniboia – among them Cuthbert Grant, sitting in judgement on his own blood and kin.[28] This was the beginning of the notorious Sayer trial which was to end any legal attempt to curb free trading in Red River.

The trial of Guillaume Sayer was also the trial of the old order which had held sway in Red River since the union of the companies in 1821. It was therefore also the trial of Cuthbert Grant. Could he – sitting on the bench as a magistrate, not only in virtue of his education and his character, but also as Warden of the Plains and chief of the half-breeds – could he by his example influence the half-breeds of Red River to accept the verdict of the court and the sentence of the law? If he could not, his usefulness would be greatly diminished, if not ended.

Grant's influence, it was soon apparent, could no longer hold the half-breeds in check. There was talk indeed of the leading free trader, James Sinclair, now being chief of the half-breeds. And the Métis of St Boniface and Pembina, the men of the main river party of the buffalo hunt, were following the lead of a newcomer, the Métis son of a Nor'West *voyageur*, Louis Riel. This elder Riel, whose famous son and namesake was to pursue a dominant role in the events of 1869-70 and again in 1885, had returned to Red River from Lower Canada in 1841. He brought with him much talk of Papineau, and of how the new Recorder in Assiniboia, Adam Thom, had written against the French in Montreal and had helped Lord Durham prepare the Report which said that the best fate for the French would be to be assimilated by the British. From Pembina the Reverend Georges Belcourt sent messages of inflammatory sympathy, and the resentment which had smouldered so long reached the point where it was ready to burst into flame. Thus the men who flocked to mass at St Boniface Cathedral that Ascension Day came armed, and after Mass they swarmed across the Red to gather in menacing array around the Court House where the court was in session.[29]

The court sat unprotected, for its president was Governor Caldwell, who thus could not command the pensioners, and neither could Captain Foss, who was still suspended from the performance of his duties. He was free to supervise the building of a summer house on his new property on a point of the Assiniboine later to be known as Armstrong's Point. So it was that the sturdy Irish veterans stood cheerfully around the gates of Fort Garry, or mingled with the Métis, or worked on their lots along the Assiniboine. Nor did Sheriff Alexander Ross, much less Sheriff Cuthbert Grant, swear in special constables. It had become tacit policy in Red River not to resist the buffalo-hunters when roused and acting as a body, as they now manifestly were.[30]

In this atmosphere of gathering defiance, the Court finished its previous cases and called Sayer before it. As the prisoner stood up, the excitement came to a head. The crowd surged forward, shouts went up, and a wild Métis demanded to be let into the Court House to shoot Judge Thom on the bench. A group led by Sinclair and escorted by Sheriff Ross, did make their way in. Thom, keeping his head and coolly defiant, asked their purpose. Sinclair replied by challenging the validity of the Court and its proceedings. Thom rebutted his arguments. The upshot was a compromise, an agreement that Sinclair might represent the prisoner and challenge the jury. He challenged no fewer than nine and their places were taken by Métis and half breeds, some from the mob outside, who sat in the jury box with their powder horns at their sides.

The trial then proceeded. Sayer explained that he had not been trading, but only exchanging gifts, Indian-fashion, with relatives. Moreover, he said, even if this were trading, Chief Trader J. E. Harriott, who was trading among the free traders as Grant had done in the twenties, had told him he might trade for furs. The jury then retired and, with a perhaps surprising and possibly pre-arranged honesty, brought in a verdict of "guilty of trading in furs," but coupled this with a recommendation for mercy in view of the culprit's belief that he had permission to trade. Thereupon Ballenden rose and professed himself satisfied with the verdict, and asked that mercy be granted and that the charges against the other three accused be withdrawn.[31]

The intent was to try to have a formal verdict and yield the rest to the clamouring crowd outside. But when the news of Sayer's dismissal without penalty was shouted from the door, the crowd took it for acquittal and drew the instant conclusion that henceforth no one would be prosecuted for trading in furs. They thought their purpose realized and raised the shout: "Le commerce est libre! Le commerce est libre!"[32] which in fact marked the end of any attempt to enforce the monopoly of the Hudson's Bay Company by resort to the courts.

Nor was this the whole programme of the Métis, for they followed up their victory on May 17 by demanding that Thom, whom they regarded as an enemy of their race, should retire from the Court, and that twelve representatives of the Métis be admitted to the Council of Assiniboia.[33] In short, their demands were revolutionary, and in them there was no place for Grant. Grant had served Simpson and the Hudson's Bay Company too long and too loyally. He could no longer be regarded as the chief of all the Métis of Red River. New leaders had risen: James Sinclair for the English half-breeds, and Louis Riel for the French Métis. Only in Grantown was Grant still chief.

The diminution of Grant's influence which was marked by the Sayer trial was quickly acted upon by Simpson. The Council of the Northern Department did not renew, for the first time in twenty-one years, his annual appointment as Warden of the Plains. Grant's unique place in the Red River colony was ending. Councillor of Assiniboia and Magistrate he remained, but his usefulness as a check on the free trade was over. Even on the Council his position as representative of the people of mixed blood was henceforth to be shared, as the Reverend Louis Laflêche was appointed in that capacity in 1850. This was the beginning of a process which was to bring a number of half-breeds to the Council table, among them some of Grant's Grantown neighbours.

The old order was changing in another respect. Grant had always believed himself the seignior of Grantown. He believed that his people held their lands of him. But the new interest in land titles caused by the free trade quarrels led Chief Factor Ballenden to challenge Grant's belief. In 1850 he convinced Grant that his proud claim was groundless. Ballenden wrote to Simpson:

> Fort Garry, Red River Settlement
> 13th February 1850
>
> Private
>
> Dear Sir George,
>   . . . In the Settlement, in so far as regards the Company's affairs, all goes on quietly. – Provisions of all kinds are abundant and the proximity of the Buffalo has given the more improvident of the Half Breeds a Supply of fresh meat, of which they would, otherwise, have been much in want this spring. – Here, as elsewhere, there is a Scarcity of Fur bearing animals: but I think we have got our share. – Our Returns are indeed equal, if not superior, to those of last year at this date. – At Pembina, Mr. Setter is doing but little, but his opponent, so far as I can learn, is doing still less. – At Red Lake the Indians are literally starving. –
>   During the last week or more, we have been rather gay here. – The Bishop of Ruperts Land & Mr. Thom have each given a party and Mr. Logan has issued his Cards for one also. – I attended at the two former and as I am invited to the latter, I shall be there also

if circumstances do not prevent me. – I think I must give something like a Return also, altho' I would rather not. –

Since I wrote you Grant and I have come to an amicable arrangement. – He gives up his absurd claims to Seignorial rights and acknowledges that the people of the White Horse Plains are in no respect different, in so far as regards their lands, from the other Settlers. – This is all well, but allow me again to request that you will not only recommend, but also urge on, the preparation of, the Title deeds as corrected. – I am particularly anxious on this subject, as I think it has been too long neglected, and as I know it will, in the eyes of the Settlers, give value to that which they considered almost valueless, – their lands...

Yours Most truly
(Signed) JOHN BALLENDEN[34]

The career of Grant was ending; the history of Grantown and its people was to go on.

CHAPTER X

THE LAST YEARS OF GRANTOWN

The changes wrought by the events of 1849 produced no change in Grant's relations with his neighbours in Grantown or in the course of life there.

An interesting event of the early fifties was the marriage of his daughter Elizabeth. It was not always easy in Rupert's Land to find a suitable mate when young people were ready for marriage. Sometimes parents had to seek far afield, and such was the case with Cuthbert Grant's daughter Elizabeth. Thus when Grant received a letter from York Factory acquainting him of the interest of young William McKay in his daughter, he and his family thought it worth considering as William McKay Sr was the master of a post at Trout Lake, and he and his wife were people of fine character. Because of the distances involved it might take several years to make the necessary arrangements. The following correspondence tells of the courtship. In January 1849, James Hargrave had written from York Factory to his old friend on behalf of one of his men, Mr W. McKay as follows:

Y.F. 17 Aug/49

C. Grant Esq/R.R.
My Dear Grant –

I enclose a letter from Mr. W. McKay, one of my post servants the subject of which was made known to me this summer. His son and your Daughter Elisabeth it seems had formed a reciprocal attachment to each other some time ago – and altho like others they kept this to themselves – yet now the young fellow has come forward in a manly frank manner and requests permission of me "to take a wife." He is a lad so far as I have known of a good character – is prudent and saving having wages as an asst. interpreter in the amount of £20 p. an. Should you approve of the proposal and that your daughter is still unengaged – I see myself no objection to his settling in life. And could your daughter come here next spring under the wing of a carefull and respectable freighter such as Mr. Mowat, I would take care of her in the Factory until her intended arrived from Grant Lake – when I would unite them as man and wife – agreeably to the rites of the Country & of England.

With kinds regards to my old friend Mrs. Grant now & always.
                                    My Dear Grant
                                    most faithfully yours
                                          J. H.[1]

Grant replied to the above in June, 1850:

                                    Grantown 3rd June, 1850.

J. Hargrave Esquire
My Dear Sir,
        Your kind favour of the 17th Augt came safe to hand on
the arrival of the fall boats as well as an enclosed letter from
Mr W. McKay regarding his Son William demanding my
daughter Elisabeth for a wife. Now, after the character you give
me of the young man's good behaviour etc. there lies no difficulty in complying to his request, but the devil is to get the girl
to consent to go down alone and unprotected for she's not
acquainted with any of the freighters, and her mother is also
against it. But if the young man could be permitted to come and
pass 2 or 3 days with us, no doubt all these present difficulties
would be done away with, so you see how the land lies.
        I shall not attempt to intrude on your present time and give
you nothing but dismal news, so trusting this will find you
enjoying your usual good health and spirits
                                    I am
                                    Your ever faithful affate sert
                                    Cuthbert Grant[2]
Mrs. Grant begs to be kindly remembered to you.

Elizabeth's reluctance was overcome at length, perhaps by a visit
from the young man. Nevertheless the final arrangements took some
time to complete, for the reply to a letter sent one year could not be
expected until the next. It was 1853 therefore before the marriage
took place and no doubt Grant gave his daughter a fine wedding.

At this date it is difficult to recover the details of the wedding, but
a very old Indian told Margaret Complin of Regina that in his youth
he was guide to the early missionaries at Norway House. Once in his
youth when he was with one of the missionaries on a trip they lodged
for several days with Cuthbert Grant, who took them in in spite of
the fact that the wedding festivities of his daughter were going on.
This was probably Elizabeth's wedding, as his anecdote is of the same
year. He told of a large cavalcade arriving at Grantown after the

ceremony in St Boniface – long ribbons flying from the rosettes which decorated each individual's costume. He said that a large ox had been killed and roasted and that the festivities kept on with much gaiety and dancing for several days.[3]

These festivities were not the only occasion for rejoicing in Grantown during these years. At long last Bishop Provencher's efforts to provide not only spiritual ministration but schooling for the mission had borne fruit. The Reverend L. Laflèche was now resident at Saint-François-Xavier and, except when with the hunt, could keep a school for the boys. In 1850 the Grey Sisters who had come to St Boniface in 1844 were able to send two sisters to reside at Saint-François. The fact that the convent school at once had eighty pupils shows how much Grantown needed and wanted such a school.

Life was hard for the sisters. At first they had to sit on their beds, when resting, for want of chairs. For economy, they burned their candle only while reading; prayer and meditation took place in the dark. And one young sister wrote despondently that in Saint-François even the fence posts leaned in the direction of warm, sociable and longed-for St Boniface. The sisters had known much hardship in founding a convent in St Boniface, but as time went on the pressure which Grant brought to bear upon them to extend their work to Grantown, coupled with his promise to build them a house, resulted in 1850 in the coming of Sr Marie Eulate Lagrave and Sr Hedwidge Lafrance to start a new convent at Saint-François-Xavier.

When Bishop Provencher asked for sisters to found this new school, Sr Lagrave offered her services. She said that as she and Sr Lafrance had already pioneered in founding the St Boniface convent, they should do the same at Grantown. She felt that as they had experience they would be better able to meet the even harsher conditions expected there.

M. le Curé Laflèche lodged the sisters in the old presbytery built by l'Abbé Poiré in the 1830's. Some sixty children attended the first school. Many of them spoke Sioux and Cree and wanted the sisters to teach them to sing and read in French. Late in September of that same year Sr Fizette joined them as "Institutrice" to the school.[4]

At Grantown they had greater distances to travel, for as always the sisters were appealed to in time of sickness. Indians came and camped for months, and often became their charges. This work in addition to the number of pupils and scant accommodation taxed their resources to the utmost.

These gains for civilization at White Horse Plain, the slowly ripened fruit of the example Grant had set his people when he founded Grantown, are confirmed but modified by the Red River census of 1849. In that year there were 914 people at White Horse Plain. They owned 521 horses, 569 cattle, 36 ploughs, 394 carts, and one windmill. But they farmed only 526 acres, only 228 more than in 1833. In 1833, with a population of only 294, and 298 cultivated acres, there had been more than one acre a person, while in 1849 there was little more than one-half acre a person under cultivation.[5] This last fact reflected the slowly apparent truth that Grant's attempt to settle the Métis had been only partially successful. The need to continue the great hunts, the profits of hunting, and the lure of the wild life of the plains had kept his people the plainsmen and warriors they had been in his youth.

It was perhaps well, as it was inevitable, that they should have remained so. In 1851 the precarious peace with the Sioux was ended by a clash between the hunters and the Sioux which is known in the history of White Horse Plain as the Battle of the Grand Coteau.[6] There on July 12, 1851,[7] the Red River hunt, in two parties, encountered some hundreds of Sioux. The Grand Coteau is the eastern edge of the long escarpment at which the second steppe of the northern plains begins, and it forms the watershed between the Missouri and the Assiniboine. The hunt was therefore on the borders of Sioux territory within the United States, and consequently subject to attack.

There is no evidence of Grant having been present at the encounter. Neither is there any that he was elsewhere. But it is most unlikely that he would not have been mentioned if he had led his people at this time. What was present was the discipline and spirit Grant had instilled in the Métis.[8]

In June of 1851 the St Boniface or main river party, accompanied by the Reverend Albert Lacombe going for the first time to the plains where he was to serve out his ministry, travelled south to a rendezvous with the Pembina party. From Pembina the combined parties set out west on June 16 to a rendezvous with the buffalo-hunters of Saint-François-Xavier. The parties numbered three hundred and eighteen hunters. With them were their able-bodied women, with children too small to be left in the settlement, for it was the women who cut up and dried the meat, made the buffalo-hide sacks, and prepared the pemmican.[9] The total number of persons was thirteen hundred with eleven hundred carts.[10]

On June 15 the White Horse Plain party left Saint-François-Xavier, accompanied by its missionary, the Reverend Louis François Richer Laflêche, grand vicar of Bishop Provencher and himself later to be famous as Bishop of Three Rivers. The party was small, numbering only two hundred carts and sixty-seven hunters, with an unknown number of women.[11] It was led by a nephew of Cuthbert Grant, Jean Baptiste Falcon, a son of the bard of the Métis.[12]

It seems evident that the Métis of St Boniface and Pembina and those of Saint-François-Xavier were acting independently of one another, as Hind says they were in 1852.[13] It may be conjectured that the cause of the separation was the rejection by the Métis of St Boniface and Pembina of Grant's leadership following the troubles surrounding the Sayer trial of 1849.[14] But they had to plan mutual support in the event of attack by Sioux. It was known that the Sioux were planning to attack the hunt, and it was therefore important to give them no advantage.[15]

The rendezvous was kept safely on June 19 or 20. A general council was held, not only for the usual election of officers, but also to discuss "the route the two camps would have to follow to keep apart sufficiently from one another so as not to injure each other's hunt."[16] The decision was made to divide, but to move, as a single camp moved in parallel columns, along parallel routes at twenty to thirty miles from one another. The parties were to keep in touch and come to one another's help in the event of attack by the Sioux. There was an express agreement, clearly something novel, that on no pretext would any Sioux be allowed to enter either camp.[17]

After the council, both parties advanced out into the plains towards the southwest, veering off a little from the lands of the Sioux in so doing.[18] According to Lacombe's account, they travelled and hunted together, or in close proximity, for some days,[19] until perhaps June 28. When they did separate, it does not appear whether the White Horse Plain party was to the south or north of the main party. It is natural to suppose that it would have taken the northern route, as the one less exposed to attack by the Sioux, and the rest of this narrative rests on this assumption, which admittedly could be erroneous. The main party encountered some Sioux shortly after parting company but, according to the previous agreement with the small party, did not allow them into camp, and chased them away.[20] The Saint-François-Xavier camp was warned at once.

For some days after that encounter, which must have taken place about June 30, the two parties travelled and hunted without incident. Their parallel routes must now have been towards the land between the headwaters of the Cheyenne River and the big bend of the Souris. The main party was travelling near the Maison du Chien, or Dog Den Butte, a well-known landmark on the outlying ridge of the Coteau de Missouri that was known as the Grand Coteau. They were on the march on Sunday, July 13, by permission of Lacombe in order that on Monday they might run some buffalo which had been reported to be near. While the camp was on the march, a small party of Sioux tried to cut off some stragglers.[21]

The evening before, Saturday, July 12, the Saint-François-Xavier camp reached a spot on the Grand Coteau of the Missouri which cannot now be determined precisely.[22] On the assumption made above that it had followed a northern route, and assuming also that the two parties had kept roughly parallel after their separation, it would be twenty to thirty miles north of the Maison du Chien.

The scouts had just topped the first "butte," and the party had just climbed to the top of the first terrace of the Coteau, when they sighted a large camp of Indians. They at once signalled a warning to the carts below. Falcon promptly ordered camp to be made on a spot that could be easily defended and sent five hunters forward with a spyglass. These rode boldly and carelessly, Métis-fashion, to the top of the nearest high bluff.[23] There they saw that the camp was that of a very large band of Sioux (the number of warriors is estimated in the various accounts at twenty-five hundred).[24] These figures are no doubt greatly exaggerated, but serve to indicate how impressed all the Métis and their companions were by the size of the band.

The five scouts, having scorned concealment, now scorned any other precaution. They proceeded to ride towards the camp. At once a party of twenty Sioux rode out to meet them. When the two met, the Sioux surrounded the Métis and invited them to go to the camp in a way that left no doubt that they were considered prisoners. There seemed to be nothing for it but to go peacefully. But two Métis suddenly kicked their buffalo-runners into a gallop and broke away and escaped under fire back to the carts. Three – James Whiteford, one of the three McGillis boys in the party, and one Malaterre[25] – were held by the Sioux.

The Métis camp, when they saw the fugitives riding hard down the slope, sprang to arms. Falcon and Laflêche called the hunters together: with the boys of twelve years old, there were seventy-seven men who could handle a gun.[26]

The Sioux who had pursued the two escaping hunters then approached the camp of the Métis and parleyed with some of them. They insisted that they had no warlike intentions and that the three captives would be freed on the morrow. They protested that they were hard up and in need of help. They would come the next day with the prisoners and only a small party, in the hope of receiving some presents.[27]

With that they rode off, but Laflêche and the Métis were convinced that they were insincere and meant trouble.

They therefore began to make ready to receive an attack and, when three Sioux horsemen were seen approaching, they sent ten mounted men to meet them and keep them from observing the camp and its defences. The customary courtesies were exchanged, but the Sioux kept at a distance and departed. The Métis were convinced that a surprise attack had been intended then and that they had foiled it.[28]

The decision was now taken to fight without further parley, even if this meant, as they feared it did, that the three captives would be killed. It was thought better to sacrifice them and save the party than to risk all.[29] While they did not know how many Sioux they faced, they knew the camp was a very large one; it seemed to them unlikely, careless as the Métis customarily were of odds in conflict with the Sioux, that they would be able to beat off the the attack of hundreds of the boldest fighters on the plains.

They therefore resolved to sell their lives dearly, and if possible to hold out until succour came from the main party. The carts were placed in a circle, wheel to wheel, with the shafts tilted in the air. Poles carried to make frames on which buffalo-meat was dried were run through the spokes to make the carts immovable.[30] Packs, hides, saddles, and dried meat were piled between and under the carts to complete the barricade.[31]

The purpose of the barricade of carts was not to form shelter behind which the hunters would fight. It was meant to fence in the cart-ponies and oxen and to break up the charge of the Sioux horsemen.[32] The carts formed a corral, but gave little protection against gun-fire or arrows. For that purpose trenches were dug under the carts, and here the women and children took shelter. But the men dug trenches, or rifle pits (here one meets the rifle pits of Batoche) out in front of the barricade. Their purpose was to hold the Sioux out of range of the carts and the draft animals.[33] The women and children were reasonably safe in their trenches, but if the draft animals were killed, the party would perish on the plains without further attack by the Indians.

After darkness two men were sent to carry the news of the threatened attack to the main party and to ask for help. Although the camp police kept a special guard that night, Laflêche and the hunters stayed up to watch the eclipse of the moon, of which he had warned them, spread its black shadow over the silver slopes of the Coteau.[34]

The next morning, Sunday, July 13, "having exhorted and confessed all those who presented themselves," Laflêche celebrated Mass and distributed the sacrament "to all who desired to die well."[35]

When these final preparations were completed, the scouts were seen to signal that the Sioux were coming. When they appeared along the crest of the Coteau, it was not the few horsemen promised the night before, but an army -- the whole manpower of the great Sioux camp, their war-ponies of piebald and pinto and chestnut vivid on the skyline, their gun-barrels and spear-points glinting in the fierce sunlight of the plains.

At a signal the Sioux host halted. Was it possible they did not mean to attack? The Métis had held their buffalo-runners ready in the cart circle for a sally. Now thirty of the hunters rode out to accost the Sioux and warn them to keep their distance from the camp.[36]

The three prisoners could be seen in the midst of the Sioux. Mc-Gillis, on seeing the thirty approach, suddenly kicked his horse into a gallop and, escaping his startled captors, joined the Métis band. Daring as was his action, he was in terror and besought his friends not to laugh at his being afraid. There were, he gasped, two thousand Sioux who meant to attack them.[37]

The Métis rode up to the advance guard of the Sioux, made them some presents, and requested them to go away.

The Sioux ignored both the presents and the request. They could and would take all the camp had to yield, and had brought out some carts to haul away the booty. They began to push forward.

The Métis at once wheeled away and rode hard for the camp. The Sioux tried to head them off, hoping to overwhelm the camp by entering with the hunters in their retreat. But they were too slow, and the hunters re-entered the cart circle, left their horses, and ran for their rifle pits.[38]

The Sioux came charging in, hoping to brush aside the flimsy barrier of the carts and break up the circle. At their head rode a young chief, "so beautiful," Falcon said in after years, "that my heart revolted at the necessity of killing him."[39] He shouted to the Sioux brave to turn away, but he rode on, the war-cry ringing from his lips. Falcon shot him off his horse, and the Métis hunters fired in volley.

Here and there a Sioux warrior whirled from his saddle and tumbled into the grass; the others pulled their ponies around and galloped back to the main body.

Inside the circle Laflêche had donned his surplice with the star at the neck, and had taken his crucifix in his hand. His tall white figure passed around the carts as he encouraged the warriors and soothed the children. All that day he prayed amid the fighting and exhorted his people from a cart rolled into the centre of the circle – a prairie Joshua. He did not, he told a friend later, take a gun himself, but he had a hatchet handy, resolved that if the Sioux reached the carts he would fight beside his Métis warriors.[40]

A brief pause followed the first charge, but was ended almost at once. Whiteford and Malaterre were guarded by an American living with the Sioux.[41] This man now told them to make a dash for it. He would, he said, only pretend to shoot at them. Whiteford kicked his horse, perhaps the best runner on the plains, into a gallop and rode, weaving and swaying through a poplar grove, down the slope towards the camp. Malaterre, knowing his horse was too poor to carry him clear, first shot at the nearest Sioux and actually hit three. He then rode for his life, but was soon brought down by a storm of balls and arrows. His body, bristling with shafts, was dismembered and his remnants waved at the Métis to terrify them. But Whiteford escaped unharmed; and with true Métis bravado, he checked his flight and shot down a pursuing Sioux. Then he was welcomed wildly within the cart-circle, where he joined the defenders. His old mother, who had been weeping for a son she believed doomed, ran to him and said: "My son, if you are tired, give me your gun and go and get some sleep. Let me fire a shot at those rascals out there!"[42]

There was no time for sleep for anyone. The mass of the Sioux now closed in and surrounded the camp, as Laflèche wrote, like a waistband.[43] Indian-fashion, they did not charge in a body. They crept forward, sniping; they made sudden dashes; now and then excited braves would come charging in on horseback, and swerve off shooting from the saddle, or under their horses' necks. It was exciting, it was dangerous, but it was not the one thing that might have brought victory to the Sioux, the overwhelming of the Métis by their numbers. The Métis were therefore able to hold them off from the cart-circle, firing steadily as targets offered, themselves offering no target. Most of the Sioux bullets fell short of the cart-circle; all their arrows did. Only occasionally did a horse rear, or an ox bellow as a shot went home. And up the sun-scorched slope, the Sioux began to feel the bite of the telling Métis fire. Warrior after warrior, "like choice game," writes Dugas, "was offered up with the sure hand of the priest practised at the sacrifice." Some of the stricken warriors turned over quietly in death, some leaped in their death throes, "strewing the yellow prairie with their heaving bodies."[44]

The fight was too hot for them. Indians, and even the warlike Sioux, would never suffer casualties as Europeans would. It was not a matter of courage, but of the conventions of warfare. In battle the

Indian saw no merit in death, however brave. The Sioux now drew back to take account of the nature of the contest they had engaged in. Their shame grew as they viewed the small numbers of the Métis and the fragility of their defences. Their shame turned to anger. Whooping and yelling, the infuriated warriors charged in on their straining ponies, swerving, checking, striving always to kill or stampede the stock in the corral. But their fury produced no giving-way. Laflèche still cheered his people from the cart in the cart-corral. Falcon, steady, earnest, fired with his men, and moved among them to direct their fire. With him was his sister Isabella; when he went around the rifle pits, she took his gun and fired for him, not without effect.[45]

The second assault failed like the first, and still the Sioux had not used their numbers to make a mass charge and overrun the gun-pits and the barricade of carts. Sullenly the Sioux began to withdraw, one by one or in small groups. The more stubborn or more daring kept up a sniping fire and tentative sallies from time to time. But after six hours all were wearied of the unrewarding battle. A chief was heard to cry: "The French have a Manitou with them. We shall never come to the end of them. It is impossible to kill them."[46] Such was the effect of Laflèche's courage. And in fact not a Métis had been killed in the action, although they had lost twelve horses and four oxen.[47] The Sioux had suffered losses they thought heavy, and now began to load their wounded into the carts they had brought to carry away the plunder of the Métis camp. They had also to regain their courage and replenish their ammunition.[48] A heavy thunder-storm completed their discomfiture, and it was followed by a mist which made it impossible to shoot.[49]

Moreover, their scouts, thrown out towards the main Métis body at the Maison du Chien, had brought in reports that had to be considered.[50] The two hunters sent on Saturday might have encountered the Sioux scouts and returned to camp. But two young Métis had panicked and fled from the camp towards the main party.[51] Would they bring the main party to the help of the besieged camp?

The Métis themselves had the same question to consider. When the Sioux withdrew, the hunters rode out over the battle field, where they saw many traces of the hurt inflicted on the attackers. Eight Sioux had been killed and many wounded, as was shown by the blood-stained grass and the waters of two nearby ponds.[52] There they found the mutilated body of the unfortunate Malaterre pierced by three balls and sixty-seven arrows. They buried him there on the prairie.[53]

On the next day, July 14, the Sioux were expected to attack, as they had not withdrawn far but had kept raising the war-whoop around the camp during the darkness. A council was held, and the decision was taken to try to join the main party.[54]

It was a decision to retreat in the face of an enemy yet undefeated and in overwhelming numbers, one of the most dangerous operations of war. The Métis planned and executed it brilliantly. Four mounted parties were sent out a mile from the line of march, one ahead, one behind, and two on the flank towards the Sioux. They were to signal any approach of the Sioux by two scouts galloping past one another on a butte, the best known of all the plains signals of the buffalo-hunters. The carts were to advance in four columns so placed that, by two wheeling quickly, a square could be formed rapidly. Then the cart-corral could be formed, the barricade stiffened with the poles, and the hunters fan out for the fight.[55]

After an hour's march, the scouting party behind was seen to make the signal of two horsemen crossing on a butte. The Sioux, who had been shouting around the camp during the night, were in pursuit. At the signal the columns halted and wheeled into position, the ponies and oxen were taken out of the shafts, and the carts run into the circle. The Métis had learned even more vividly from the loss of stock they had suffered in the first day's fight the need to conceal their stock and hold the Sioux at a distance. The cart-ring was now formed of two lines of carts; then at three chains from the barricade of carts the hunters hastened to throw up their rifle pits well out from the cart-ring.[56] The Sioux were perhaps less numerous and less fiery than the day before, but they closed in none the less on the cart-corral and pressed the attack for five full hours.[57] Once more Laflêche exhorted his people to remember their faith and their ancestry; once more Falcon and Isabella aided the Métis marksmen in the heat and dust and drifting smoke.

Finally the firing slackened and the war cries died away. Once more a thunder-storm was rolling up over the Coteau.[58] A Sioux chief rode up, upraised palm out in the gesture of peace, and demanded to be allowed to enter the camp. He was told to leave quickly, if he did not wish to be left on the prairie. He replied with dignity, before retreating, that the Sioux had had enough; that they were going away; that, henceforth and forever, they would never again attack the Métis.

Then the whole war party, mounted and yelling a last defiance, war plumes flying and lances waving, put itself at a gallop, and charged in single file around the cart-ring, firing a last tremendous volley of gun-fire and arrows from the backs of their straining ponies. It was the heaviest volley of the two-day battle.[59] Then the cloud of horsemen streamed over the shoulder of the Coteau and vanished. As they vanished the rain broke in torrents.

The weary Métis thought that they must have suffered losses from the tremendous discharge but, as the men ran in from the rifle pits, it was found that only three were wounded and those but slightly. As they rejoiced, the first party of hunters from the main party, warned by the fugitives, came pounding over the prairie.[60] They had been dispatched post-haste early that morning by Father Lacombe.[61] The main body came up later.

With the three hundred and eighteen fresh hunters of the main party were as many Saulteaux warriors. With those of White Horse Plain camp, they numbered seven hundred men, a force sufficient to scatter the enemy. The Sioux, it was known from their increasing use of arrows, were short of ammunition as well as discouraged by their defeat. Many of the hunters demanded that they should be pursued and chastised. But Laflèche and Lacombe, with the majority of the hunters, were against further fighting. Better to be merciful and complete the hunt, they decided.[62] The Métis resumed their hunt, but first they raised on the plain a tall pole bearing a letter to the Sioux. What was in the letter no one has recorded.

In the whole adventure they had lost only the unhappy Malaterre, and in the two actions not one man, woman or child. They had lost, it is true, twelve horses and four oxen, but not enough to prevent them moving over the plains. The Sioux, it was reported later, had lost eighty men, besides many wounded, and sixty-five horses.[63] By the standards of Indian warfare, this was a heavy defeat, and in fact it ended the long warfare of the Métis and the Sioux.[64]

The Métis thereafter were masters of the plains wherever they might choose to march. The action of the Grand Coteau showed that they could fight and move on the plains even in the face of superior numbers of Sioux, perhaps the most formidable warriors of all the North American plains tribes. Their conduct of the march of the cart-brigade, their plains-craft, their battle tactics – from the firing from the saddle to the use of the rifle pit – were brilliant by any standard of warfare. Small wonder that the British officers who knew them spoke longingly of using them as cavalry.[65] Or that that veteran of Europe's wars, Captain Napoleon Gay, after his service with Riel in 1870, tried to train his volunteer cavalry in the Franco-Prussian war as Métis mounted riflemen![66]

The battle of the Grand Coteau was perhaps the proudest memory of the Métis nation.[67] It symbolized their highest endeavour as a people. Nothing more conclusively proved their mastery of the plains by which they lived. It stands midway between the collision at Seven Oaks and the black day of Batoche, when the Canadian militia did what the Sioux had not done and overran the Métis rifle pits. And finally it demonstrates that the boundary of Canada and the United States was not a mere astronomical line, but a real boundary marked by the clash of peoples and cultures, the border of the park belt and the grassland, of the prairie and the plain, where the Métis of Red River continued the old feud of Cree and Saulteaux with the Sioux, and helped, in the blind and primitive working of history with geography, to prepare for the different histories in western North America of Canada and the United States.

Since Grant was not at the Grand Coteau but had remained at White Horse Plain that summer to lead the old folk to Grant's Lake for the goose hunt, then with what mingled pride and regret he must have heard of the great fight which so brilliantly vindicated the fighting skills of the Métis – pride at the achievement, regret at his absence. And how strange that this epic of Métis valour did not stir Pierre Falcon to compose another of his ballads! In many ways the Grand Coteau was the apex of the Métis nation, their supreme achievement as a people who had learned to live on and by the plains. Yet its story is little known, its actors are nameless, it was not celebrated in the songs of the Métis, nor fully celebrated in their legends.

The curious obscurity which veils the great feat of arms of the hunt of 1851 seems indeed to hang over the last years of Grant's life. He continued to live as principal man and magistrate at Grantown. One vivid glimpse of him and his hospitality as chief man of his settlement is given in the letters and journals of Mr W. W. Kirkly of the Church Missionary Society. In December 1852, Kirkly set out from Fort Garry to Portage la Prairie where in 1850 the Reverend Wm. Cockran had begun an Anglican mission. Kirkly stopped at White Horse Plain and described his stay as follows:

It was about seven o'clock when we reached here and finding it impossible to reach the house we had intended, we determined to remain at the first which seemed to offer means of shelter to us and our horses. Presently we came to one, occupied by a Mr. Grant, and who is a Magistrate and chief man among the Roman Catholics, and of the Plain, though we neither of us knew him; yet on being assured by our guide that he was a very hospitable man, we made bold to call upon him. He was not in, but after waiting a short time he came, and at once gave us a cordial welcome, assuring us, as Rebekah did Abraham's servant, that there was room for us and provender for our cattle. We thankfully accepted his kind offer.

Dec. 29, 1852 – We rose between five and six this morning, intending to go as far as the house which we thought of reaching last night, before breakfast; but our kind host, hearing us on the move, arose and ordered the domestics to prepare breakfast for us; and by the time we were ready a hot comfortable meal was prepared, which was very welcome before starting out in the cold.[68]

Yet Grant, now fifty-nine years of age, was not entering on any decline of his powers. He was not becoming a prematurely old man, who stayed at home from the hunt to care for the old people. In 1852 he went to the plains again, perhaps to ensure that his people did not lack his leadership if the Sioux renewed their attack. But the hunt returned in peace in August, as did the fall hunt. It was this year, it may be noted in passing, that the White Horse Plain hunt went out by itself without going to the general rendezvous. It may have been because the Grand Coteau gave them assurance that they could deal with the Sioux alone; it may be that the buffalo herds were now so far to the west that the shortest route to them was up the Assiniboine to the Souris.

Grant indeed was so active that he was thinking of resuming his old role of licensed free trader.[69] This was partly because his fortunes needed repairing since he had lost his salary as Warden of the Plains, and partly because since 1849 the free trade had spread rapidly, checked only by commercial competition from the Hudson's Bay Company. Accordingly Grant addressed himself to Simpson, whom he had served so loyally for the past thirty years.

Grantown 26th May 1853

Sir Geo. Simpson
    Gov. of Ruperts Land
Dear Sir
    I fear, though, I hope, without sufficient ground, that this session may be your last for coming among us, I am, therefore anxious to appeal once for all to your often tried kindness, because now the council of Ruperts Land contains hardly any of my old friends.
    I have long thought, that I could promote the Company's best interests by trading again under its sanction. I was of this opinion even before the competition of the Americans had begun

to show itself across the lines; and if so, how much stronger must my opinion be now, when this competition has lasted so much longer, and spread so much farther than could have been at first expected. In fact, the present state of things appears to be such as to render the assistance of individuals, who can be depended on, necessary to the company; and at the same time it seems to remove the objection, which certainly had weight some years back, that the employing of middlemen would tempt others to engage in the same business without authority. If this be so in general, I flatter myself, that my services in this way might be more valuable than those of most other persons.

But to enable me to serve the Company with effect I should require the command of a little capital. I see no other way of getting this but your powerful help. I should be glad to accept a composition in lieu of an annuity the more so as very few indeed of those, who know my claims are likely after this to have any voice in the management of affairs. All things considered, I should think that seven years of my present *income*, say, in round numbers £1200, would be a reasonable amount, to be paid in such a way as may be agreed on between us. I shall merely add that I do not wish to have the whole immediately, nor the whole in cash at all, but part in money and part in goods, say (first) £200 to be paid down in cash now. (secondly) Goods to the value of £500, at York Factory prices to be delivered this fall at York Factory. (thirdly) Goods to the Value of £500 at London prices to be sent out by the ship next year.

Hoping to see you personally soon.

> I have the Honor to be
> Dear Sir
> your ever grateful and obliged
> Humble Servant
> (Signed) Cuthbert Grant.[70]

Grant's request was reasonable enough, for his next-door neighbour, Urbain Delorme, was already launched on the career that was make him one of the chief plains traders, and a little down the river scal Bréland was following suit. It would seem that Simpson did not ree at once, for a year later in June of 1854 they were to have met Fort Garry to discuss Grant's affairs. But Grant's health did not low him to leave Grantown: he had suffered a fall from a horse and as not making a good recovery. Simpson wrote him not unkindly.

Cuthbert Grant, Esq. (Grantown)

Fort Garry 29th June, 185.

My dear Sir,

I have received your letter of 26. inst. & am very sorry t
learn that the impaired state of your health prevents your con
ing down here and that consequently I shall not have the pleasur
of seeing you this season. I shall hope to have better accounts
you in the course of the autumn.

I am not prepared to give you an immediate reply to th
points you have brought under my notice in reference to you
salary as Warden of the Plains. The arrangement to which yo
refer was made thirty years ago, & although I have in my min
a general recollection of the terms, it is necessary to refer
documents not in my possession here, in order to refresh m
memory as to details. I shall look into the matter after my retur
to Canada, and communicate with you further thereon hereafte

I am much obliged by your kind enquiries after my healt
which I am thankful to say continues good. Wishing you
speedy recovery,

I remain &c. &c. (Sd) G. SIMPSON[71]

Grant did not recover. One can feel the awed hush that must ha
fallen over Grantown – their beloved seignior "Mr Grant" had suffere
a serious accident – and as the days went by their concern grew. Sma
groups stood about the open doorways of the village, and occasional
a messenger went to or from the big white house where he lay. F
days this atmosphere of fearful expectancy hung heavily over th
village, until the news went out on July 15 that he was dead; the
anxiety gave way to sorrow.

That funeral of July 16 was long talked of around the fires
Grantown. Their friend and counsellor through all the years wou
lead the Métis no more. He was buried with full pomp and ceremon
The bell tolled solemnly as the long cortege filed to the church. T
parish record stands:

On the 16th of July 1854 our priest buried in the church of th
parish along the wall of the right side body of Cuthbert Gra
Esquire who died yesterday at the age of 61. He was the husba
of Dame Marie MacGillis. Were present Pierre Thibert, Jose
Guilliout & Louis Gariepy and many others who did not si
(Signed) J. B. Thibault, Pres.[72]

The parish accorded him its greatest honour. He was buried beneath the altar of the church he had helped to found, where his dust lay mingled with that of his seigniory. With Grant died Grantown, as the name then gave way to that of the parish, Saint-François-Xavier. But his memory remained green among his people – the bravery, the dash, the kindness, the dignity of "Mr Grant." No man, writes the historian of the Métis, Dr Marcel Giraud, did so much, or set such an example, to civilize the Métis of the plains of Rupert's Land.[73] We may let that stand as Grant's sufficient and abiding epitaph.

EPILOGUE

As time went by the whole country became settled, and the needs which had given Grantown importance in the Red River economy passed away. There are still landmarks which speak of the early days, and names such as Grant's Point and Sayer's Creek which recall the men of those days. The village remains today – a little hamlet along the river – and its centre is still near the site of Grant's big white house.[1]

After Grant's death life at Grantown continued in the pattern which its seignior had established, but as the years passed the mother settlement's two pressing needs for food and protection, which Grantown had been established to meet, were no longer present. The march of civilization and increased farm productivity removed finally the twin purposes of its founding, and Grantown lost some of its *raison d'etre*. For with the advance of settlement and the coming of law and order to the plains, Grant's brave buffalo hunters were no longer needed for protection; and with new links with the outside world, the hamlet was no longer needed to provide food from the hunt. But there were many ways in which the settlement remained little changed through the years. There was still the church, the convent and the big white house on which the village centred; but now that Grant was gone the name of Grantown gradually fell into disuse, and it came to be called by the name of the parish, Saint-François-Xavier, which name it continues to bear.

Pascal Bréland, Grant's son-in-law, was a man of especially fine character and of influence among the Métis. He represented the people of Saint-François-Xavier in the first legislature of Manitoba. The Bréland family never left Red River, and through this family Cuthbert Grant has many direct descendants living in the Winnipeg area today.

As they grew up the rest of Grant's children became scattered. Sons and daughters married and went west, and one son, Charles, moved to North Dakota where he reared a large family.

It is interesting to know that today Grant's life work still goes on through another Cuthbert Grant. He is a grandson of Charles Grant and great-grandson of Cuthbert Grant of Grantown. He and his wife are engaged in educational work among the Indians and Métis, teaching arts and crafts and other subjects on a reservation in the state of North Dakota.

NOTES

In citing sources the following abbreviations have been used:

H.B.C.A.– Hudson's Bay Company Archives
(All citations are by the courtesy of the Governor and Commitee.)

P.A.C. – Public Archives of Canada

P.A.M. – Public Archives of Manitoba

S.P. – Selkirk Papers.

Notes to Chapter I

That the protection which the men of Grantown provided for the whole colony at Red River was gratefully recognized in the parent settlement at The Forks in indicated by an experience of one of his grandsons. When Cuthbert McKay, son of Cuthbert Grant's daughter Elizabeth, used to walk along the bank of the Red River to attend college in Winnipeg, an old lady who was one of the original settlers would never let him pass without offering him some treat, saying, "We all remember that we never slept quiet in our beds until your grandfather and his brave Métis came to settle near us."

Isaac Cowie, *Company of Adventurers* (Toronto: William Briggs, 1913), p. 170.

Letter from A. S. Morton to Margaret Arnett MacLeod, October 21, 1938: "Fortunately we had time to run down to Grant's house, a creek (Aspen Creek) about 20 rods to the south (of the fort) from which they would get their water, as the Assiniboine is about half a mile to the west, a ridge running parallel with the river and the fort on a beautiful slope where the hill slips into a wide river-flat. But I found that the fort had been plowed in. The man on whose farm it stands said that it had been partially plowed in by his predecessor but that he had plowed in two cellars that were there. These probably were the deep cellars of the ice houses. There was a mass of bones scattered round, such as one sees where forts are plowed in, and we picked up a brass button of a uniform such as the proprietor would wear. We were pleased at this, for it acts as a confirmation of the story of the farmer. . . . So that is the end of Cuthbert Grant's house."

See also his *History of the Canadian West to 1870-1871*, p. 432; see also C. M. Gates, *Five Fur Traders of the Northwest*, p. 96n.

4 George Bryce, "The Pre-Selkirk Settlers of Old Assiniboia," *T.R.S.C.*, XII, 3rd Ser. (1918), p. 156.

5 W. S. Wallace, "Strathspey and the Fur Trade," in *Essays in Canadian History*, edited by R. Flenley (Toronto, 1939), pp. 284-287.

6 M. Giraud, *Le Métis canadien* (Paris, 1945), p. 548 and p. 751. The debt of the authors to M. Giraud's monumental work is gratefully acknowledged.

7 Register of Presbyterian Church of St Gabriel Street, Montreal. The two boys have been confounded by

some writers, and Cuthbert given his brother's birth date of 1791 and his name – James, as a second name. Still others have implied that Cuthbert's birth was even earlier than his brother's.

8 These details are taken from Wallace, "Strathspey and the Fur Trade," pp. 283-287.

9 P.A.M., *The New Nation*, Feb. 4, 1870.

10 It is of interest to note that Miss Evelyn Grant of Nairn, Scotland, who died in 1948, was the last representative of the Grants of Letheredie in the past generation, and that the best known descendant was Admiral of the Fleet, Sir Roderick McGrigor, R.N. (Ret.), who died December 5, 1959.

11 Alexander Mackenzie, *Voyages from Montreal*, etc. (New York, 1802), p. 8.

12 Harold Innis, *Peter Pond, Fur Trader and Adventurer* (Toronto, 1930), pp. 107-8.

13 E. Coues, *New Light on the Early History of the Greater Northwest*, II (New York, 1897), p. 511.

14 C. M. Gates, "John McDonell's Journal," *Five Fur Traders* (Minneapolis, 1933), pp. 114-5; A. S. Morton, *History of the Canadian West to 1870-71* (Toronto [1939]), p. 433.

15 Robert Campbell, *History of the Scotch Presbyterian Church* (Montreal, 1887), p. 107. Campbell confused the son with the father.

16 L. F. R. Masson, *Les bourgeois de le nord-ouest*, II, pp. 23-24.

17 Campbell, *Scotch Presbyterian Church*, p. 107.

18 Wallace, "Strathspey and the Fur Trade," pp. 286-287.

19 Archives of the Superior Court, Montreal; (see Chapter V below).

20 Archives of the Superior Court, Montreal; (see Chapter VI below).

21 United Kingdom: *Papers Relating to the Red River Settlement* (London, 1819), Report of W. B. Coltman

to Sir John Sherbrooke, May 20, 1818, p. 146.

Notes to Chapter II

1 Ross Cox, *The Columbia River*, II (London, 1832), p. 252.

2 W. S. Wallace (ed.), *Documents Relating to North West Company* (Champlain Society, 1934), p. 505.

3 Morton, *Canadian West*, pp. 531-543.

4 For a description of the fort, see Morton, *Canadian West*, p. 432; United Kingdom: *Papers Relating to Red River*, 166, Coltman to Sherbrooke, May 20, 1818.

5 Wallace, *North West Company*, p. 493; E. E. Rich (ed.), *Colin Robertson's Correspondence Book* (Hudson's Bay Record Society, 1939), pp. 238-9.

6 William Douglas, "New Light on the Old Forts of Winnipeg," *Transactions of Historical Society of Manitoba*, III (II), p. 42.

7 From tradition related to Mrs A. N. MacLeod. But see R. Fleming, *Minutes of the Council of the Northern Department* (Toronto: Champlain Society, 1940), pp. 446-7.

8 Recounted to Mrs A. N. MacLeod by descendants of Grant.

9 P.A.M., S.P., Fidler's Journal, May 22, 1815.

10 Edwin James, *Thirty Years of Indian Captivity of John Tanner* (Minneapolis: Ross & Haines, Inc., 1956).

11 W. L. Morton, *Manitoba: a History* (Toronto: University of Toronto Press, 1957), chap. iii.

12 Morton, *Canadian West*, p. 544.

13 *Ibid.*, pp. 510 and 553.

14 The best account of Selkirk's attempt to begin the settlement of Red River is still Chester Martin's *Lord Selkirk's Work in Canada* (Oxford, 1916), chap. iii. The whole

story has been told in J. P. Pritchett's admirable *The Red River Valley, 1811-1849* (Toronto, 1942). For Selkirk's settlement at Baldoon, see Martin, *Lord Selkirk's Work*, chap. ii, and P. C. T. White, *Lord Selkirk's Diary, 1803-1804* (Toronto: Champlain Society, 1958).

Notes to Chapter III

1 E. H. Oliver, *The Canadian North-West: Its Early Development*, I, pp. 56-57; P.A.M., S.P., Fidler's Journal.

2 Morton, *Canadian West*, p. 555.

3 Fleming, *Minutes of the Council of the Northern Department*, pp. 446-7.

4 See the account in Morton, *Canadian West*, pp. 558-564.

5 E. E. Rich (ed.), *Simpson's Athabasca Journal* (Hudson's Bay Record Society, 1938), pp. 454-5.

6 *Ibid.*, p. 432; Wallace, *North West Company*, pp. 429-30; 464-5.

7 P.A.M., S.P., f. 12, pp. 316-18, r. 12, pp. 685-688; f. 12, p. 726.

8 P.A.M., S.P., Journal of Miles Macdonell, f. 16, p. 899.

9 *Simpson's Athabasca Journal*, pp. 468-9.

10 Morton, *Canadian West*, p. 569.

11 *Simpson's Athabasca Journal*, pp. 449-50; Wallace, *North West Documents*, p. 464.

12 P.A.M., S.P., Fidler's Journal, July 28, 1814.

13 The ideas were apparently wholly new, and invented on the spot by the Nor'Westers: P.A.M., S.P., f. 12, p. 739, an account of the events of June, 1815.

14 P.A.M., S.P., Fidler's Journal, June 22, 1815. The custom of making native "captains" goes back at least to Champlain.

15 *Ibid.*, Sept. 1, 1814.

16 Martin, *Selkirk's Work*, p. 80.

17 *Red River Papers*, "Sketch" by Miles Macdonell, p. 31.

18 *Ibid.*, p. 32.

19 P.A.M., S.P., Fidler's Journal, May 26, 1815.

20 *Ibid.*, May 22, 1815.

21 *Ibid.*, June 7, 1815.

22 *Red River Papers*, p. 34.

23 P.A.M., S.P., Miles Macdonell's Journal, pp. 17, 35-36.

24 *Ibid.*

25 *Red River Papers*, p. 35.

26 P.A.M., S.P., Fidler's Journal, June 24, 1815.

27 Ross Mitchell, *Medicine in Manitoba* (Winnipeg, 1954), p. 31.

28 P.A.M., S.P., Fidler's Journal, June 25, 1815.

29 *Ibid.*; also *Red River Papers*, p. 172.

30 Alexander Macdonell, *Narrative of the Transactions in the Red River Country* (London, 1819), p. 289.

31 "Introduction," *Robertson's Correspondence Book*.

32 P.A.M., S.P., A Journal (from internal evidence, Robertson's), f. 17, 381, Aug. 20, 1815.

33 Nothing more is known of Lamar than appears in these events.

34 P.A.M., S.P., A Journal, f. 17, 387-89.

35 *Ibid.*, f. 17, 393 and f. 17, 396.

36 *Ibid.*, f. 17, 398; 17, 400.

37 P.A.M., S.P., James Sutherland's Narrative.

38 *Ibid.*

39 P.A.M., S.P., A Journal, f. 17, 422.

40 *Robertson's Correspondence Book*, p. 241.

41 Oliver, *Canadian North-West*, I, 42-3.

42 Nothing more is known of Holte than appears from his part in these events.

43 Nothing more is known of Rogers than appears in these events.

44 P.A.M., S.P., A Journal, f. 17, 442.

45 P.A.M., S.P., p. 8895. The original is in French; the translation is by W. L. Morton.

46 P.A.M., S.P., A Journal, f. 17, 460; f. 17, 481; f. 17, 483.

47 P.A.C., North West Papers, Semple to Grant, Feb. 2, 1816; quoted in Cameron MacMillan, "The Struggle of the Fur Companies in the Red River Region, 1811-1821." (Unpublished thesis of University of Manitoba, 1955).

48 Alexander Macdonell, *A Narrative*, p. 57; E. E. Rich (ed.), *The Letters of John McLoughlin from Fort Vancouver*, I (Toronto: Champlain Society, 1941), pp. 351-2; Wallace, *North West Company*, p. 490.

49 P.A.M., S.P., pp. 8896-7.

50 *Ibid.*, pp. 8898-9.

51 P.A.M., S.P., Sutherland's Narrative.

52 *Ibid.*

Notes to Chapter IV

1 P.A.M., S.P., A Journal, Mar. 12, 1816, 17, 489.

2 *Ibid.*, 17, 491.

3 *Ibid.*

4 *Ibid.*, 17, 492.

5 *Ibid.*, 17, 493-7.

6 *Ibid.*, 17, 500.

7 P.A.M., S.P., 1, 187; 1, 698; 17, 974; 18, 027; 18, 037; 18, 045.

8 P.A.C., North West Papers, Holte to Pritchard, Apr. 14, 1816; quoted in Macmillan, "Struggle of the Fur Companies," p. 99.

9 Macdonell, *Narrative*, p. 58.

10 P.A.M., S.P., A Journal, Apr. 10, 1816, 17, 506; on Semple's attitude, see *Red River Papers*, 182, Coltman to Sherbrooke, May 20, 1818.

11 P.A.M., S.P., Sutherland's Narrative.

12 P.A.M., S.P., A Journal, Apr. 8, 1816, f. 17, 506.

13 *Ibid.*, ff. 17, 514-24.

14 P.A.M., S.P., Sutherland's Narrative; Macdonell, *Narrative*, pp. 59-61.

15 P.A.M., S.P., Sutherland's Narrative; Macdonell, *Narrative*, p. 61.

16 Macdonell, *Narrative*, p. 62

17 P.A.M., S.P., Sutherland's Narrative; Macdonell, *Narrative*, 63; also S.P., Pambrun's Narrative, 12, 303; and A Journal, 17, 521; also *Red River Papers*, p. 181.

18 Macdonell, *Narrative*, p. 65; P.A.M., S.P., A Journal, 17, 525.

19 Macdonell, *Narrative*, pp. 68-9; Giraud, *Le Métis Canadien*, p. 593.

20 Beaver House, H.B.C.A., B22/A119.

21 *Ibid.*; Macdonell's *Narrative*, pp. 69-70.

22 P.A.M., S.P., A Journal, 17, 534.

23 *Ibid.*, ff. 17, 541-3.

24 The details are from *Red River Papers*, pp. 183-4.

25 *Ibid.*, p. 183.

26 *Ibid.*, p. 184 and p. 196.

27 P.A.M., S.P., A Journal by Sheriff Macdonell.

28 *Ibid.*

29 *Red River Papers*, p. 189.

30 These details are deduced from the imperfect details of movements and numbers in the deposition on pp. 189-90 of *Red River Papers*.

31 *Ibid.*, p. 185; also P.A.M., S.P., A Journal.

32 *Robertson's Correspondence Book*, pp. 206-7.

33 *Red River Papers*, p. 122, J. B. Coltman to Governor Sherbrooke, May 14, 1818; the encounter, wrote Coltman, was "next to a certainty" accidental.

34 The scene is suggested by details on pp. 185 and 190 of *Red River Papers*; also in P.A.M., S.P., 2,597 *et seq.*, J. Pritchard to Selkirk, Aug. 22, 1816.

35 *Ibid.*, p. 87, evidence of John Pritchard, that Boucher was "most insolent in tone."

36 *Ibid.*, p. 188. The weight of evidence agrees with Coltman's conclusion that Semple's party fired first, but probably as a warning.

37 *Ibid.*, evidence of Pritchard as told by Grant, p. 88, and p. 186, on which Coltman says Grant's deposition No. 216 (never printed or found) agrees substantially with Pritchard's statement on this point.

38 *Ibid.*, p. 186. There is conflict of evidence as to whether Semple or Holte was hit first. The account in

the text seems more probable; in any event, the difference was a matter of seconds.

39 *Ibid.*, p. 191, evidence of Cuthbert Grant.

40 P.A.M., S.P., A Journal, 17, 589-97.

41 *Red River Papers*, p. 122, Coltman to Sherbrooke, May 14, 1818.

42 *Ibid.*, p. 186.

43 *Ibid.*, p. 192.

44 P.A.M., S.P., 18, 557; *Macdonell's Narrative*, p. 78.

45 See *Encyclopedia Canadiana*, III, "Pierre Falcon."

46 Translation by Professor Robert Walters of the University of Manitoba.

47 P.A.M., S.P., A Journal, 17, 589-97.

48 Chas. N. Bell, *Lord Selkirk's Settlement and the Settlers* (n.p., n.d.), 19; some accounts in old age of eyewitnesses.

49 *Red River Papers*, p. 89. Grant's concern for the safety of the colonists was long gratefully remembered by the women of Kildonan, as told to Mrs A. N. MacLeod by many descendants, particularly Rev. Cuthbert McKay.

That original inventory of goods was in the Charter Room in Lord Selkirk's home at St Mary's Isle, Kirkcudbright, Scotland, having been found later by Lord Selkirk at Fort William. Dr John Perry Pritchett, author of *The Red River Valley, 1811-1849*, saw it there and was impressed with Grant's painstaking efficiency in the matter. He says: "It is a very curious document, written on the backs of five large sheets of printed texts such as might be used for religious instruction in schools. It is headed, 'List of Goods, Utensils, etc. Belonging to the Colony of the Red River Settlement taken by the North West Clerks, Métis etc. on the 20th of June 1816.' Every page is signed, 'Received, Cuthbert Grant, Clerk of the North West Company.'

And as far as it is possible to add up the inventory, the number of articles amounts to 7,429 with many of them counted in dozens or pairs." The historian Gunn relates that Grant had two copies of this inventory made, one of which he gave to Acting-Governor Macdonell as he left with the settlers in the boats, and one for his employers.

50 *Red River Papers*, p. 89.

Notes to Chapter V

1 *Trial of Charles de Reinhard, 1818* (Montreal, 1819), p. 115.

2 *Ibid.*, p. 117.

3 *Simpson's Athabasca Journal*, p. 444; *Robertson's Correspondence Book*, pp. 225-8.

4 *Reinhard's Trial*, p. 15.

5 *Ibid.*, p. 117.

6 *Ibid.*, p. 118, evidence of Reinhard.

7 P.A.M., S.P., 3324 *et seq.*, Narrative of Frederick Damien Heurter.

8 M. A. MacLeod, *Songs of Old Manitoba* (Toronto, 1960), pp. 10-15. Translation by Robert L. Walters; the "Doctor" was Dr John McLoughlin.

9 Nothing more is known of D'Orsonnens than his service with Selkirk.

10 P.A.M., S.P., Journal of Miles Macdonell, Dec. 10, 1816 to Jan. 10, 1817.

11 P.A.M., S.P., Heurter's Narrative.

12 P.A.M., S.P., Macdonell's Journal, Jan. 4, 1817.

13 *Robertson's Correspondence Book*, p. 217, June 21.

14 P.A.M., S.P., Heurter's Narrative.

15 *Ibid.*

16 P.A.M., S.P., Macdonell's Journal, Mar. 2, 1817.

17 *Ibid.*

18 P.A.M., S.P., Macdonell's Journal, Mar. 2, 1817.

19 P.A.M., S.P., Heurter's Narrative; Giraud, *Le Métis Canadien*, p. 607.

20 P.A.M., S.P., Macdonell's Journal, June 18, 1817.

21 *Ibid.*, June 19 and 20.
22 *Ibid.*
23 *Ibid.*, June 21.
24 *Ibid.*
25 *Simpson's Athabasca Journal*, p. 442; Wallace, *North West Company*, p. 457.
26 P.A.M., S.P., Macdonell's Journal, June 22.
27 *Ibid.*, July 3.
28 *Ibid.*, July 5.
29 *Ibid.*, July 9 and 19; also p. 3,802, Coltman to Selkirk, July 16, 1819.
30 Giraud, *Le Métis Canadien*, p. 611.
31 *Red River Papers*, p. 194; also p. 122, Coltman to Sherbrooke, May 14, 1818 and May 20, 1818.
32 *Ibid.*
33 Giraud, *Le Métis Canadien*, p. 610. This deposition, No. 216, although frequently referred to in Coltman's Report in *Red River Papers*, is not, as already noted, printed there, and later intensive search has failed to produce it.
34 P.A.M., S.P., Sherbrooke to Bathurst, Nov. 27, 1817: *Red River Papers*, p. 110.
35 *Reinhard's Trial*, p. 3.
36 *Records of the Superior Court of Montreal*.
37 *Reinhard's Trial*, pp. v, vi and xi.
38 P.A.M., S.P., Selkirk to Solicitor-General Uniacke, May 12, 1818; Uniacke to Selkirk, May 16; Selkirk to Uniacke, June 9.
39 P.A.M., S.P., J. Allan to S. Gale, June 18, 1818.
40 P.A.M., S.P., Selkirk to Uniacke, June 30, 1818.
41 *Red River Papers*, 194.
42 P.A.M., S.P., J. Allan to S. Gale, June 20, 1818.
43 See the crushing denunciation in Pritchett, *The Red River Valley*, pp. 213-214.
44 *Red River Papers*, p. 194.
45 *Ibid.*, p. 122.
46 *Ibid.*
47 *Ibid.*

Notes to Chapter VI

1 *Robertson's Correspondence Book*, p. 284.
2 P.A.M., S.P., Mathiez to Selkirk, Aug. 2, 1819.
3 *Robertson's Correspondence Book*, p. xciv.
4 *Ibid.*, p. 284 *et seq.*
5 P.A.M., S.P., Macdonell to Selkirk, Jan. 19, 1819.
6 *Robertson's Correspondence Book*, pp. 295-6.
7 *Ibid.*, p. 296.
8 *Simpson's Athabasca Journal*, pp. 456-7; Wallace, *North West Company*, p. 485. See the new evidence in Marjorie Wilkins Campbell, *McGillivray, Lord of the Northwest* (Toronto, 1962), pp. 296 and 300.
9 P.A.M., S.P., 7, 588, Geo. Simpson to A. Colvile, May 20, 1822.
10 *Ibid.*
11 P.A.M., S.P., Simpson to A. Colvile, May 20, 1822.
12 *Ibid.*; *Simpson's Athabasca Journal*, p. 437.
13 P.A.M., S.P., Simpson to Colvile, May 20, 1822; Simpson alleged that Dumoulin was inciting the Métis to resist the Company.
14 W. H. Keating, *Narrative of an Expedition to the Source of St Peter's River*, II (London, 1825), 42-43.
15 *Simpson's Athabasca Journal*, p. 441.
16 Beaver House, H.B.C.A., D.3/3, Simpson's Journal, 1821-22, Feb. 26, 1822, quoted by kind permission of the Governor and Committee of the Hudson's Bay Company.
17 *Ibid.*
18 P.A.M., S.P., Simpson to A. Colvile, May 20, 1822.
19 Beaver House, H.B.C.A., D.3/3, Simpson's Journal, 1821-22, June 1-7, 1822.
20 *Records of the Superior Court of Montreal*.

21 H.B.C.A., D.4/88, Simpson at York Factory, Sept. 1, 1825, quoted in Marcel Giraud, *Le Métis Canadien* (Paris, 1945), p. 713.

22 E. James, *Thirty Years of Indian Captivity of John Tanner* (Minneapolis, 1956), pp. 273-75.

23 Information given M. A. MacLeod by old people of Saint-François-Xavier.

24 Beaver House, H.B.C.A., B.239/K/1 f. 35d.

25 Beaver House, H.B.C.A., D.4/2, p. 111.

26 Beaver House, H.B.C.A., D.4/118, f. 29d. Letter No. 92.

27 Beaver House, H.B.C.A., A.34/1, p. 133.

28 Beaver House, H.B.C.A., B.239/K/1, f. 33.

29 See R. M. Ballantyne, *Hudson's Bay* (2nd ed.; Edinburgh and London, 1899), pp. 131-137.

30 Beaver House, H.B.C.A., B.239/K11, f. 33.

31 Merk, *Fur Trade and Empire*, p. 203.

32 P.A.M., S.P., f. 8, 221, Simpson to A. Colvile, Jan. 27, 1824.

33 Beaver House, H.B.C.A., B.239/K/1, f. 51d.

34 P.A.M., S.P., f. 8, 221, Simpson to Colvile, Jan. 27, 1824.

35 Bulletin de la Société Historique de Saint-Boniface, *Lettres de Monsignor Joseph-Norbert de Saint-Boniface*, III (St Boniface, 1913), 78-79.

36 *Ibid.*

37 P.A.M., S.P., Simpson to A. Colvile, Jan. 27, 1824.

38 P.A.M., S.P., Simpson to A. Colvile, May 31, 1824.

39 Beaver House, H.B.C.A., D.4/3, Simpson to McTavish, Jan. 4, 1824.

40 Beaver House, H.B.C.A., D.4/8, pp. 14-16.

1 Beaver House, H.B.C.A., B.239/c/1, Simpson to McTavish, Jan. 7, 1824.

Notes to Chapter VII

1 The above was the account compiled by Mrs A. N. MacLeod from various versions of the legend.

2 G. P. de T. Glazebrook, *The Hargrave Correspondence, 1821-1843* (Toronto, Champlain Society, 1938), p. 11.

3 All details in the accompanying paragraphs are from notes of M. A. MacLeod's made from the reminiscences of old inhabitants of Saint-François-Xavier.

4 P.A.M., S.P., 8,221, Simpson to A. Colvile, May 31, 1824.

5 Giraud, *Le Métis Canadien*, p. 715.

6 *Provencher Letters*, I, p. 121.

7 Giraud, *Le Métis Canadien*, p. 844.

8 Beaver House, H.B.C.A., B.235/2/5, Fort Garry Journal, Aug. 13 and 18, 1824.

9 *Ibid.*, Feb. 18, 1825.

10 E. E. Rich (Ed.), *Letters of Eden Colvile* (Hudson's Bay Record Society, 1956), p. xliv, fn. 2.

11 Beaver House, H.B.C.A., B.235/a/5, Fort Garry Journal, Feb. 18, 1825.

12 F. Merk, *Fur Trade and Empire*, fn. 162-163.

13 Beaver House, H.B.C.A., B.235/a/6, Fort Garry Journal, Aug. 4, 1825.

14 Reminiscences of Saint-François-Xavier people.

15 Beaver House, H.B.C.A., B.235/2/6, Fort Garry Journal, Apr. 8, 1825.

16 See Merk, *Fur Trade and Empire*, p. 46 and p. 351.

17 For Simon McGillivray, Junior, see *Simpson's Athabasca Journal*, p. 451; Wallace, *North West Company*, p. 471.

18 Beaver House, H.B.C.A., D.4/13, ff. 68, 68d.

19 Beaver House, H.B.C.A., D.4/6, ff. 26, 26d, 27, 27d.

20 Beaver House, H.B.C.A., B.235/2/7, Fort Garry Journal, Aug. 26, 1826.

21 Beaver House, H.B.C.A., D.4/89, F.103, Simpson to Governor and Committee, Oct. 16, 1826.

22 G. M. McMorran, *Souris River Posts* (Souris, n.d.), p. 13.
23 Beaver House, H.B.C.A., B.235/a/7, Fort Garry Journal, Jan. 4, 1827.
24 Giboche is not otherwise known.
25 Beaver House, H.B.C.A., D.4/90, f. 30, 30d, Simpson to Governor and Committee, July 25, 1827.
26 *Ibid.*, also B.235/a/8, Fort Garry Journal, June 30 and Aug. 31.
27 Beaver House, H.B.C.A., B.235/2/9, Fort Garry Journal of Geo. Taylor, Oct. 27, 1827.
28 Beaver House, H.B.C.A., B.235/a/9, Geo. Taylor's Journal, Nov. 6, 7, 8, 1827.
29 *Ibid.*, Fort Garry Journal, Dec. 31, 1827.
30 *Ibid.*, Mar. 15, 1828.
31 *Ibid.*
32 Beaver House, H.B.C.A., 4/90, f. 30, 30d, Simpson to Governor and Committee, July 25, 1827.
33 Beaver House, H.B.C.A., B.239/K/1, 132, Minutes of Council of Northern Department, July 2, 1828.
34 Beaver House, H.B.C.A., B.235/a/11, Fort Garry Journal, June 10 and Aug. 31, 1828.
35 Beaver House, H.B.C.A., B.22/e/3, Brandon House, May 6, 1829.
36 *Ibid.*
37 T.P.L., Hargrave MSS, Hargrave to Grant, Sept. 5, 1842.
38 *Provencher's Letters*, pp. 122, 127, 130, 132
39 Beaver House, H.B.C.A., B.235/a/12, June 9 and Aug. 29.
40 *Ibid.*, f. 4, Sept. 17, 1829.
41 Alexander Ross, *The Red River Settlement* (London, 1856), pp. 145-146.
42 *Provencher's Letters*, p. 131.
43 *Ibid.*
44 P.A.M., *Garrioch's Journal*, I. Isabella was one of the beautiful daughters of the famous Daniel Mackenzie, who refused to allow her to marry a half-breed such as Garrioch was.
45 While settlers on the Red River had hay privileges, so far as is known these settlers of Grantown are the only people who had sugar privileges also. Their sugar-lots were on the Rivière aux Ilets de Bois, which was later renamed the Boyne, and were near where the town of Carman stands today. Each family had its own preserve on which other families did not trespass, and after the season was over each family left its simple sugar-making paraphernalia of iron pots, wooden ladles, etc., right on their claim where they remained until the owners returned the next spring.

Notes to Chapter VIII

1 E. E. Rich, *History of the Hudson's Bay Company, 1670-1870*, II (London, 1959), 515.
2 T.P.L., Hargrave MSS, Simpson at Fort Garry, to Donald Ross at Norway House, Dec. 19, 1831.
3 E. Coues, *New Light on the Northwest*, I, 99 and 193.
4 *Ibid.*, p. 191; see also p. 226.
5 See Olive Knox, "The Red River Cart," *The Beaver* (March, 1942), pp. 39-43.
6 I. I. Stevens, *Reports of Exploration and Surveys . . . from the Mississippi to the Pacific Ocean*, I (Washington, 1855), 65-67.
7 Morice, *Catholic Church in Western Canada*, I, 126.
8 There are numerous descriptions of the organization of the hunt. Perhaps the best is that by Louis Riel in A. H. de Tremaudan's *La nation métisse*, pp. 438-39.
9 See Alexander Ross's account in the *Red River Settlement*, pp. 256-57.
10 See Margaret Arnett MacLeod, "A Note on the Red River Hunt," *Canadian Historical Review* (June 1957), pp. 129-130.

11 T.P.L., Hargrave MSS, J. D. Cameron, Fort Alexander, to Donald Ross at Norway House, Feb. 7, 1834; Jas. Hargrave, York Factory, to J. G. MacTavish, Moose Factory, Dec. 1, 1834.

12 Giraud, *Le Métis Canadien*, p. 803.

13 See Chapter X.

14 See W. L. Morton, "Introduction," *Letters of Eden Colvile, 1849-1852* (London: Hudson's Bay Record Society, 1957); also his "Introduction," *The Red River Journal of Alexander Begg* (Toronto: Champlain Society, 1957).

15 T.P.L., Hargrave MSS, Thos. Simpson, Fort Garry, to Donald Ross, Norway House, Dec. 19, 1831.

16 Morice, *Catholic Church in Western Canada*, I, 141.

17 *Provencher Letters*, III, 140.

18 *Ibid.*, pp. 136-37, July 16, 1834.

19 Register, Saint - François - Xavier Church.

20 Beaver House, H.B.C.A., D.4/101, p. 4, Geo. Simpson to Governor and Committee, July 21, 1834.

21 *Ibid.*

22 G. P. de T. Glazebrook (ed.), *The Hargrave Correspondence* (Toronto: Champlain Society, 1938), p. 121.

23 E. H. Oliver, *The Canadian North-West*, I, 274.

24 *Ibid.*, p. 270.

25 *Ibid.*, p. 280.

26 *Ibid.*, p. 286.

27 The remainder of this chapter is taken from *The Beaver*, Summer, 1956, pp. 4-7.

28 See Grace Lee Nute, "James Dickson: A Filibuster in Minnesota in 1836," *Mississippi Valley Historical Review*, Sept., 1923, pp. 127-141.

29 *Report of Canadian Archives*, 1936, p. 459.

30 The sword is now a valued possession in Margaret Arnett MacLeod's home. She first saw it in a farmhouse to which it had been removed from Grant's home a generation after his death. It was lying on a kitchen table, where it had just been placed after being used to cut weeds by the roadside. Later, it was identified for her by the Master of Arms at the Tower of London as a British general's sword issued in 1810.

31 See Margaret Arnett MacLeod, *Songs of Old Manitoba*, p. 27, for a translation into English.

Notes to Chapter IX

1 Ross, *Red River*, pp. 242-252.

2 *Ibid.*, pp. 258-259.

3 *Ibid.*, pp. 268-269.

4 Beaver House, H.B.C.A., D.3/2, p. 40, Simpson to Governor and Committee, June, 1841.

5 T.P.L., Hargrave MSS, Finlayson to Hargrave, July 30, 1842.

6 Ross, *Red River*, pp. 325-30.

7 Details from the Register of Saint-François-Xavier.

8 P.A.M., Red River Census, 1843.

9 Morice, *Catholic Church in the Canadian West*, I, 195.

10 *Provencher Letters*, Provencher to Bishop of Quebec, June 25, 1840.

11 Dom Bénoit, *Vie de Monseigneur Taché*, I (Montreal, 1894), 87.

12 Pritchett, *The Red River Valley*, chap. xxiii; J. S. Galbraith, *The Hudson's Bay Company as an Imperial Factor* (Toronto, 1955), chap. xv; W. L. Morton, "Introduction," *Letters of Eden Colvile* (London: Hudson's Bay Record Society, 1957).

13 T.P.L., Hargrave MSS, Jas. Hargrave, York Factory, to Grant.

14 *Ibid.*, N.F., Fort Garry, to Jas. Hargrave, York Factory, July 30, 1842.

15 Ross, *Red River*, p. 325.

16 P.A.M., Garrioch's Journal, IV, f. 204.

17 Garrioch's Journal, V, May, 1845, to Jan., 1846, *passim*.

18 Oliver, *Canadian North-West*, I, p. 318. Stoves for the personal use of settlers were exempt.

19 It is to be noted that among the free traders Garrioch lists there are no names from White Horse Plain.

20 United Kingdom: *Parliamentary Papers: Hudson's Bay Company*, 1849, pp. 1-5.

21 Rich, *Colvile Letters*, p. lxvi.

22 *Ibid.*, p. lxxiii.

23 Provencher Letters, Provencher to Bishop of Quebec, June 16, 1846.

24 Parish Register, Saint-François-Xavier, Sept. 1848.

25 J. M. Reardon, *George Anthony Belcourt*, pp. 84-85.

26 *Provencher Letters*, Provencher to Bishop of Quebec, July 18, 1848, and Aug., 1848.

27 Rich, *Colvile Letters*, pp. lxxxiii-lxxxvi.

28 P.A.M., "Record of the Quarterly Court of Assiniboia."

29 Rich, *Colvile Letters*, p. lxxxiii.

30 *Ibid.*, p. lxxxv.

31 P.A.M., "Record of the Quarterly Court of Assiniboia."

32 Ross, *Red River Settlement*, p. 376.

33 Rich, *Colvile's Letters*, pp. lxxxvii-lxxxix.

34 Beaver House, H.B.C.A., D.5/27, ff. 253-254.

Notes to Chapter X

1 T.P.L., Hargrave MSS, Jas. Hargrave, York Factory, to Grant, Aug. 17, 1849.

2 *Ibid.*

3 Viscount Milton and W. B. Cheadle, *North-west Passage by Land* (London, 1865), pp. 49-50, describe a later Grantown wedding.

4 Morice, *Catholic Church in Western Canada*, I, 233.

5 P.A.M., *Red River Census*, 1849.

6 The surviving accounts so far as they are known to the authors are as follows:

   1) A letter from Rev. L. F. R. Laflêche, dated September 4, 1851, and published by Arthur Savaete, *Vers L'Abîme* (Paris, n.d.), pp. 182-184.

   2) A letter of Father Albert Lacombe, O.M.I., dated March 11, 1852, and published in *L'Echo de Saint-Justin*, X (10) August, 1931.

   3) With this, on pp. 193-201 of *Vers L'Abîme*, is a supplementary account "based on the knowledge of" Abbé Georges Dugas.

   4) A passage in the "Journal of Rudolph Friederich Kurz" published in Bulletin 115, Bureau of Ethnology, Smithsonian Institution, pp. 191-192.

   5) A letter from Father Lacombe, dated January 1852, published in *Les Cloches de Saint-Boniface*, 1917, p. 61.

   6) François-Xavier Falcon's account of a battle, seemingly that of 1851, but said to have taken place in 1853. This was written in 1940.

   7) The account of Abbé Georges Dugas in his *Histoire de l'ouest canadien* (Montreal, 1906), pp. 119-130. Dugas does not give his sources, but his abundance of vivid detail makes it clear he has talked to those who had been present.

   These will be referred to hereafter as: Laflêche, Lacombe 1, Lacombe 2, Dugas 1 (L'Histoire, etc.), Dugas 2, Kurz, Falcon.

   This account appears in Transactions of the Manitoba Historical Society, III.

7 As there is some doubt as to the year of the fight, it is good to know that there was, as Rev. L. F. R. Laflêche reported, an eclipse of the moon on the night of July 12-13, 1851.

8 See, for example, the admiring account in Cowie, *The Company of Adventurers*, pp. 324-325.

9 Margaret Arnett MacLeod, "A Note on the Red River Hunt," *Canadian Historical Review* (June, 1957), pp. 129-130.

10 Lacombe 1.

11 Laflêche; Dugas 1; Dugas 2.

12 Falcon. It is usually said that the captain of the White Horse Plain camp was unknown, but Falcon's evidence is accepted here as probably true. It is certain that Cuthbert Grant was not present.

13 H. Y. Hind, *The Red and Assiniboine Exploring Expedition*, II, 179 and 283-284.

14 W. L. Morton, "Introduction," *Letters of Eden Colvile*, (Hudson's Bay Record Society, 1957) pp. lxxxii-lxxxvi.

15 Dugas 2, p. 120.

16 Lacombe 1.

17 *Ibid.*; Dugas 1.

18 Lacombe 1. The movement of the two parties has been estimated as follows for this work:

Saint-François-Xavier Party leaves Saint-François on June 15 and reaches rendezvous in four days, i.e. on June 19.

St Boniface and Pembina Parties leave Pembina on June 16 and go to rendezvous.

That is, the first marches three days and the latter four.

Allowing a march of 15 miles a day, the parties would meet near the traditional rendezvous of Calf Mountain or Star Mound (Note that St F. Party was there first, i.e., the smaller party moved faster.)

A council was held here, perhaps also later. This would consume June 20, and perhaps another day later.

The three parties then travelled and hunted together for some days, but had been separated, it would seem, for two weeks before July 12.

Say, then, they hunted and travelled together June 22 to June 28.

Allowing an average day's march of 7½ miles, hunting and travelling, this would take them 60 miles southwest from Calf Mountain.

The St F. party then separated from the two larger parties.

The larger party had travelled and hunted 14 days to reach a point near the Dog's House. At 7½ miles a day, this would be 150 miles further, a total march of 280 miles from the present site of Winnipeg (by Pembina). The distance from Winnipeg to the region of the Dog's House is 200 miles.

The St F. party, not having gone by Pembina, would possibly be some miles farther west, having travelled 235 miles since June 15.

Thus the days and route of travel, so far as they are accounted for in the documents, roughly agree with the actual distance.

19 *Ibid.*

20 Dugas 1.

21 Lacombe 1; E. Coues, *New Light on the Northwest*, I, 406 – "At three o'clock we came to the ridge of high land, which runs from E. to W., and separates the waters between the Missourie and Rivière la Souris. This ridge adjoins the Dog's House, which we could plainly see about three leagues eastward – supposed to be the highest hill for many miles. It stands nearly due S. from the S. E. bend or elbow of Rivière la Souris, and may be seen at a considerable distance. We could also discern the banks of that river to the N. about five leagues distant; and had the weather been clear, doubtless we could have distinguished the Snake's Lodge, which bears S. about 20 leagues."

22 Dugas 1.

23 *Ibid.*

24 Dugas and Lacombe say 2,000, Kurz about 2,500.

25 Dugas says Malaterre, Falcon says Whiteford.

26 Dugas 2.

27 *Ibid.*

28 Dugas 2.

29 Dugas 1, p. 123.

30 *Ibid.*

31 Kurz.

32 *Ibid.*

33 Dugas 1, p. 123.
34 Laflêche.
35 Dugas 2.
36 Dugas 1, pp. 123-4.
37 *Ibid.*, p. 124.
38 All these details are from Dugas 1, pp. 124-5.
39 Falcon.
40 Dugas 1; Laflêche.
41 Falcon says a Frenchman.
42 Dugas 1, p. 126.
43 Laflêche.
44 Dugas 2.
45 Falcon.
46 Dugas 1, pp. 127; Laflêche.
47 Kurz; it is assumed they were lost on July 13 because better precautions were taken on July 14.
48 Dugas 2.
49 Lacombe.
50 Dugas 2.
51 Dugas 1, p. 128.
52 Falcon.
53 Dugas 1, p. 128.
54 *Ibid.*
55 *Ibid.*
56 All details are from Dugas 1, p. 129, and show how he must have got them from an eye-witness who thoroughly appreciated the significance of every feature of the Métis defence.
57 *Ibid.*
58 Lacombe.
59 *Ibid.*; Dugas 1, p. 129.
60 *Ibid.*
61 Lacombe 1.
62 *Ibid.*; Dugas 1.
63 Kurz; Lacombe 2 says that only eighteen Sioux were killed. It is probable the Métis never really knew. To the Indian mind even eighteen was a heavy loss.
64 Falcon; but not of the Sioux and the Saulteaux.
65 See Colonel Crofton's report in United Kingdom, *Parliamentary Papers, Hudson's Bay Company*, 1849 (London, 1850); also Cowie's reference, *Company of Adventurers*, p. 170.

66 P.A.M., Riel Papers, Gay to Riel, Aug. 20, 1872.
67 See the account in de Tremaudan, *La nation métisse*, pp. 143-145.
68 P.A.M., *The Church Missionary Record, 1854*, p. 5.
69 As evidence that Grant, in his last years probably re-established his early trading establishment in the country west of Brandon House, we have an account of an interview with Mrs Filoman Lafontaine, who lived at Grande Clarière, Manitoba. The Souris *Plaindealer*, September 19, 1934, reports that Madame Lafontaine, who was born in the parish of Saint-François-Xavier in 1844, had spent some time at Fort Mr Grant during the early years of her life. She was able to direct those who were seeking to identify old trading post sites, to the exact location of this particular post.
70 Beaver House, H.B.C.A., D.5/37, f. 273.
71 *Ibid.*, D.4/24, pp. 472-73.
72 Parish Register of Saint-François-Xavier.
73 Giraud, *Le Métis Canadien*, p. 717.

Notes to Epilogue

1 *Saskatchewan and the Rocky Mountains* (Toronto, 1875), Lord Southesk, pp. 348, 349. Lord Southesk gives a vivid description of the Grantown of some six years later as he observed it on a Sunday, January 8, 1860. "Shortly after starting we passed the Roman Catholic Church just as the congregation was coming out. There seemed to be about 200 people, mostly men and more or less of French-Canadian blood. They have one almost invariable type of dress, which though handsome in itself, looks rather sombre in a crowd – capots of dark blue, leggings of the same, caps either of the same or of some dark

fur. The only relief to this monotony is given by a scarlet, crimson or variegated scarf around the waist, and red stripes embroidered with various coloured ribbons down the outside of the leggings. The female costume is generally dark also, and not remarkable, though with more picturesqueness about the head-dress, which is sometimes a dark shawl or blanket worn as a hood, sometimes a crimson or yellow silk handkerchief which forms a rich contrast to the glossy black hair it partly conceals.

The Fort of White Horse Plain is situated near the Assiniboine and the settlement extends itself along the banks of that river. For twenty miles almost without a break small farms run outwards from the river-side into the uncultivated but grass clad prairies. The soil seems rich, a belt of large, fine elm trees border the course of the stream, and young poplars grow in masses here and there; the ground undulates considerably in many parts, and alto-gether this settlement looks warmer and more home-like than that on the Red River near Fort Garry.

The settlers' houses are generally plain square boxes devoid of the smallest attempt at ornament; with-out a chimney even, unless a short projecting iron stove-pipe may be called so. Wood is the material invariably employed – placed hori-zontally in long logs about a foot square. Neither gardens nor sur-rounding fences are in favour, and the cottages stand all bare-faced, as boulders are strewn by a flood, or meteor stones dropped from the sky."

INDEX

American Fur Company, 131
Assiniboia, 15, 34, 116, 117
Assiniboine Indians, 7, 23, 90-91, 100
Athabasca, 9, 13, 15, 20, 31, 32, 39, 41, 74

Baie St Paul, 115, 122, 134
Baldoon, 16
Ballenden, John, 134, 136, 137-138
Belcourt, Rev. Georges, 114-115, 129, 134, 135
Boucher, François Firmin, 48, 65, 69
Boucher, Rev., 110, 114
Bourassa, Michel, 45
Bourke, John, 44, 47-49, 52, 108
Boutino, Moustouche, 45
Brandon House, 4, 11, 14, 18, 34, 42-43, 64, 65, 79, 80, 95, 99, 100, 101
Bréland, Alexandre, 93
Bréland Alex (grandson of Maria Grant), 103
Bréland, Pascal, 106, 153, 156

Cadotte, Joseph, 58, 62, 64, 66, 77
Caldwell, Maj. W. B., 134, 135
Caledon, Lord, 106, 123
Cameron, Duncan, 21, 22-24, 25-26, 27, 31, 33, 38
Cameron, J. D., 36
Canadian Jurisdiction Act of 1803, 21, 54
Cary, Capt. George M., 117
Christie, Alexander, 115-116, 118, 133, 134
Churchill [English] River, 35, 36
Clan Grant, 2
Clarke, John, 35
Coltman, W. B., 63, 64-66, 69, 70-72, 73
Colvile, Andrew, 80, 85, 86
Costello, Thomas, 54
Council of Assiniboia, 117, 133
Cowie, Isaac, 1
Cox, Ross, 9
Cree Indians, 7, 23, 71, 90-91, 151
Crees, Swampy, 26
Cuchillon, schooner, 30, 39, 75
Cummings, Cuthbert, 83, 84

Delorme, Urbain, 93, 153
de Meuron Regiment, 54, 55, 58, 61, 63, 74, 75, 77, 84, 97
de Reinhard, Charles, 54, 55, 68
Deschamps, François, 31, 49, 70
Desjardin family, 103
Desmarais, Madeline, 73, 89, 103
Destroismaisons, Rev. Picard, 88, 93, 104
Detroit, 21
de Wattville Regiment, 63
Dickson, Gen. James, 117-119
D'Orsonnens, Capt. Protais, 55, 58
Dugas, Georges, 147
Dumoulin, Rev. S. S., 78

English River, see Churchill River

Falcon, Isabella, 148, 149
Falcon, Jean Baptiste, 143, 144, 146, 148, 149
Falcon, Mary (Mme Pierre), 2, 6, 94
Falcon, Pierre, 6, 18, 56, 93, 119, 151
Fidler, Peter, 12, 18, 26, 27, 28-30, 31, 42, 64, 78
Finlayson, Duncan, 131
Finlayson, Nicol, 124
Fletcher, Lt.-Col. J. F., 63
Forks of the Red River, The, 10, 13, 14, 15, 17, 18, 22, 24, 25, 26, 33, 35, 36, 38-42, 44, 45, 53, 61, 63, 64, 73, 77, 80, 86, 90, 92, 94, 104, 105, 109, 110
Fort Albany, 12, 54
Fort Alexander, 83, 99
Fort Bas de la Rivière, 10, 15, 17, 22, 53, 54, 55, 62, 75, 99
Fort Daer, 33, 39
Fort Dauphin, 36
Fort de la Rivière Tremblante, 1, 14, 77
Fort des Prairies, 35, 36
Fort Douglas, 12, 32, 34, 40, 44, 45-48, 51, 52, 53, 58, 60, 61, 63, 64
Fort Espérance, 11, 14, 21
Fort Garry, 84, 89, 96, 99, 109, 116, 129
Fort Gibraltar, 10, 11, 15, 18, 21, 22, 25, 26, 30, 33, 34, 38, 44
Fort Hibernia, 14, 77, 78

Suggestions For Further Reading

Giraud, Marcel, *Le Métis Canadien*, Paris, 1945.

J. G. MacGregor, *Peter Fidler: Canada's Forgotten Surveyor 1769-1822*, McClelland and Stewart Ltd., Toronto, 1966.

MacLeod, Margaret Arnett, "Cuthbert Grant of Grantown," *Canadian Historical Review*, Mar., 1940

Morton, A.S., *History of the Canadian West to 1870-71*. Toronto, 1939.

Morton, W.L., "Introduction," *London Correspondence Inward from Eden Colvile, 1849-52*, London, Hudson's Bay Record Society, 1956.

Morton, W.L., *Manitoba: A History, 2nd ed*. Toronto, 1967.

Pritchett, J.P., *The Red River Valley*, Toronto, 1945.

Rich, E.E., (ed) *Simpson's Athabasca Journal*, Toronto, Champlain Society, 1958.

Rich, E.E., *Colin Robertson's Correspondence Book*, Toronto, Champlain Society, 1939.

Ross, Alexander, *The Red River Settlement*, London 1856, reprint Edmonton, Hurtig, 1972.

Writings of Margaret Arnett MacLeod (1877-19____)

A. Books and Booklets

BOOKS

Letters of Letitia Hargrave, Champlain Society, 1947

Songs of Old Manitoba, Ryerson Press, 1959

Cuthbert Grant of Grantown by MacLeod & Morton, McClelland and Stewart, 1963.

BOOKLETS

The Frozen Priest of Pembina, Nov. 1935

Bells of the Red River, 1937

Lower Fort Garry, June 1957

Red River Festive Season, Oct. 1962

B. Periodical Articles

"Life in the Early West" - Paper read before the Historic & Scientific Society, Series 111, No. 4, 1947-48

"Memorandum Regarding Affairs of York Factory," Winter Seasons, 1939-40, *Canadian Historical Review*, Mar. 1948.

"Historic Route to the Lower Fort," *Can. Library Assoc.*, Sept. 1949.

"Red River Buffalo Hunt," *Can. Historic Rev.*, June 1957

"Franklin's First Expedition as seen by the Fur Traders," *The Polar Record*, Vol. 15, 1971

C. Newspapers Pieces

"Autumn Beauty is Gracious in the Red River Valley,"
Tribune, Oct. 31, 1931

"From Tepee to Cloister," *Free Press.*, Sept. 1931

"Heights," The *Tribune*, also "Tea at the Heights," Oct. 31, 1931

"Arvid Olson's New Shirt," *Tribune*, June 11, 1932

"Spring of Yule is Abroad," *Tribune*, Dec. 17, 1932

"Stranger at the Gates," *Free Press*, March 26, 1932

"First Lady Visits Winnipeg," 1872, *Tribune*, Nov. 30, 1935

"Florence Nightingale," also "Lamp That Shone in Red River,"

"From Lady Dufferin to Lady Tweedsmuir," 1872-1935, *National Home Monthly*, Dec. 1935

"Frozen Priest of Pembina," *The Catholic World*, Nov. 1935 also issued as a booklet; also "A Trip to St. Paul in 1860," *Free Press* Jan. 1935

"He's Manitoba's Champion Fiddler," *Free Press*, Apr. 6, 1935 (Frederic Genthon)

"Lady Dufferin Tells of Western Tour," *Tribune*, Dec. 7, 1935

"Escape from the Sioux," *The Catholic World*, Nov. 1936 *Free Press*, Aug. 27, 1938

"Lamp Shines in The Red River," *Beaver*, Sept. 1936 *The Bulletin*, Calif.

"Bells That Rang in Red River," No 1 *Free Press*, Mar. 27, 1937; No 2 Apr. 3, 1937; No 3 Apr. 10, 1937; No 4 Apr. 17, 1937; No 5 missing; No 6 May 1, 1937

"From Tepee to Cloister," *The Magnificat*, May 1937

"Lady of the Steamship." *Tribune*, Apr. 24, 1937

"Red River Festive Season," Pt. 1, *Free Press*, Dec. 24, 1938; Pt. II, Dec. 31, 1938

"Company in Winnipeg," *Beaver*, Sept. 1940

"Dawson, Route," *Free Press*, Aug. 3, 1940

"Early Christmas in Red River," also "Red River Festive Season," *Manitoba Calling*, Dec. 1941

"Making Maple Sugar in Manitoba," *Free Press*, Apr. 19, 1941

"Brandon Boy's Sleigh in the Depression," *New World*, Toronto Mar. 15, 1943

"Peter Rindsbacher, Red River Artist," *Beaver*, Dec. 1945

"Fur Trader's Inn." Pt. I (George & Vulture), *Beaver*, p. 3, 1947; Pt. II, *Beaver*, p. 28, 1948

"Riddle of the Paintings," *Beaver*, Dec. 1948

"St. Andrew's-on-the-Red," *Free Press*, Oct. 8, 1949

"Winnipeg in Rompers," *Free Press*, June, 1949

"Winnipeg and the Hudson's Bay Co.," *Beaver*, June, 1949

"The City that Never Was," *Beaver*, Sept. 1950

"The Mactavishes find a Chief." *Free Press*, Mar. 3, 1951

"Ten Days In a Badger Hole," *Country Guide*, Oct. 1951

"The Christmas Holiday," *Beaver*, Dec. 1952

"Our Famous Fort that ruled the West," also "Lower Fort," *Mayfair*, Jan. 1952

"Red River's New Year," *Beaver*, Dec. 1953

"C.P.R. was born in an Icy Tent," *Free Press*, Nov. 26, 1955

"Manitoba Maple Sugar," *Beaver*, Spring, 1955

"Strathcona and Hill, C.P.R.," also "C.P.R. Was Born in a Tent," *Free Press*, Nov. 26, 1955

"Abrey's Aluminum Transit," *Free Press*, April 21, 1956

"Bard of the Prairies (Falcon)," *Beaver*, Spring, 1956

"Dickson the Liberator," *Beaver*, Summer 1956

"Legend of White Horse Plain," *Free Press*, Nov. 2, 1957

"Songs of the Insurrection," *Beaver*, Spring, 1957

"Crow Indian Girl," also "Indian Love Call," "A Western Evangeline Search" *Free Press*, May 17, 1958

"Sister Ste. Therese" also "Kidnapping of Sister Therese," *Indian Record*, Jan. 1958 *Free Press*, Apr. 5, 1958

"Western Evangeline Search," The *Globe Magazine*, June 21, 1958

"York Factory," unplaced.

Talks given by Mrs. MacLeod

Argentina   to   Twenty Club

Regional Writing   to   Can. Authors Assoc., Nat. Conv.

Lower Fort Garry   to   Twenty Club Business & Prof. Women's Conv.

Early Red River   to   Medical Faculty Club./Teachers Conv. Nov. 10, 1950

The Early Western Scene   to   Women's Canadian Club

Life in the Early West   to   Historical Soc., Wpg./Twenty Club, Oct. 19, 1949/Pen Guild, Jan. 16, 1950/Authors Assoc. Toronto/Medical Faculty Assoc. luncheon

Graduation

Research in History   to   Can. Authors Assoc., July 2, 1951

Historic Route to the Lower Fort   to   Chbr. of Industry, Game & Fish

Early Life in Red River   to   Selkirk Club

Days Before Yesterday   to   St. James Kiwanis Club/Pen Guild

Life of Women in Early Days in West   to   Arts & Science Faculty Club, Jan. 24, 1951

Ceramics   to   Women's Canadian Club, Arvida/Twenty Club

BROADCASTS

Old St. Andrews Church on the Red River, Oct. 21, 1949
John Pritchard C.B.C., undated

Lady of the Steamship, C.B.C., undated

Note on the Authors

Margaret Arnett MacLeod is a well-known writer of western history. Besides her numerous magazine articles she has written *Songs of Old Manitoba* and a series of booklets dealing with life at Red River in earlier years. In 1947 she edited *The Letters of Letitia Hargrave* for the Champlain Society, of which she has been a Council member. In *Cuthbert Grant of Grantown* she has collaborated with William Lewis Morton, formerly Professor of history at the University of Manitoba, now Vanier Professor at Trent University, Rhodes Scholar and the author of *Manitoba: a History*, *The Canadian Identity*, *Kingdom of Canada* and *The Critical Years*. His *Progressive Party in Canada* won him the Governor General's Award in 1950. He is the editor of many collections including *Monck Letters and Journals 1863-1868* (Carleton Library, No. 52).

THE CARLETON LIBRARY

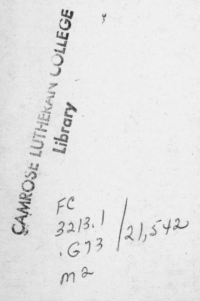

Date Due

DEC 0 7 1981		
V E E		
DEC 0 4 1984		
Oct 15 /85 9:00 AM.		
Oct 12		
Nov 12 9:00 am		
Dec 5		
NOV 2 5 1990		